THE BEDFORD SERIES IN HISTORY AND CULTURE

Slave Revolution in the Caribbean, 1789–1804

A Brief History with Documents

Laurent Dubois

Michigan State University

and

John D. Garrigus

Jacksonville University

BEDFORD/ST. MARTIN'S   Boston ♦ New York

For Bedford/St. Martin's

Executive Editor for History: Mary V. Dougherty
Director of Development for History: Jane Knetzger
Developmental Editor: Shannon Hunt
Senior Production Supervisor: Joe Ford
Production Associate: Matthew Hayes
Senior Marketing Manager: Jenna Bookin Barry
Project Management: Books By Design, Inc.
Text Design: Claire Seng-Niemoeller
Cover Design: Billy Boardman
Cover Art: Hand-colored engraving of *Toussaint Louverture fighting the French in Saint-Domingue,* ca. 1800. © Bettmann/Corbis.
Composition: Stratford Publishing Services, Inc.
Printing and Binding: Haddon Craftsmen, an RR Donnelley & Sons Company

President: Joan E. Feinberg
Editorial Director: Denise B. Wydra
Director of Marketing: Karen Melton Soeltz
Director of Editing, Design, and Production: Marcia Cohen
Manager, Publishing Services: Emily Berleth

Library of Congress Control Number: 2005931087

Copyright © 2006 by Bedford/St. Martin's

Manufactured in the United States of America.

3   2   1
k   j

For information, write: Bedford/St. Martin's, 75 Arlington Street, Boston, MA 02116 (617-399-4000)

ISBN-10: 0-312-41501-X (paperback)
        1-4039-7157-9 (hardcover)
ISBN-13: 978-0-312-41501-3

Foreword

The Bedford Series in History and Culture is designed so that readers can study the past as historians do.

The historian's first task is finding the evidence. Documents, letters, memoirs, interviews, pictures, movies, novels, or poems can provide facts and clues. Then the historian questions and compares the sources. There is more to do than in a courtroom, for hearsay evidence is welcome, and the historian is usually looking for answers beyond act and motive. Different views of an event may be as important as a single verdict. How a story is told may yield as much information as what it says.

Along the way the historian seeks help from other historians and perhaps from specialists in other disciplines. Finally, it is time to write, to decide on an interpretation and how to arrange the evidence for readers.

Each book in this series contains an important historical document or group of documents, each document a witness from the past and open to interpretation in different ways. The documents are combined with some element of historical narrative—an introduction or a biographical essay, for example—that provides students with an analysis of the primary source material and important background information about the world in which it was produced.

Each book in the series focuses on a specific topic within a specific historical period. Each provides a basis for lively thought and discussion about several aspects of the topic and the historian's role. Each is short enough (and inexpensive enough) to be a reasonable one-week assignment in a college course. Whether as classroom or personal reading, each book in the series provides firsthand experience of the challenge—and fun—of discovering, recreating, and interpreting the past.

Lynn Hunt
David W. Blight
Bonnie G. Smith
Natalie Zemon Davis
Ernest R. May

Preface

In the French Caribbean, between 1789 and 1804, slave revolutionaries transformed some of the richest plantation colonies in the world into zones of liberty and equality. Their struggle for liberation, freedom, and dignity reconfigured the political geography of the Americas and inspired others throughout the hemisphere for generations. Despite the importance of these remarkable events, however, many North American students know little about them. *Slave Revolution in the Caribbean* provides students of Atlantic, U.S., and Caribbean history with a selection of primary sources that tell the story of this revolution and introduce some of its most famous—as well as some of its little-known—protagonists. The collection invites readers to explore firsthand the complexities of this dramatic era of revolution, which historians of the Atlantic world now recognize as a crucial turning point in the history of slavery, racism, and the broader meaning of democracy and human rights.

The documents in this collection include published accounts, as well as laws and legislative debates, but also a number of archival sources. Most of these materials are known only to specialists, and many are published in English for the first time here. Through firsthand descriptions of colonial society and the revolts that destroyed it, students will learn how these revolutionaries won their freedom, transforming the colonial policies of the powerful French empire in the process. They will hear the voices not only of witnesses to the revolt, but also those of insurgents themselves. After winning freedom, former slaves struggled to define and consolidate it, and the collection presents students with a variety of perspectives on this pivotal struggle. Eventually, ex-slaves took up arms again to defend their freedom against new French government policies. The collection concludes with a range of accounts of the wars that led to reenslavement in Guadeloupe and the creation of the new nation of Haiti in 1804. These complex and diverse struggles, rife with contradictions, defined the

Age of Revolution, and throughout the collection students will see how they forced observers throughout the broader Atlantic world to respond and reconfigure their views about slavery and freedom.

The introduction uses these sources as a foundation for a narrative of the major events of this period of revolution, describing the French Caribbean colonies as they were before 1789, exploring the struggles of free people of color and slaves and the ultimate abolition of slavery, tracing the rise and struggles of military and political leaders of the revolution, exploring reactions to these events in the United States, and finally examining how France sought to regain control of the colony but instead incited an all-out war that led to the independence of Haiti in 1804.

The documents that follow—representing the perspectives of enslaved insurgents and their allies, the slave owners they struggled against, different groups within the population of the colonies, and a variety of observers in the Caribbean, Europe, and the United States—are introduced by headnotes that provide historical context. Footnotes define unfamiliar terms and elucidate contemporary references. To facilitate students' understanding of this complex era, the text includes maps of the Caribbean and Saint-Domingue, a guide to the major figures discussed in the work, a chronology of events, questions for consideration to guide reading and discussion, and a selected bibliography.

A NOTE ABOUT THE TEXT

In our translations we aimed to maintain the tone and style of the original texts while making them as clear as possible for our readers. Deciding how to translate terms used to identify individuals or groups, especially racial terms, has been particularly difficult. Not only do the meanings of such terms shift in important ways between French and English, they also had different meanings and resonances at different moments during the revolution as well as in the hands of different writers and actors. As a result we have sometimes left racial terms, particularly *nègre,* untranslated because no English term precisely captures its resonances. It could be translated as either "negro" or "black," but it was often a synonym for "slave" and therefore could have a distinct political meaning, especially during the revolution. Writers and lawmakers who used *nègre* instead of *noir* ("black") were making important implications. We have therefore left the word in

French in the documents to remind our readers how political and social contexts infuse such terms with particular meanings. In 1792 the French Revolutionary government introduced a new Republican calendar, intended to announce and exemplify the dawn of a new age. (The Haitian government did the same thing in 1804.) The French Revolutionary calendar began with "Year 1" in September 1792, with the establishment of the French Republic, and subsequent calendar years began in September also. The months all received new names as well, such as "Thermidor" and "Pluviôse." In documents that used the Republican calendar, we have maintained the dates as they were, while providing the equivalents in the Gregorian calendar in brackets. In several documents, we have translated and included as footnotes the authors' original annotations; these are indicated with asterisks (*). We have also included our own numbered notes to clarify or provide context for certain words or passages.

ACKNOWLEDGMENTS

We would like to extend our deepest thanks to those who have accompanied us as we have put together this collection. Patricia Rossi and Lynn Hunt first invited us to contribute to the Bedford series, and Shannon Hunt has marvelously shepherded the manuscript from its early drafts through to its final form. We were lucky to have encouraging and insightful reviewers comment on the manuscript: Edward L. Cox, Rice University; Evan Haefeli, Tufts University; Eric Martin, Lewis-Clark State College; David P. Geggus, University of Florida; Franklin W. Knight, Johns Hopkins University; and Jeffrey Shumway, Brigham Young University. Our thanks go to Sue Peabody, who shared with us a translation of one of the documents reproduced here. At Michigan State University, Eric Duke helped us to format the manuscript, and Monica Del Valle skillfully reread and corrected some of our translations. A grant from the Sesquicentennial Research Fund of Michigan State University provided financial support for the completion of this project. Ami Richards helped with some of the research and, at a deeper level, inspired the way part of this book is written, as did Katharine Brophy Dubois.

Contents

Maps

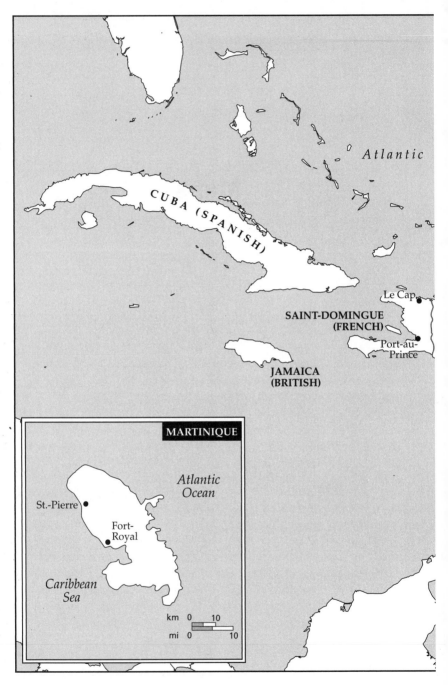

Map 1. The Caribbean in the Revolutionary Era

2

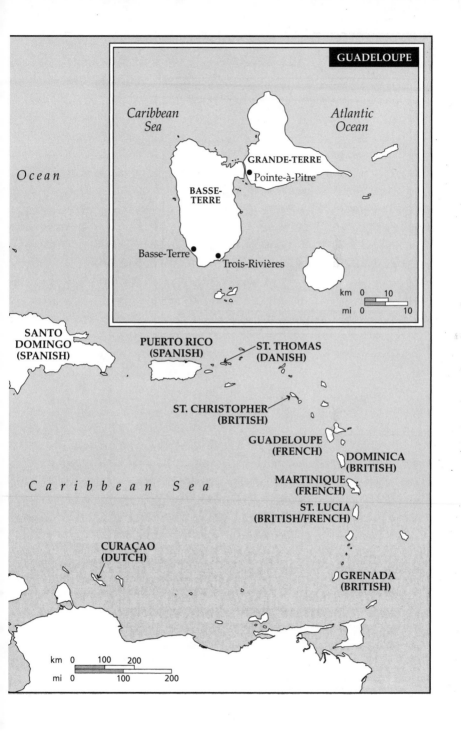

GUADELOUPE

Caribbean
Sea

Atlantic
Ocean

Ocean

GRANDE-TERRE

BASSE-
TERRE

Pointe-à-Pitre

Basse-Terre

Trois-Rivières

km 0   10
mi 0   10

SANTO
DOMINGO
(SPANISH)

PUERTO RICO
(SPANISH)

ST. THOMAS
(DANISH)

ST. CHRISTOPHER
(BRITISH)

GUADELOUPE
(FRENCH)

DOMINICA
(BRITISH)

MARTINIQUE
(FRENCH)

C a r i b b e a n   S e a

ST. LUCIA
(BRITISH/FRENCH)

CURAÇAO
(DUTCH)

GRENADA
(BRITISH)

km 0   100   200
mi 0   100   200

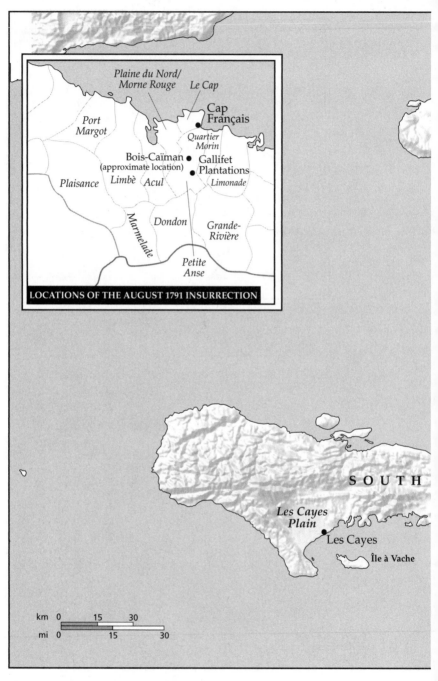

Map 2. Revolutionary Saint-Domingue

4

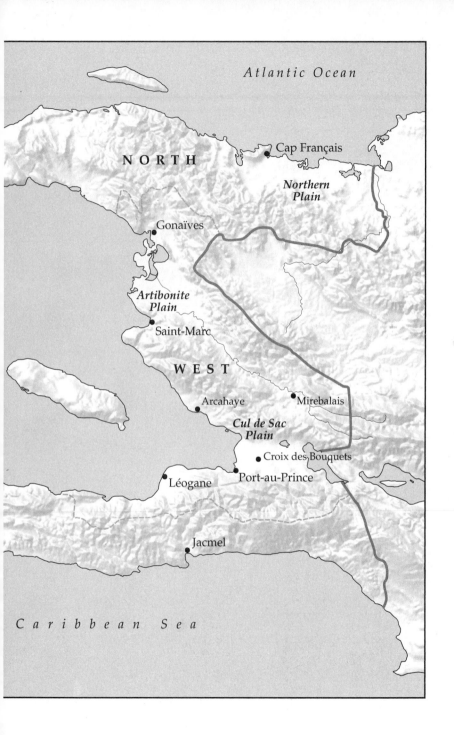

Atlantic Ocean

N O R T H

Cap Français

*Northern
Plain*

Gonaïves

*Artibonite
Plain*

Saint-Marc

W E S T

Arcahaye

Mirebalais

*Cul de Sac
Plain*

Croix des Bouquets

Léogane

Port-au-Prince

Jacmel

C a r i b b e a n   S e a

PART ONE

Introduction: Revolution, Emancipation, and Independence

In the wake of Columbus's crossing the Atlantic in 1492, trade between Europe, America, and Africa profoundly transformed economies and societies on all three continents. As indigenous civilizations were conquered and decimated, colonists in some parts of the New World established plantations focused on the production of agricultural commodities that would be consumed in Europe: tobacco, cotton, indigo, and, most important, sugar. From the beginning, these plantations depended on forced labor, sometimes of indigenous captives and indentured Europeans. But planters eventually shipped millions of enslaved Africans to plantations across the Atlantic, where they worked and died to satisfy Europe's new tastes. The two most important plantation zones in the Americas were Brazil and the Caribbean; they consumed, quite literally, the vast majority of enslaved peoples brought from Africa during the nearly four centuries of the trans-Atlantic slave trade. During the seventeenth and eighteenth centuries, the Caribbean became a crucial source of sugar for several northern European empires, supplying an expanding consumption of this addictive food and driving economic expansion and social change in the process.

In the eighteenth century, the French Antilles far outstripped the British and Spanish West Indies in both population and production. France's colonies included Martinique and Guadeloupe in the eastern

Caribbean and Guiana on the north coast of South America. But its most important possession was Saint-Domingue. The most profitable plantation colony in the New World, this territory was the size of Maryland and produced 40 percent of Europe's sugar and 60 percent of its coffee. In the process, it consumed more enslaved workers from Africa than did any other New World society after Brazil. Life on the plantations of Saint-Domingue was brutal, and a third to a half of those slaves who survived the crossing from Africa died within a few years of their arrival. Discipline was maintained through regular use of torture and terror against the enslaved. Some workers resisted by escaping the plantations, and some struck back by using poison against their masters. Nevertheless, most whites in the colony, like those elsewhere in the Americas, felt confident that they were in control of their slaves.[1]

However, in August 1791, a massive slave revolution began in Saint-Domingue. Launched by a carefully constructed coalition of African and island-born plantation workers, the insurrection forced France to proclaim the end of slavery throughout its empire in less than three years. In 1802, when Napoléon's troops attempted to restore the old colonial system, soldiers of African descent who had been French citizens for half a decade fought back in both Guadeloupe, where they were defeated by the French, and Saint-Domingue, where they emerged victorious. On January 1, 1804, their leaders transformed Saint-Domingue into an independent American nation. They called it Haiti, the name once used by the indigenous inhabitants. In doing so, they announced that they had not only secured their freedom and independence, but had also avenged the long-dead indigenous communities that had been decimated and enslaved after Columbus arrived.

The revolutionary transformation in the French Caribbean during these years had a profound impact in the Atlantic world. It led directly to a major reconfiguration of imperial power in the Americas, since it was Napoléon Bonaparte's defeat in Haiti that caused him to sell France's territory of Louisiana to the United States. Ironically, therefore, Haiti's freedom led to the expansion and solidification of slavery in the United States as new slave states were created in the territory of the Louisiana Purchase. The plantations and slave society in Cuba also expanded dramatically in the wake of the Haitian Revolution, providing sugar that Haiti no longer shipped across the Atlantic.

At the same time, the revolution also struck a resounding blow against the institution of slavery and the racial ideologies used to protect and justify it. The 1791 uprising in Saint-Domingue is the only such revolt that succeeded in destroying slavery in the society where it took place. And it did more than that: It propelled the radical expansion of French citizenship, which was extended to more than a half-million men and women of African descent in the Caribbean. For, as a direct result of the slave revolution in Saint-Domingue, the National Convention abolished slavery in the French empire on February 4, 1794. Emancipation was therefore confirmed in Saint-Domingue but also instituted in Guadeloupe and French Guiana—and even briefly in Saint Lucia during a French occupation—although not in Martinique, which was occupied by the British starting in 1794. During the 1790s, men of African descent sat in the various French parliaments as representatives of the colonies. In a dramatic shift from traditional forms of imperial governance, French laws were to be applied uniformly across the empire. Although emancipation created new forms of racism and coercion and was ultimately reversed in Guadeloupe and Guiana, its example posed a dramatic challenge to the existing imperial order, as did the creation of Haiti as an independent black state.

The era of slave revolution in the French Caribbean was a turning point in the history of the Atlantic slave system. It was an essential part not only of the history of the islands but also of the history of New World slavery, of U.S. history during the early republic, of Latin American independence, and of the emergence of the nation-state in the nineteenth century. It came in the wake of, and was influenced by, the successful revolt of the North American colonies, and it was intimately tied to the revolutionary transformation of continental France during the same period. Colonial institutions transferred revolutionary ideas across the Atlantic in both directions. The complex interaction of events and decisions in France and the Caribbean produced new conceptions of democracy, human rights, and citizenship. Indeed, it is difficult, if not impossible, to understand either set of transformations without understanding the other. The slave revolutions of the Caribbean, then, were an integral part of the "Age of Revolution," whose political, economic, and cultural shock waves resonate to the present day.

THE FRENCH CARIBBEAN
IN THE EIGHTEENTH CENTURY

France established its first Caribbean outpost in 1625 on the tiny island of Saint Christopher (today, Saint Kitts), where the English had arrived late the previous year. It took ten more years for royal officials to organize the colonization of the larger islands of Martinique and Guadeloupe, whose native Carib people had kept the Spanish at bay for more than a century. Colonists in these islands planted tobacco and, very early on, submitted to a ruling hierarchy, first in the form of colonization companies and, starting in 1674, under direct royal rule.[2]

French Saint-Domingue, in contrast, began as outlaw territory. In the early seventeenth century, Spain had forced its colonists to abandon the western portion of their colony of Santo Domingo; the high mountains dividing the island made it impossible for Spanish authorities to prevent Dutch merchants from trading with ranchers and farmers along the long western coastline. Once vacant, however, this coast—and the thriving livestock herds left behind by the Spanish—attracted a mostly male population of adventurers, naval deserters, castaways, and indentured servants fleeing the French colonies of Guadeloupe and Martinique. Hunting wild cattle and selling leather and *boucan* (smoked meat) to passing ships, they became known as buccaneers. After 1640, as the population of livestock declined, the buccaneers increasingly turned to piracy.[3]

French authorities claimed leadership of these men and in 1664 sent a governor to oversee colonization of the island of Tortuga and the nearby coast of Spanish Santo Domingo. The French settlers called the island Saint-Domingue, and this became the name of the colony they established on its western side. The French navy used the buccaneers in attacks on Spanish-American forts but also encouraged immigration by colonists more interested in growing tobacco, indigo, or sugar. In the 1690s, French authorities began giving naval commissions to pirate chiefs to get them to disband their crews. Some of the wealthiest used the looted Spanish silver to buy the land and slaves they needed to become planters.

Saint-Domingue followed a trajectory already traced in Martinique and Guadeloupe, where planters tried a variety of different crops but ultimately focused on sugar. The exigencies of sugar production would shape life in all three colonies during the eighteenth century. Unlike tobacco or cotton, sugar must be dramatically transformed after it is planted and harvested. After nine to fifteen months of growth, ripe sugar cane must be crushed within a few days of being cut, or the sugar produced will be of inferior quality. The cane juice must then be expertly boiled and processed for days before the sucrose solution will crystallize. For this reason, even as early as 1700, a sugar plantation was as much a factory as a farm. Planters invested in expensive refining equipment, counting on years of profitable crops. The more land they could plant and the more workers they had tending and processing the cane, the faster they could recoup their outlay. Sugar was most profitable for the biggest planters and for those who could bend their workers to the industrial discipline that the crop imposed.

Though it was settled decades after Martinique and Guadeloupe, Saint-Domingue soon became France's most significant possession. By the middle of the eighteenth century, the colony was the world's largest sugar exporter, producing more sugar than all of Britain's West Indies colonies put together. There were a number of reasons for Saint-Domingue's productivity. The colony was ten times as large as Martinique and Guadeloupe combined, and its fertile coastal plains were large enough for eighteenth-century sugar estates to reach their maximum size. Planters invested heavily in their estates; in 1763, for instance, when the colony received permission to export a more profitable kind of refined sugar to France, the wealthiest planters rapidly upgraded their refineries. The colonial administration also funded irrigation projects that transformed arid zones into prime land for sugar cultivation. By the end of the century, nearly every sugar district in Saint-Domingue had a laboriously negotiated irrigation network that not only watered the fields but also powered expensive water mills that crushed canes more efficiently than animal-powered machines. This sugar industry, furthermore, had a broad impact on the French economy. Up to three-quarters of the plantation products imported by France from its colonies were reexported to other European countries in a trade that produced an important merchant class in the port cities.[4]

Saint-Domingue was divided into three provinces, whose separation and varied geography made them almost like different colonies. High mountain ranges divided French Saint-Domingue from Spanish Santo Domingo and also divided the French provinces from one another, making travel between them by land very difficult. The north province contained the colony's commercial capital, Le Cap, then also referred to as Cap Français and now called Cap Haitien. Located on the major Atlantic sailing routes and surrounded by the fertile northern plain, Le Cap became the largest city in Saint-Domingue. As the place where most French immigrants and African captives first touched Caribbean soil, Le Cap was a truly Atlantic city. In many ways, it was more connected to France than the official colonial capital, Port-au-Prince. With governors and other high administrators maintaining residences there and the colony's leading cultural institutions—theaters, printing presses, a scientific academy—located there, Le Cap was the showplace for private and government architecture by the 1780s.

On the far side of the island, Saint-Domingue's south province was the most isolated from Atlantic commerce. A journey to the southern coast from France involved sailing around a treacherous peninsula and took commercial captains far out of their way. For this reason, the south was more connected to other parts of the Caribbean than to France. Southern planters sold their produce to Dutch, British, and eventually U.S. ships, violating French law. They also bought many of their slaves as contraband. Colonists in this region were poorer, more likely to be Creole (that is, born in the colonies), and less likely to abandon their estates for life in Europe. There was also a large and deep-rooted population of free people of color in the province; indeed, in many parishes they outnumbered whites.[5]

The west province, sheltered by the colony's two peninsulas, was home to the capital city of Port-au-Prince. Though less convenient for shipping than the north province, the west province contained the colony's largest plain, at Croix des Bouquets. The focus of massive investment after 1750, the west had more plantations than the north, not only in sugar but also in coffee and indigo, by 1789.[6]

In the early years of colonization in the French Caribbean, as in other New World societies, plantations were worked by a mixture of indentured servants from Europe and slaves imported from Africa. But as the sugar economy expanded and gobbled up most of the land in the French islands, the number of indentured servants declined rapidly. Planters in Martinique and Guadeloupe turned so rapidly to enslaved African men and women that by the 1650s, about a decade after sugar was introduced, black slaves outnumbered free colonists there. By the eighteenth century, slaves made up approximately 90 percent of the population on both islands. This pattern of racial domination and exploitation allowed colonists to reap great profits from their plantations, but it created profound social and political tensions.

Saint-Domingue's sugar barons invested in human power as well as in their estates. They commonly described their wealth not in terms of cane acreage or tons of sugar exports, but instead in terms of the hundreds of enslaved workers they controlled. The pace of slave imports into Saint-Domingue, which was the major destination of most French slavers, expanded dramatically in response to the sugar boom. Between 1700 and 1725, Saint-Domingue recorded annual imports of approximately 2,000 men, women, and children. The average number doubled in the next twenty-five years and then doubled again from 1751 to 1775. In 1777 slave ships disembarked roughly 22,000 Africans, and by 1790 the number reached an all-time annual high of nearly 48,000. Surviving records show that Saint-Domingue imported 685,000 Africans between 1700 and 1791, up to half of them in the last fifteen years of this period. The number, furthermore, does not account for the many slaves brought into the colony illegally by slavers who operated between Caribbean islands. Constant imports were needed because between 5 and 10 percent of Saint-Domingue's plantation slaves died of overwork, malnutrition, disease, and harsh treatment every year. Europe's insatiable appetite for expensive sugar and the growing efficiency of the slave trade meant that exporting an extra barrel or two of sugar would more than pay for replacing the Africans sacrificed to the cane.[7]

By 1790, after several years of record-breaking African imports, there were at least a half-million slaves in Saint-Domingue; they outnumbered white colonists by more than ten to one. Up to two-thirds of the slaves, and therefore a majority of the people of the colony, were African-born. Early on, a majority hailed from West Africa and were usually referred to in the colony as *Aradas*. This group was ultimately outnumbered, however, by arrivals from west-central Africa, often from the kingdom of the Kongo and surrounding regions. They were referred to as *Congos* in the colony. Religious ideas and practices, languages, agricultural techniques, political ideologies, and military knowledge and experience (notably among Congo slaves, many of whom were veterans of central African wars of the late eighteenth century) were all brought into Saint-Domingue, shaping its culture, landscape, and ultimately the course of its revolutionary transformation.[8]

On the plantations themselves, the imbalance between the enslaved and the white masters and overseers was extreme. Sugar plantations were much larger on average than plantations that cultivated cotton or tobacco, as did most in the U.S. South. The average sugar plantation had about two hundred slaves, but in the colony's two largest sugar zones, the northern plain behind the city of Cap Français and the Croix des Bouquets plain behind Port-au-Prince, over three hundred men, women, and children worked hundreds of acres on the largest estates. Some investors controlled as many as a thousand people on neighboring properties. On many large plantations, the planter, a bookkeeper, a plantation manager, a sugar refiner, and perhaps a surgeon were the only whites directing the work of three hundred slaves. Smaller plantations might have only one or two resident whites. The severe discipline necessary to control these workers made plantation life unpleasant for Europeans, especially unseasoned newcomers. About a quarter of Saint-Domingue's planters lived in France, leaving the disagreeable business of administering their tropical properties to managers. It was even more common for colonists to leave their wives and families at home in France. Only those whites born in Saint-Domingue—who, like slaves born in the colony, were called Creoles—were likely to live on estates with their wives and legitimate children.[9]

The treatment of slaves in the French Caribbean was, in principle, governed by *The Code Noir* (Document 1), which was issued by King Louis XIV in 1685. In practice, however, planters and managers ignored many of the provisions of this document, particularly those that provided protection to the slaves. Violence was a central part of plantation society in Saint-Domingue, Martinique, and Guadeloupe. Masters and their employers maintained estate discipline through the regular torture and execution of rebellious field workers. They often meted out punishments publicly to terrorize other slaves, forcing them to watch and sometimes participate. Provisions in *The Code Noir* that limited acceptable forms of torture to whipping were never effectively enforced. This violent order was, of course, not unique to the French Caribbean; British planters in nearby Jamaica, for instance, had the same life-and-death power over their slaves.

During their long working days, Saint-Domingue's plantation slaves were divided into specialized work gangs and usually labored under the supervision of other slaves. These *commandeurs* (drivers), who were named by the planter or manager, were often island-born. They formed the core of a plantation's slave elite, which might include a dozen other skilled individuals deemed reliable by the master, such as carpenters, blacksmiths, cart drivers, and barrel makers. Planters tended to appoint only men to such positions. They were generally exempted from field work. On many estates, therefore, women made up more than half of the first work gang, which performed the heaviest labor like digging the wide shallow ditches where the cane would be planted.[10]

Domestic work was the only relatively privileged area in which women predominated. Like the *commandeurs* in the fields, a slave woman often supervised the slaves who worked in the master's house. Housekeepers frequently performed sexual work for their master as well. Because Europeans came to Saint-Domingue not to settle but to make their fortunes, nearly every colonist took a mistress, frequently a slave. It is difficult to generalize about these relationships. Masters reinforced their power by raping slave women, using sex as a weapon, but sometimes they also established long-term ties with enslaved women, fathering mixed-race children and often freeing them. Enough colonists did free their sons and daughters from slavery that royal officials counted roughly 24,800 free nonwhites in the colony, alongside 30,800 whites, in 1789. At least several hundred of the free people of color were wealthy planters and merchants. Members of this free colored elite owned and exploited slaves much like whites did. Identifying themselves as French colonists, they played a critical role in destabilizing colonial society after 1789. Though most were not opposed to slavery, their attack on racism opened the way for the slave revolt that became the Haitian Revolution.[11]

Many free people of color got a foothold in the economy of the colony by cultivating not sugar but two other important crops: indigo and coffee. Although the production of indigo dye required heavy field labor and a delicate refining process, only a few dozen slaves were needed to do the work. After 1760, coffee became Saint-Domingue's second most important plantation crop. Because coffee needs cooler temperatures than sugar, most of the new plantations were built in the hills, where sugar cane could not be planted. Like indigo, coffee could be profitably grown with far fewer slaves than needed for sugar. The median size of Saint-Domingue's coffee plantations was thirty-three slaves.[12]

Although they owned the largest enslaved population in the Caribbean, Saint-Domingue's planters also boasted one of the most secure slave regimes in the region. The security of the master class rested on cooperation between whites and free people of color. In the 1730s, a local police force called the *maréchaussée* was founded to supplement the colonial militia in the policing of the slaves. From its very inception, the *maréchaussée* used free men of color for the difficult physical work of patrolling the roads, searching slave huts, and chasing escapees in the trackless interior. In the 1770s, furthermore, as the number of human imports from Africa continued to rise, colonial governors—who found that both island-born whites and French immigrants would revolt rather than accept increased militia duties—ordered free colored militiamen to help the constabulary with slave-policing duties.

These free men of color, however, received little reward for their contribution to the security of the colony; indeed, their recruitment into military service was part of an administrative project to increase the separation between white and free nonwhite individuals in the colony. Since the 1600s, a number of locally respected free people of color had been treated as full citizens and allowed to serve as militia officers and work as doctors. French immigrants to the colony sought their daughters and sisters as wives. But by the late eighteenth century, they were subjected to an increasing number of laws that discriminated against them because of their African descent. Attempting to prove themselves as virtuous Frenchmen, hundreds of free colored militiamen volunteered to join royal French troops to fight in the American Revolution in 1779. After being poorly treated by their own officers at the battle of Savannah, their most determined leaders decided to petition royal officials in France for changes in the colonial racial laws. However, only after the beginning of the French Revolution did free colored activists find the opening they needed to press for equal rights.

Poor whites in Saint-Domingue also had grievances that would explode during the early years of the French Revolution. After France lost Quebec in the Seven Years War that ended in 1763, immigration to Saint-Domingue had increased dramatically. Though some of these new colonists grew prosperous planting coffee, most dreams of quickly making an "American" fortune were frustrated. Wealthy planters owned much of the land and dominated local society. The military commanders who ran the colony's government treated unemployed and propertyless colonists harshly. These immigrants, whom the slaves mocked with the name *petits blancs,* resented the royal administrators, the established white planters and merchants, and the wealthy mixed race families, who were scorned for their African ancestry but had successful plantations, farms, and businesses. Poor colonists wanted opportunities, even if those came at the expense of groups they believed to be unfairly privileged.

The wealthiest white planters and merchants in Saint-Domingue had their own complaints against the colonial system. Many resented France's trade laws, which prohibited them from selling their sugar directly to the profitable foreign market and from buying slaves from foreigners. They spoke out against "ministerial tyranny"—the idea that French officials in Versailles could overrule Saint-Domingue's elites in commercial or political matters that colonists understood best. In 1784 and 1785, for instance, they bitterly opposed a royal attempt to humanize slave conditions with a law that would require planters to provide workers with a minimum of food, clothing, and rest. The Supreme Council of Le Cap refused to register the decrees, and they were never put into practice. In 1787, the royal government responded by shutting down the Council of Le Cap, an action that left many colonists bitter and frustrated about their lack of input in colonial government.

The debate over these reforms presaged the conflicts and accusations that would become commonplace during the revolutionary years. Some administrators, as well as Enlightenment writers Louis-Sébastien Mercier and Denis Diderot, warned that the unchecked brutality of planters might provoke a slave revolution and argued that the state had the duty to reign in their abuses (Document 2). Planters insisted that violence was necessary to keep the slaves in check and that the intervention of the state in master-slave relations—an intervention they saw as "abolitionist"—was likely to stir up a slave insurrection. Masters and administrators were not the only ones attentive to these debates, it seems. Starting in 1791, many slave insurgents presented themselves as defenders of the king of France, probably at least in part because of royal attempts to better their living conditions.

Interestingly, eighteenth-century Saint-Domingue had a comparatively small rebel tradition until 1791. Neighboring Jamaica, for instance, had at least eight major slave uprisings between 1673 and 1766, as well as the formation of strong "maroon" communities of escaped slaves that forced the British to sign peace treaties with them in the 1730s. Large and aggressive maroon groups did not exist in Saint-Domingue, in part because there were few parts of the colony that were not settled with plantations, even in the mountains. Saint-Domingue's maroons may have been less militant than those in Jamaica because the French colony was so large and had so many legally free people of color. Despite requirements that all free people of color be able to prove their liberty, there were many isolated parishes where an escapee could eke out a living as a peasant, hunter, or cattle smuggler. Maroon groups did not play a significant role in preparing the 1791 uprising. But the ongoing practice of short-term escape from plantations did help create connections between slaves on different plantations. So did the religious rituals that brought slaves together, one of which was described in a famous passage by the Martinican-born lawyer and writer Médéric-Louis-Élie Moreau de Saint-Méry (Document 3).

Saint-Domingue's most significant episode of prerevolutionary slave resistance began around 1752, when the charismatic slave Makandal was alleged to be poisoning whites and their livestock in the north province. This rumor created a kind of hysteria among colonists. Although they captured and executed Makandal in 1758, his ability to create networks of resistance linking workers on different plantations provided an example for the successful revolt of 1791. The stories that circulated about his exploits both among masters and slaves helped keep alive the idea that a dramatic change in the social order was possible.

Saint-Domingue's rapid transformation from a near-empty frontier to a densely populated economic powerhouse made it ripe with tensions and fissures. The plantation economy transformed the landscape, and the circulation of products, people, and ideas integrated the colony's port towns into the Atlantic world as well. The white population was divided in complex ways, and many whites were waiting for an opportunity to transform their relationship with France and improve their economic possibilities. Free people of color, many of them wealthy and content with the economic order, were frustrated by legal discrimination and hoped to challenge the racial order. Most important, the vast majority of people—the enslaved—lived under a brutal regime, and many were ready to revolt when they saw an opening. By the late 1780s, then, the stage was set for an intertwined set of struggles over the status of free people of color, administration of the colonies, and the question of slavery itself.

THE REVOLUTION BEGINS, 1789–1791

In July 1789, slaves began gathering on the docks in Saint-Pierre, Martinique. They were mobilized by a rumor that the king of France had freed them and that local authorities were attempting to quash news of the decree. Many refused to work, and two threatening letters demanding freedom were delivered to the governor (Document 4). This uprising took place before news from Paris of the fall of the Bastille arrived in Martinique. But slaves were aware of the calling of the Estates General—a body of elected representatives of France's nobility, clergy, and "Third Estate" (the rest of the population) that assembled to advise the king—and of abolitionist activity in France, both of which seem to have spurred on their hope of imminent liberation. The revolt was quickly suppressed, but it was the first of a series of such revolts.[13]

The slaves were not the only people who were eager to participate in the revolutionary changes in the French empire. In 1787, King Louis XVI announced plans to hold a meeting of the Estates General to address France's fiscal crisis. Absentee planters hoped to represent

Saint-Domingue in the body and began to form committees in France, but royal officials rebuffed them. Nevertheless, in late 1788 and early 1789, without official approval, colonists on the island formed assemblies to write suggestions for reform and elect representatives. These men traveled to Paris to press for admittance into the Estates General, but they too encountered opposition. In 1788, Jacques-Pierre Brissot, a writer and abolitionist, had started an antislavery group called the Société des Amis des Noirs (Society of the Friends of the Blacks), modeled after a group founded in London the year before. Members lobbied for the abolition of the slave trade and the gradual elimination of slavery in the colonies, pointing out that the claim of the planter representatives that they represented the entire population of Saint-Domingue was absurd and misleading.

Though the colonial deputies did not get the number of seats they requested, six were admitted to the meetings at Versailles by July 1789. By this time, part of the Estates General had boldly transformed itself into a National Assembly, claiming to represent the will of the entire nation and openly confronting the king. Soon, representatives from Martinique and Guadeloupe were also admitted to the body. By then, the questions of tax reform that had driven the initial calling of the Estates General had ballooned into much broader political questions about citizenship and representation. On August 26, 1789, the delegates approved the Declaration of the Rights of Man, which delineated a sweeping array of rights meant to provide the foundation for the writing of a French constitution. Planters and their friends in Paris described this document as the "terror of the colonists," a potential threat to slavery. Alarmed by the direction of the French Revolution, they formed a society to monitor and intervene in the situation, called the Club Massiac after its meeting place, the Hotel Massiac in Paris. One of the members published the "Overview of the Constitution of Saint-Domingue," arguing that Saint-Domingue was not part of France but rather a self-ruling province.[14]

Saint-Domingue's wealthy men of color were more enthusiastic than most planters about the revolutionary changes, which gave them a chance to step up demands for an end to racial discrimination. Vincent Ogé, a wealthy merchant from Cap Français, was in Paris on business. In late August at the Hotel Massiac, he presented an argument in favor of granting rights to free people of color, stressing the need "to preserve our properties and to stop the disaster that threatens us." Perhaps to convince the conservative white members of the club that they needed free colored allies, Ogé was deliberately unclear about his stance on slavery. Nevertheless, he did evoke the danger of a slave revolt. "Is liberty made for all men?" he asked. "I believe so. Must it be given to all men? Again, I believe so." He hinted that he had his own proposal to avoid bloodshed. The members of the Club Massiac, however, had little to say to Ogé or to Julien Raimond, another free man of color who also presented his ideas.[15]

Meanwhile, several dozen Parisian free people of color—mostly artisans and servants—met with Étienne-Louis-Hector Dejoly, a French lawyer and member of the Society of the Friends of the Blacks. In September, Raimond and Ogé joined this group and, along with Dejoly, were elected its leaders. They petitioned the Constituent Assembly (which had replaced the National Assembly), pointing out that the colonial deputies from Saint-Domingue who had been admitted in July did not represent the free people of color because only whites had participated in their election (Document 5). The assembly's Verification Committee began hearings to investigate the issue. The testimony and submissions of the free people of color brought Raimond in contact with the Abbé Grégoire, a priest and deputy from eastern France who was well known for his position that Jews should be recognized as French citizens. Grégoire quickly became a vocal supporter of the free colored cause, using Raimond to educate himself about the colonial situation. In December of 1789, Grégoire published a pamphlet supporting the demands of the free people of color, as he did again the following year with his "Letter to Those Who Love Mankind" (Document 7).

Facing mounting controversy over free colored citizenship, the Constituent Assembly voted to form the Colonial Committee to study colonial representation. Chosen on March 4, 1790, it was mostly composed of deputies favorable to planter interests. On March 8, the committee recommended that the colonies be allowed to write their own constitutions. When the Parisian free colored group and its allies pushed for a clear statement of whether men of color would be allowed to participate in this process, the committee produced the "Instructions of March 28," which again avoided the racial issue (Document 6). Planters took this as a victory, assuming that they had the right to exclude free people of color from their assemblies. But Vincent Ogé believed that, since the document didn't list race among the criteria for voting, he and other propertied men of color were qualified to participate in the elections for a new Colonial Assembly.

The most restless group in Saint-Domingue in the first twelve months after the passage of the Declaration of Rights was made up of the colony's poor whites. Colonial elections in late 1789 had given a voice to a population of white immigrants, soldiers, and plantation employees who deeply resented the royal government and the wealthy planter class. Meeting in the town of Saint Marc in 1790, a Colonial Assembly dominated by these so-called radical whites criticized the royal governor, threatened to abolish the high interest rates that French merchants charged colonists, and demanded a strict application of the laws discriminating against free people of color. These actions angered not only the free people of color but also the royal officials and commercial interests in the colony. In early August 1790, the governor used royal troops reinforced by free colored militiamen to shut down the Saint Marc Colonial Assembly. While eighty-five members of the assembly went to France to appeal their case to the Constituent Assembly, sympathizers calling themselves "Patriots" rallied in towns across Saint-Domingue against what they described as a "counterrevolutionary" coalition of rich whites and free people of color with the royal government. But on October 12, 1790, the Parisian legislature ruled against the Saint Marc Colonial Assembly, whose actions were seen as a dangerous bid for colonial autonomy. Nevertheless, French legislators also conceded that they would not pass any laws about colonial civil rights unless specifically asked by the colonists, once again avoiding a decision on the free colored question.

Meanwhile, Vincent Ogé, who had secretly left France for Saint-Domingue, wrote a letter insisting that the colonial governor allow free colored voters to participate in local elections. When the governor flatly denied Ogé's requests, Ogé gathered several hundred friends and neighbors in the parish of Grand Rivière. After turning back a unit of the Cap Français militia twice their number, Ogé's troops had to flee before a second force five times larger than they were. Retreating to the east, they crossed over into Santo Domingo, where Spanish authorities returned them to the French. Ogé and twenty-three others were publicly executed in Cap Français in February 1791 (Document 8).

By spring 1791, the unrest caused by radical whites in the Saint Marc Colonial Assembly and the violence Ogé had provoked began to worry deputies in the Paris Constituent Assembly. Many were alarmed by the increasing chaos in colonies that were highly important to France's economy and were dismayed by radical whites' demands for colonial autonomy. In April 1791, news arrived in Paris of yet more trouble in Saint-Domingue: poor white Patriots in Port-au-Prince had convinced newly arrived French troops to join them in revolutionary action against the "tyrannical" royal government. In a riot, crowds killed Colonel Mauduit Duplessis, the royal commander of the city. The Patriots took over the city, and the royal government moved to Cap Français.

Faced with this volatile situation, in May 1791 deputies in the Constituent Assembly crafted a compromise that they hoped would provide both order and justice. They decided to send more troops to Saint-Domingue. They understood, however, that those reinforcements needed specific instructions about the vexed question of free colored citizenship. While many colonial whites in Paris had been vociferously resisting granting rights to free coloreds, Julien Raimond had continued energetically demanding an end to discrimination and the granting of political rights to his class (Document 9). He had powerful supporters. Speaking before the assembly, the influential deputy Maximilien Robespierre stressed that he saw no difference between the rights of Frenchmen and the rights of colonial free men of color. Even representatives from port cities were increasingly sympathetic to Raimond's argument that his class was Saint-Domingue's best hope.

On May 15, 1791, contradicting its earlier decision to not legislate civil rights in the colonies, the National Assembly voted to give full French citizenship to free men of color whose mothers and fathers had both been free and who owned sufficient property (Document 11; see Figure 1). The color line had been broken, and colonial advocates in Paris immediately sent warnings to the colony. The news infuriated the colonial Patriots, who vowed to fight a measure they blamed on French abolitionists. Especially in Port-au-Prince, many radical whites loudly announced that they would never accept free colored citizenship. Wealthy free men of color rejoiced; but as they realized that colonists in France were delaying arrival of the new law, they began to arm themselves. In June and July, fighting broke out between groups of radical whites and free coloreds in Port-au-Prince as well as on the nearby Cul-de-Sac plain. The situation was less tense in Cap Français, where the Patriots had less influence. Indeed, Le Cap was preparing for the meeting of the new Colonial Assembly in August when smoke began to rise from the northern plain.

Figure 1. *Mortals Are Equal.*

This anonymous engraving, probably produced in 1791, presents an allegorical representation of the granting of rights to free men of color. The original caption explains the image as follows: "Reason, characterized by a woman with the sacred fire of the love of the fatherland on her head, places the white man and the man of color at the same level. Behind him is a cornucopia, a banana tree, and fertile countryside. He is leaning on the Rights of Man and holds in his other hand the Decree of May 15 concerning the free people of color. Reason is being pushed by Nature, who is wearing a crown of fruit and has fourteen breasts. She is standing on a goatskin bag from which are emerging the demon of Aristocracy; of Egoism, which through its avarice wants to have everything; Injustice; [and] the demon of Discord or of Insurrection, ready to cross the ocean, which is in the background."

Bibliothèque Nationale.

23

FROM SLAVE REVOLUTION TO EMANCIPATION, 1791–1794

By the middle of 1791, the French Caribbean had been wracked by political conflict for two years. Enslaved people had been watching and had occasionally taken action: They had rebelled in Martinique in 1789, and they attempted to organize insurrections in Guadeloupe in April 1790 and at Port-Salut in the southern province of Saint-Domingue in January 1791. In the latter two cases, however, conspiring leaders were arrested before they could set their plans in motion. Many planters worried that revolutionary and abolitionist ideas would inspire more plots; others remained convinced of the fidelity and servility of their slaves.

The struggles on both sides of the Atlantic had not yet produced any changes in slavery itself. It seemed possible that the institution would survive the French Revolution, as it had the American Revolution a decade earlier. But the course of Caribbean history changed dramatically in August 1791, when a massive and well-coordinated insurrection began in Saint-Domingue's north province. The speed and fury of the uprising shocked and overwhelmed planters, many of whom believed that their slaves did not have the capacity to carry out such a revolt. Many whites were killed on their plantations, while the rest fled to the safety of Le Cap. Workers burned cane fields, ransacked houses, and destroyed plantations' industrial machinery (Documents 13 and 14).

The revolt was planned, quite effectively, by delegates from plantations throughout the northern plain, many of them drivers on the plantations, who met on August 14 in the woods near a plantation. At a religious ceremony that probably took place a week later at another location, conspirators apparently used a sacrifice to seal their pact (Document 12). Originally planned for the night of Wednesday, August 24, probably because insurgents hoped to capture Le Cap and destroy the planter assembly that was gathering there, the insurrection broke out two days early when some conspirators acted prematurely. Despite several attempts, the rebels were not able to take Le Cap, but they did quickly gain control of much of the northern plain. In the first two weeks of the rebellion, slaves rose up in twenty-three of the twenty-seven parishes in the north province, destroying over two hundred sugar plantations and twelve hundred coffee estates. Though the rebels were initially about a thousand strong, whites counted between ten and twenty thousand by early September. In the weeks following the August uprising, they managed to consolidate their gains and transform themselves into a powerful insurgent army that held out against repeated counterattacks by French troops and volunteers and took many prisoners (Documents 15 and 17).[16]

Enslaved Africans were a vital part of the rebellion in the north, but the movement's leaders were mostly creole slaves who had been born in the colony. There were also a number of free men of African descent—most of them free black (that is, not of mixed European-African ancestry)—among the insurgent's early leaders. The most famous of these was Toussaint Bréda, who would soon take the last name Louverture. He had been born in slavery but was a free man by 1779, growing coffee on leased land and using rented slave workers. But the free colored population in the north was quite divided, and many joined in the effort to put down the rebellion.

Even as revolt spread across the north, white Patriots in the south and west provinces refused to accept the May 15, 1791, decree giving civil rights to wealthy free men of color. The latter, meanwhile, were not willing to yield the rights Paris had given them. In September 1791, members of the two groups clashed, as they had a few months earlier, in the plain outside Port-au-Prince, arming slaves to help them. In October, they negotiated a peace, but this broke down in November when news arrived from Paris that the Constituent Assembly in Paris had canceled the limited free colored political rights it had granted in the May 15 law. Into early 1792, groups of free coloreds and whites continued to fight in the region. Alarmed at the rapid disintegration of estate discipline caused by the recruitment of slaves into these battles, wealthy planters in key districts abandoned the urban Patriots and negotiated their own treaties with local men of color. In these treaties, the whites acknowledged that free men of color should have access to full political rights.[17]

As these events were transforming Saint-Domingue, much was changing in Paris as well. In 1791, the Constituent Assembly had written and approved France's first written constitution. These deputies then stepped down, and a group of newly elected representatives took their place to rule France, with King Louis XVI as a constitutional monarch. Among the new legislators was the abolitionist Jacques-Pierre Brissot. Brissot and his supporters criticized Louis XVI's administration and argued that French revolutionaries needed to liberate the rest of Europe. They crafted a response to the news of insurrection in Saint-Domingue, which incited a range of reactions from political figures in Europe (Documents 18–20). The strategy of the Brissotins was to present Saint-Domingue's free men of color as the best defense against the growing slave rebellion. Under their influence, on April 4, 1792, the Legislative Assembly in Paris voted another colonial law, reversing the September decree of the Constituent Assembly (Document 21). The law now extended citizenship to all free men of color, urging them to join with other colonists in repressing the rebel slaves.

The Legislative Assembly had sent three revolutionary commissioners to Saint-Domingue in late 1791. They had begun negotiations with the rebel leaders Jean-François and Georges Biassou, who proposed a deal in which the French would free a certain number of prominent insurgents, while the rest would return to the plantations (Documents 16 and 17). The negotiations, however, had broken down relatively quickly, and the war continued. In June 1792, Paris sent troops to Saint-Domingue under the command of a second team of commissioners, whose assignment was to oversee the controversial extension of citizenship to the free people of color granted in the April 4, 1792, decree and to crush the insurrection and restore slavery. The assembly appears to have chosen at least two of the new commissioners for their opposition to colonial racism. Léger Félicité Sonthonax, the leader of the commission, knew Brissot well and had written an article supporting the extension of rights to free people of color. Another commissioner, Étienne Polverel, had also worked on behalf of free colored rights. Arriving in Saint-Domingue in September 1792, the new commissioners soon came to rely heavily on the newly enfranchised men of color, promoting them to both military and administrative positions. One of the new citizens, Laurent Jolicoeur, petitioned for the freedom of one of his slaves, in the process drawing on Enlightenment theater and reconfiguring ideas of racial identity and sexuality in interesting ways (Document 23). Whites complained about this "favoritism," but the colony soon faced a challenge even greater than just defeating the rebel armies.[18]

On August 10, 1792, revolutionaries in Paris had arrested King Louis XVI and Queen Marie Antoinette after discovering their secret correspondence with the Austrian emperor, against whom France had declared war on April 20. In September, the Legislative Assembly proclaimed France a republic. Its members then stepped down for the election of a new set of representatives. This new body, known as the National Convention, began to write a new constitution that eliminated the monarchy and placed all power in the hands of the legislators. The legislators also tried the former king for treason, and he was executed on January 21, 1793. This act led to war with England and Spain. Both kingdoms had their own Caribbean colonies, and soon the imperial war spread to Saint-Domingue.

Since the early days of the slave revolt, some Spanish colonial leaders had been unofficially supporting Saint-Domingue's rebel slaves. In May 1793, Spain expanded these efforts and began to award commissions and uniforms to the leaders of the ex-slave armies and to give land and liberty to their soldiers. In June, Toussaint became a Spanish officer. The British navy, meanwhile, blocked French ships from traveling to the Caribbean. In September 1793, at the invitation of counterrevolutionary colonists, British troops from Jamaica invaded Saint-Domingue, taking control of parts of the west and south provinces. In the eastern Caribbean, meanwhile, counterrevolutionary planters were also making overtures to the British. Slaves in the town of Trois-Rivières in Guadeloupe took advantage of this when they rose up and killed their masters, presenting their action as a defense of the besieged French Republic (Document 22).[19]

As Saint-Domingue was being invaded, a new governor, Thomas François Galbaud, arrived from France. People in Cap Français who criticized Sonthonax's reliance on the free men of color rallied around the conservative Galbaud, who was the son of a planter. When Sonthonax had Galbaud arrested on suspicion of plotting against him, the governor's supporters in Le Cap took up arms. Close to losing the colony's most important city to this counterrevolution, Sonthonax offered amnesty and freedom to the rebel bands camped in the surrounding plain in exchange for help against the revolution's enemies. (See Figure 2.)

A few thousand rebels accepted this offer and stormed into Le Cap, turning the tide against Galbaud's forces. Thousands of terrified colonists fled to North America, many taking their slaves. Meanwhile, desperate for more support in the battle against the Spanish and the British, Sonthonax steadily expanded his offer. On July 11, he announced that the families of all those who fought for France would also be freed. There were increasing calls for a much bolder move: the abolition of slavery throughout the colony. On August 29, 1793, after a major demonstration in Cap Français, Sonthonax declared the end of slavery in the north province (Document 24). In the south and west provinces, Sonthonax's colleague Polverel had similarly extended freedom to slaves fighting on the side of the revolution. In September and October 1793, as the British invasion began, he issued general emancipation decrees in these other two provinces.[20]

In Paris, the National Convention was also facing external war and

Figure 2. *The Armed* Nègre.

This engraving by a little-known artist named Fougea shows an armed father and son leaving their house, presumably on their way to fight for their freedom. On their door is pinned a paper that says "Decree of the [either *Court* or *Convention*] that returns liberty to the men of color." If the partial word is *Convention,* this would clearly date the image to 1794; if the word is *Court,* it might refer to the 1792 decree giving political rights to free men of color. The composition suggests a clear relationship between the decrees in Paris and the actions of slaves in the Caribbean. The image is heavily gendered in the way it contrasts the manly father and son with a weeping mother and child. The different genders of the children, for instance, are curiously emphasized in anatomically exaggerated representations of their bodies.

internal rebellion. In this period known as the Terror, deputies purged conservatives and even moderates like Brissot from their ranks, hoping to save the new French republic from internal and foreign enemies. It was in this context that news of the abolition of slavery in Saint-Domingue arrived in Paris, carried by the African-born free black Jean-Baptiste Belley and two other representatives from the colony. On February 4, 1794, the National Convention ratified the decisions of Sonthonax and Polverel, officially ending slavery throughout all French territories (Document 26). A mission was soon dispatched to the eastern Caribbean, where both Martinique and Guadeloupe had just been occupied by the British, to carry the decree of emancipation to the other French colonies. The new Constitution of 1795 contained specific antislavery language and affirmed that the colonies would have the very same laws as France itself. Henceforth, in principle, no geographical or ethnic limits could exclude people from being and acting as French citizens.

Within a few short years, the slave insurgents who rose up in Saint-Domingue in 1791 had managed to win both freedom and citizenship for all enslaved people in the French Caribbean. But the question of precisely what these new rights would mean would animate new conflicts and debates on both sides of the Atlantic in the years to come.

DEFINING EMANCIPATION, 1794–1798

In June 1794, news of the National Convention's decree of abolition was carried to the eastern Caribbean by an energetic commissioner named Victor Hugues. With only fifteen hundred soldiers accompanying him, Hugues boldly landed in Guadeloupe and, using emancipation as a weapon, rallied the island's enslaved and free people against the British and the counterrevolutionary colonists who supported them. Purging local society of royalists with a portable guillotine he had brought from France, Hugues nevertheless tried to keep the plantation system viable by requiring ex-slaves to work in the cane fields. This labor, he insisted, was how Guadeloupe's new citizens would repay the debt they owed the revolution for their freedom (Document 27).[21]

Hugues did, however, incorporate many former slaves into the island's government and military. Joined by prorevolutionary whites and former free men of color, these new citizen-soldiers gave Guadeloupe a powerful military force, which Hugues used to attack the

British on neighboring islands. French forces joined with local insurgents in Saint Vincent, Grenada, and Saint Lucia, conquering the latter for a brief period and forcing the British to send a major expedition across the Atlantic to counter French advances.

In addition to these military campaigns, Hugues authorized captains of private ships to serve as proxies for the French navy, attacking other ships and bringing their cargoes back to Guadeloupe. The revolutionary privateers, many of them heavily crewed by men of color who were ex-slaves, crippled Caribbean commerce for much of the time Hugues was in power. As many of the captured ships were North American, this privateering led to a conflict between the United States and France in the late 1790s. But Hugues's activities, together with events in Saint-Domingue, helped spread the political influence of the French Revolution in the Caribbean, contributing directly and indirectly to slave uprisings and pro-French revolts in Curaçao, on the Venezuelan coast, and in the British colony of Dominica. Martinique remained in the hands of the English, so slavery was maintained there. But one former slave in Guadeloupe succeeded in spreading emancipation when she managed to bring her brother, still enslaved in Martinique, to freedom (Document 28).[22]

As in the eastern Caribbean, the convergence of imperial war and internal conflict also shaped post-emancipation Saint-Domingue. But after 1794 the commanding figures were not European agents like Hugues, but instead men of African descent from the colony itself. In particular, Toussaint Louverture dominated political life in Saint-Domingue from 1794 until 1802.

For several months after Sonthonax's August 1793 emancipation proclamation, it seemed uncertain whether the French republic would hold on to Saint-Domingue. Although some insurgent leaders joined the French as soon as abolition was decreed, even in the north province most of the most important black generals, notably Louverture, remained allied with the Spanish (Document 25). In May 1794, however, apparently after he learned of the ratification of abolition by the National Convention, Louverture deserted the Spanish and joined the French. It was a turning point for the revolution in Saint-Domingue.

Louverture became one of the most important French officers fighting the Spanish and the British, who continued to pour resources and troops into the colony in the hope of securing it for their own empires. In 1795, after its forces had been mostly driven from northern Saint-Domingue, Spain signed a peace treaty with France. The

British were harder to get rid of. Yet by 1796, victories by Louverture and by André Rigaud, the free colored commander of the southern peninsula, were beginning to turn the tide against the British.[23]

By 1798, Louverture's military leadership had given French armies control over the north and west provinces of Saint-Domingue. His political skills, meanwhile, helped him cement his position as the leading French officer of color. Louverture was key among those who helped the French foil a March 1796 attempt by the commander of Cap Français, Colonel Jean-Louis Villatte, to overthrow the French general Étienne Laveaux. Villatte, described as a mulatto and suspected of racism toward black soldiers like Louverture, apparently hoped to ally himself with André Rigaud. For his help in defeating Villatte, Louverture was promoted to commander of the west province in May 1796. In 1797, the revolutionary government in Paris made him Saint-Domingue's top-ranking officer.

Yet Louverture saw himself as a political leader, not just a general. He began to maneuver against French officials who might overrule him, convincing Sonthonax to return to France in 1797, for example. In the same year, he acted with bold independence by negotiating directly with the British and Americans, despite the fact that the French government was in open conflict with both. This diplomacy achieved its goals, allowing Saint-Domingue to trade with Jamaican and U.S. ports so that coffee and sugar from the revived plantations could be exchanged for foreign goods, including guns and ammunition. The economic independence represented a kind of insurance, making it possible for Louverture to negotiate with a French government he was increasingly wary of.

As the 1790s wore on, the political leadership of France grew increasingly conservative, and exiled planters who opposed emancipation steadily gained more power over colonial policy. African-born Jean-Baptiste Belley eloquently defended emancipation (Document 30), as did Louverture and his ally Étienne Laveaux, who played a crucial role in passing a 1798 law that was meant to consolidate emancipation in the French Caribbean (Documents 31–33). Louverture also prepared for the potential conflict with France.[24]

In his growing independence, Louverture may have been influenced by the example of André Rigaud in the southern peninsula. The region had always been separated from the north province and from direct communication with France by geography. After the British occupation of much of the western province, this isolation increased, and the south essentially became a separate state: Rigaud established a quasi-autonomous government there, either out of necessity, as he claimed, or ambition, as others maintained. He named local officials, set up his own police system, and infuriated visiting French officers by practically expelling them from the province. Like Hugues in Guadeloupe, Rigaud also used his power to force former slaves to continue working on their plantations.

Indeed, when they abolished slavery in 1793, Sonthonax and Polverel had implemented a series of labor regulations meant to keep former slaves working on their plantations, where they were to be paid with part of the commodities they produced. This was not the kind of freedom that former slaves had envisioned, and many resisted the restrictions on their labor and movement (Document 29). But both Rigaud and Louverture were convinced that the export economy had to be maintained, and they continued to enforce and refine the plantation policies of Sonthonax and Polverel. Moreover, each leader ensured that his top officers controlled the best of the estates. In economic terms, their policies were a success: By the late 1790s, Louverture managed to rebuild much of Saint-Domingue's economy, dramatically increasing coffee exports and beginning a recovery in sugar production as well.[25]

Despite the similarities of their regimes, Rigaud and Louverture ultimately came into conflict. Unlike Toussaint, whose father was African, Rigaud was the son of a French colonist and an African woman. He had risen to prominence in a region that was home to many wealthy free people of color before the revolution. As the French government in Saint-Domingue increasingly relied on Toussaint and other soldiers who had been born into slavery, their growing influence in the colony sparked resentment from mixed-race leaders who had been the first beneficiaries of revolutionary racial reforms. For their part, Louverture and other black generals accused Rigaud and other men of color of perpetuating the whites' racist attitudes. Although his experience as a free man and his economic ideology were similar to those of Rigaud, Louverture's power stemmed in part from his ability, as a black man who had led the fight against slavery, to speak for hundreds of thousands of ex-slaves.

In 1799, the struggle between these two ambitious generals resulted in a civil war that Louverture described as a conflict between mulattos and blacks. Accusing Rigaud of insubordination and insurrection, Louverture began to amass troops in July 1799 for an invasion of the southern peninsula. Louverture's most effective lieutenant, Jean-

Jacques Dessalines, led forty-five thousand men against Rigaud's fifteen thousand. Ships from the U.S. Navy blockaded the key port of Jacmel on the southern coast, which held out until well into summer 1800. Only on August 1, 1800, after thirteen months of brutal war and two days after Rigaud had sailed for France, did Toussaint enter the southern capital of Les Cayes. Later writers described Dessalines's men executing ten thousand of Rigaud's men at the end of the struggle. Although this was probably an exaggeration, the victory over Rigaud did cause great racial and regional bitterness.[26]

This victory, and another over the Spanish in 1801 that gave him control of the eastern part of the island, allowed Toussaint to consolidate his rule of Saint-Domingue. He took advantage of new political developments in France in doing so. In 1799, a coup d'état orchestrated by Napoléon Bonaparte created a new regime known as the Consulate. The regime produced a new constitution for France that, in an important break with its predecessor of 1795, stipulated that it did not apply to France's overseas territories. The idea of the need for particular laws for the colonies had been a mainstay of proslavery planter politics during the early 1790s. Its resurgence in Bonaparte's 1799 constitution caused many in the Caribbean to fear that the French government was considering a return to slavery.

In the next years, Bonaparte developed an ambitious plan to revitalize France's American empire through the restoration of the sugar plantation economy in Saint-Domingue. The reacquisition of the Louisiana Territory from the Spanish, which Bonaparte completed in 1800, was part of this broader plan. Bonaparte wanted to stop U.S. merchants from supplying provisions to the French Caribbean colonies, as they had done—for the most part illegally, ignoring French laws against such trade—throughout the eighteenth century. Instead, he wanted the French colony of Louisiana to support the reconstructed sugar economies of the Caribbean. In 1801, successful peace negotiations with Britain spurred Bonaparte's New World projects. The end of the war with the British meant that the armies of ex-slaves in the French islands would no longer be as necessary as they had been since 1794. This encouraged France to confront the power of Louverture and other Caribbean leaders. Bonaparte's choices during this period, however, ultimately led to an outcome quite different from his plan: Rather than expanding the French empire, he was forced to relinquish not only Saint-Domingue but also Louisiana, transforming the history of the United States in the process.

THE HAITIAN REVOLUTION AND THE UNITED STATES

The revolution in the Caribbean came in the wake of the struggle for independence in North America. Ideas of sovereignty expressed through the American Revolution played a role in Saint-Domingue, notably by inspiring whites who wanted to win economic independence from Europe while maintaining slavery. Throughout the eighteenth century, French Caribbean colonies were intimately tied to the U.S. economy, so the actions of U.S. merchants and politicians influenced the course of the Haitian Revolution in various ways.

Events in the French Caribbean, meanwhile, had complex implications for the United States. Communication and movement between North America and the Caribbean was constant and widespread, so news traveled fast. In a slave society like the United States, particularly in the southern states, the emergence and ultimate success of a slave revolution frightened slave owners and inspired slaves, so many local administrators tried to control and suppress Caribbean news they believed to be subversive and dangerous.[27] Starting in 1791 and in successive waves in 1793, 1803, and 1809–1810 (when exiles from Saint-Domingue were expelled from Cuba and fled to Louisiana), thousands of refugees from the French Caribbean came to U.S. ports. While most were white planters, up to a third were of African descent, including both slaves and free people of color, whose presence raised complex issues about slavery and race. They had an important impact in the towns where they settled, such as Philadelphia, Charleston, and New Orleans (Document 35).

If the Haitian Revolution represented a threat to the U.S. social order, it also offered an economic opportunity. European wars in the 1790s limited the travel of French ships across the Atlantic, and the colonies in the Caribbean became even more dependent on U.S. merchants than they had been earlier. Although trade was consistent throughout the period, the administrations of John Adams and Thomas Jefferson took different approaches to relationships with the revolutionary regimes in the Caribbean. Adams was interested in commerce with Saint-Domingue, sending an envoy to work with Toussaint Louverture and allowing U.S. Navy ships to help Louverture in his battle against Rigaud, blockading the port of Les Cayes. Adams also had a political interest in supporting Louverture. From roughly 1798 to 1800, the United States and France were embroiled in the Quasi-War, incited in large part by Victor Hugues's French privateers, who captured U.S.

merchant ships heading to British islands. Helping Louverture was a way Adams could hurt the French. Indeed, when the U.S. Congress broke off trade relations with France, it made an explicit exception for Saint-Domingue, claiming that the government there was essentially autonomous. The United States sustained Toussaint as traders brought provisions and military supplies that helped him solidify his regime. The French general Charles-Victor-Emmanuel Leclerc, who led Bonaparte's expedition to the colony in 1802, blamed U.S. merchants for making Louverture's war against the French possible.

Adams's actions made his successor, Thomas Jefferson, uneasy. Jefferson's responses to events were complex and evolved over time, but he tended to see Haiti primarily as a threat to the plantation societies of the United States (Document 34). He particularly worried that slaves in the United States would find inspiration in Saint-Domingue's violent revolution, as the Richmond slave Gabriel apparently did in planning a short-lived 1800 revolt. When Jefferson came to power in 1801, he quickly reversed Adams's policies. After Haiti declared its independence in 1804, Jefferson established a policy of diplomatic isolation toward Haiti that would last until 1862. The United States also launched an economic boycott of Haiti in the early 1800s, although trade between the two countries grew once again during the early nineteenth century. In 1804, even abolitionists like Charles Brockden Brown seemed uneasy at the emergence of an independent black nation (Document 36). But many abolitionists, especially African Americans, celebrated Haiti as an enduring symbol of black victory and dignity, and its example continued to inspire slave rebellion in the United States.

WAR AND INDEPENDENCE

Like the abolition of slavery in 1793, the transformation of revolutionary Saint-Domingue into the independent state of Haiti resulted from complex political choices made on both sides of the Atlantic. The central actors were Napoléon Bonaparte and Toussaint Louverture, though it was Toussaint's generals, particularly Jean-Jacques Dessalines, who ultimately led their nation to independence.

Upon receiving news of France's 1799 constitution, Louverture made a bold move: Without approval from Bonaparte, he convened a handpicked committee in March 1801 to write a new constitution for Saint-Domingue (Document 37). This group included no ex-slaves, but rather Julien Raimond and two other men of color, three whites, and four representatives from the Spanish part of the island. Although the document confirmed that slavery was permanently abolished in the colony, it also maintained the policy of requiring former slaves to continue working on plantations. It made Louverture governor-for-life and allowed him to rule the colony's internal affairs. Still, this was no declaration of independence: Louverture believed that the colony needed to maintain ties to one empire or another. Even as he prepared for the worst, like other leaders in the Caribbean at the time, he may have hoped that France would ultimately stay true to the principles of its revolution and support freedom in the Caribbean.

Instead, Bonaparte's regime forced the men of African descent who had risen to power during the revolution to make difficult choices between political equality and freedom on one hand and loyalty to France on the other. In 1800, Bonaparte dispatched Admiral Jean-Baptiste Raymond de Lacrosse to Guadeloupe, which had been governed by a series of administrators sent from Paris since Victor Hugues' departure in 1798. Many of the island's officers, soldiers, and plantation workers feared that Lacrosse would restore slavery. In this climate, the admiral's suspicion of Guadeloupe's brown and black soldiers led to a revolt in October 1801 that drove him to the neighboring island of Dominica.

In 1802, the French general Antoine Richepance arrived at the head of a French expedition and found that hundreds of plantation laborers had fled their estates, anticipating the return of slavery. Although an army officer of color turned the island over to Richepance on his arrival, others fought against what they saw as a return of slavery. The leader of the rebels was the Martinican-born Louis Delgrès, who issued a powerful proclamation explaining his followers' struggle (Document 38). After fierce fighting, Delgrès led a group of his soldiers up the mountain to a plantation on the slopes of the Matouba volcano in southern Guadeloupe. Surrounded by the French and determined not to surrender, they ignited their casks of ammunition and shouted "live free or die" as the explosions rang out (Document 39). With a year, Richepance restored slavery in a brutal campaign that killed and deported as many as ten thousand Guadeloupeans of all colors, close to one-tenth of the population. Slavery was also reestablished in French Guiana, and it was maintained in Martinique when the British handed the island back to the French.[28]

A parallel expedition commanded by Bonaparte's brother-in-law Charles-Victor-Emmanuel Leclerc was sent to Saint-Domingue, land-ing there in February 1802. Although Toussaint and his generals initially fought the invasion, in May Toussaint formally agreed to retire from the military. His army became part of Leclerc's force and began to help it arrest plantation workers who had fled their estates. Toussaint was far from universally popular in Saint-Domingue. Some of his former officers had urged his arrest, and many former slaves resented his insistence on bringing Saint-Domingue back to full plantation production. Yet Leclerc, still worried about Toussaint's influence, summoned Toussaint to a meeting, had him arrested, and sent him in irons to France. Toussaint died in a mountain prison in April 1803.

Toussaint's deportation did not immediately incite a new uprising. Indeed, some people believed that the reestablishment of slavery was inevitable and sought to secure individual freedom for themselves (Document 42). It was Leclerc's attempt to disarm thousands of former slaves that renewed the fighting. Fleeing the estates to join already existing guerrilla bands in the hills, these cultivators became freedom fighters who threatened France's plans for Saint-Domingue. Leclerc relied heavily on black and mulatto troops and their officers, most notably Louverture's top lieutenant Jean-Jacques Dessalines, to hunt down the guerillas. As resistance grew in late summer 1802, however, more and more black and colored officers defected or led their own revolts. The arrival of a ship carrying prisoners from Guadeloupe to be sold as slaves confirmed the rumors of revolt and repression there (Document 40).[29]

In mid-October, high-ranking officers began to defect openly to join the ex-slave fighters. On November 1, 1802, Leclerc died of yellow fever, a disease that killed thousands of his European soldiers. Assuming command, his successor Donatien Rochambeau (the son of the Count Rochambeau who led the French troops supporting Washington at Yorktown) took the war to a new level of cruelty, bringing in man-eating dogs from Cuba and executing women as well as men. In part because of this cruelty, the tide had turned against the French by early 1803. The slow disintegration of French rule was evocatively described by Leonora Sansay (under the pseudonym Mary Hassal), who returned to the island with her husband after Leclerc's arrival and later fled into exile in Cuba like many other whites (Document 41).

As bad news from Saint-Domingue began to arrive in Paris, Bonaparte decided to cut his losses. Reversing his plans for an expanded French empire in the Americas, he decided instead to cede Louisiana to the United States. His offer to sell the entire territory surprised U.S. envoys in Paris, who were on a mission to try to purchase just the port of New Orleans from France. But Bonaparte understood that, without Saint-Domingue, Louisiana would be worthless to him. Ironically, then, the actions of former slave soldiers and officers in Saint-Domingue led to one of Thomas Jefferson's greatest successes, opening the way for a massive expansion of the United States and its slave system in the early nineteenth century.

While crushing guerrilla leaders who would not accept his authority, Dessalines managed to unite officers from various forces in May 1803. He created a new flag, symbolically ripping the white panel out of the French tricolor flag and combining the blue and red to symbolize the unity of blacks and men of color in pursuit of liberty. The officers who joined Dessalines in ever increasing numbers described French cruelties and the need for racial unity as they sought to convince their comrades to switch sides (Document 43). Out of approximately forty-three thousand European soldiers (who were accompanied by up to forty thousand sailors), no more than eight thousand escaped Saint-Domingue in December 1803. More than half of these men died as prisoners of the English, who by 1803 were again at war with France.[30]

On January 1, 1804, in the town of Gonaïves, Dessalines summoned his leading generals to a public ceremony at which he formally declared the independence of the territory that France had called Saint-Domingue. By choosing to name this new state Haiti, which had been used by the indigenous inhabitants of the island at the time Columbus arrived, and which was resurrected by independence-minded white colonists in the 1780s, Dessalines signaled his hope of establishing an authentic New World nation. Already in 1803 he was describing his troops as the indigenous army, and he later proclaimed that he had "avenged America." Yet he also realized that Haiti was not yet a united nation. Racial divisions threatened the coalition that had defeated France, as did tensions between men and women born in the island and those born in Africa.[31]

Perhaps for this reason, Dessalines rejected the philosophical declarations of independence drafted by his various secretaries, including one based on the ideas of Thomas Jefferson. Instead, on the evening of December 31, 1803, he ordered Louis Boisrond-Tonnerre, a man born free to a wealthy family of color and educated in France, to write a different kind of declaration that would remind all Haitians why they had rejected France. The same themes of unity against European racism and colonialism and a broad definition of the new country as a refuge for enslaved people of all kinds also shaped the Haitian constitution of 1805 (Documents 44 and 45).

THE LEGACY OF THE HAITIAN REVOLUTION

Haiti was the second independent state in the Americas and can be considered the first in Latin America. Its attempt to create a national community of the enslaved and dispossessed had an important impact on the emergence of other nation-states in the Atlantic world. The loss of its treasured colony in the Caribbean transformed France, which was in the midst of formulating itself in terms of its "white" identity, to which Haiti's self-proclaimed "black" nationhood was in some ways a direct response. The defeat of Napoleonic designs in the Caribbean opened the way for the sale of Louisiana to the United States. Meanwhile, the emergence of a neighboring black republic and the arrival of thousands of French colonial refugees strengthened the already existing racial ideology in the United States. Others, notably free people of color and slaves throughout the Americas, saw Haiti as an inspiration. Indeed, Simon Bolívar and other leaders of the Latin American wars of independence took military aid and political advice about emancipation from Haiti.

There was, not surprisingly, a strong negative reaction to this era of revolutionary transformation in the French Caribbean. Ten years of war left many dead—not only more than 100,000 British and French soldiers, but also many more residents of the colonies. Perhaps as many as 150,000 people died in Saint-Domingue in 1802–1803 alone, following a long decade of death and destruction. Yet the Atlantic slave system continued to thrive as sugar production expanded in Cuba and Brazil to make up for the production lost in Haiti. The Haitian Revolution had a mixed impact in the British Caribbean. Though some defended the right of the slaves to rebel, proslavery advocates on both sides of the Atlantic successfully deployed the specter of "another Haiti" in opposing attempts to ameliorate the conditions of the slaves, at least for a time.[32]

Haiti itself was politically isolated after 1804. It eventually gained official recognition from France in 1825 only in return for the payment of a large and debilitating indemnity that would weigh heavily on the finances of the state. During the nineteenth century, a successful coffee economy developed in Haiti, and many people were able to live decent lives farming small plots of land. Still, life for many Haitians was difficult. Environmental degradation, already a problem during the eighteenth-century plantation boom, worsened over the years as a growing population attempted to survive on limited land. Although there were several periods of stability during the nineteenth century, external political and economic pressures and internal conflicts contributed to often-violent leadership struggles. In struggles between autocratic forms of rule and the democratic aspirations of many of the nation's citizens, the former all too often won. The U.S. occupation of 1915–1934 and the fuller reintegration of Haiti into a changing global economy worsened the situation during the twentieth century.

Today, the Haitian Revolution is still proudly remembered in Haiti, and its leaders are venerated as founding heroes of the nation. People in Guadeloupe, Martinique, and metropolitan France remember the period in different ways. Slavery was not permanently abolished in Guadeloupe and Martinique until 1848; but rather than celebrating this date, Antilleans increasingly invoke the memory of those who fought for freedom against the French in 1802. The history of this resistance is called upon in the complex debates about the future of these islands, which are today (as they were during the revolution), departments of France. But the inheritance of the struggles that shaped this period is also found throughout the Atlantic world. The enslaved revolutionaries of the French Caribbean were the first to win universal freedom for their society, and in so doing they became founders of a larger struggle against slavery and racism.

NOTES

[1] David P. Geggus, "Urban Development in 18th Century Saint-Domingue," *Bulletin du Centre d'histoire des espaces atlantiques,* 5 (1990): 197; Philip D. Morgan, "The Cultural Implications of the Atlantic Slave Trade: African Regional Origins, American Destinations, and New World Developments," *Slavery and Abolition,* 18, no. 1 (1997): 132–33.

[2] This and the following paragraphs draw on overviews of the development of the French Caribbean in Laurent Dubois, *A Colony of Citizens: Revolution and Slave Emancipation in the French Caribbean, 1787–1804* (Chapel Hill: University of North Carolina Press, 2004), chap. 2, and *Avengers of the New World: The Story of the Haitian Revolution* (Cambridge: Harvard University Press, 2004), chap. 1.

[3] On piracy see Kris Lane, *Pillaging the Empire: Piracy in the Americas, 1500–1750* (London: M. E. Sharpe, 1998).

[4] See Robin Blackburn, *The Making of New World Slavery: From the Baroque to the Modern* (London: Verso, 1997), 394–439.

[5] John Garrigus, "Color, Class and Identity on the Eve of the Haitian Revolution: Saint-Domingue's Free Colored Elite as *colons américains,*" *Slavery and Abolition,* 17 (1996): 20–43.

[6] Alexandre Stanislas de Wimpffen, *Haiti aux XVIIIè siècle,* ed. Pierre Pluchon (Paris, 1993), 174–75.

[7] Data on slave imports into Saint-Domingue are drawn from the *DuBois Slave Trade Database* (Cambridge: Cambridge University Press, 1999); see also Robert Stein, *The*

French Slave Trade in the Eighteenth Century: An Old Regime Business (Madison: University of Wisconsin Press, 1979).

[8]On African contributions to the Haitian Revolution, see John Thornton, "African Soldiers in the Haitian Revolution," *Journal of Caribbean History*, 25, nos. 1 and 2 (1991): 58–80, and "I Am the Subject of the King of Kongo: African Political Ideology and the Haitian Revolution," *Journal of World History*, 4, no. 2 (Fall 1993): 181–214.

[9]David Geggus, "Indigo and Slavery in Saint-Domingue," *Plantation Society in the Americas*, 5, nos. 2 and 3 (Fall 1998): 200; David Geggus, "Sugar and Coffee Cultivation in Saint-Domingue and the Shaping of the Slave Labor Force," in *Cultivation and Culture: Labor and the Shaping of Slave Life in the Americas*, ed. Ira Berlin and Philip Morgan (Charlottesville: University of Virginia Press, 1993), 73–98, 74; on absentee ownership, see Wimpffen, *Haiti aux XVIIIè siècle*, 174–175.

[10]The classic study of slave life in the French Caribbean colonies is Gabriel Debien, *Les esclaves aux Antilles françaises, XVIIème–XVIIIème siècles* (Gourbeyre: Société d'Histoire de la Guadeloupe, 1974).

[11]David Geggus, "The Major Port Towns of Saint-Domingue in the Later Eighteenth Century," in *Atlantic Port Cities: Economy, Culture and Society in the Atlantic World, 1650–1850*, ed. Franklin W. Knight and Peggy K. Liss (Knoxville: University of Tennessee Press, 1990), 102.

[12]Geggus, "Sugar and Coffee," 76.

[13]See David Geggus, "The Slaves and Free Coloreds of Martinique during the Age of the French and Haitian Revolutions: Three Moments of Resistance," in *The Lesser Antilles in the Age of European Expansion*, ed. Robert Paquette and Stanley Engerman (Gainesville: University Press of Florida, 1996), 280–301.

[14]Florence Gauthier, "Comment la nouvelle d l'insurrection des esclaves de Saint-Domingue futelle reçue en France (1791–1793)," in *L'insurrection des esclaves de Saint-Domingue (22–23 août 1791)*, ed. Laënnec Hurbon (Paris: Karthala, 2000), 18; Pierre Pluchon, *Le premier empire colonial, des origines à la Restauration* (Paris: Fayard, 1991), 798.

[15]*Motion faite par M. Vincent Ogé jeune à l'Assemblée des colons habitants de S. Domingue à l'hôtel de Massiac, place des Victoires* (Paris, n.d.), 1, 5–6. This and the following paragraphs draw on two excellent studies of the debates in Paris between 1789 and 1791: Gabriel Debien, *Les colons de Saint-Domingue et la Révolution: Essai sur le Club Massiac (août 1789–août 1792)* (Paris: Armand Colin, 1953), 18–19, and Yves Benot, *La Révolution française et la fin des colonies* (Paris: Découverte, 1989). See also Yvan Debbasch, *Couleur et liberté: Le jeu du critère ethnique dans un ordre juridique esclavagiste* (Paris: Dalloz, 1967).

[16]Carolyn E. Fick, *The Making of Haiti: The Saint Domingue Revolution from Below* (Knoxville: University of Tennessee Press, 1990), 98–109; David Geggus, *Haitian Revolutionary Studies* (Bloomington: Indiana University Press, 2002), 81–92.

[17]See Debbasch, *Couleur et liberté*, 202–208.

[18]On Sonthonax, see Robert Louis Stein, *Léger Félicité Sonthonax: The Lost Sentinel of the Republic* (London: Associate Universities Presses, 1985).

[19]Geggus, *Haitian Revolutionary Studies*, 125, 174.

[20]Fick, *The Making of Haiti*, 162–68.

[21]Dubois, *A Colony of Citizens*, chaps. 7–8.

[22]Anne Pérotin-Dumon, "Ambiguous Revolution in the Caribbean: The White Jacobins, 1789–1800," *Historical Reflections/Reflexions historiques* (Canada), 13, nos. 2 and 3 (1986): 510–13, and *La ville aux îles, la ville dans l'île: Basse-Terre et Pointe-à-Pitre, 1650–1820* (Paris: Karthala, 2000), 254.

[23]On Louverture's about-face, see Geggus, *Haitian Revolutionary Studies*, 119–35.

[24]Gaétan Mentor, *Histoire d'un crime politique: Le Général Victor Mentor* (Port-au-Prince: Gaétan Mentor, 1999), 25; Pierre Pluchon, *Toussaint Louverture* (Paris: Fayard, 1989).

[25] Carolyn Fick, "Emancipation in Haiti: From Plantation Labour to Peasant Proprietorship," *Slavery and Abolition,* 21, no. 2 (August 2000): 11–40; and Mats Lundahl, "Toussaint Louverture and the War Economy of Saint Domingue, 1796–1802," *Slavery and Abolition,* 6, no. 2 (September 1985): 122–38.

[26] Pluchon, *Toussaint Louverture,* 265–72; Fick, *The Making of Haiti,* 205–6.

[27] See Julius Scott, *The Common Wind: Currents of Afro-American Communication in the Era of the Haitian Revolution* (Ph.D. diss., Duke University, 1986).

[28] Dubois, *A Colony of Citizens,* 353–62, 393–401, 404.

[29] See Beaubrun Ardouin, *Études sur l'histoire d'Haïti suivies de la vie du général J.-M. Borgella,* ed. François Dalencour (Port-au-Prince: 1853; Chez Dr. François Dalencour, 1958), 5, 63.

[30] The survival numbers are from Pierre Pluchon's notes accompanying Pamphile de Lacroix, *La Révolution de Haïti* (Paris: Karthala, 1995), 20. Pluchon/Lacroix estimate the European military force at sixty thousand, but the more widely accepted number of forty-three thousand comes from Claude B. Auguste and Marcel B. Auguste, *L'Expédition Leclerc, 1801–1803* (Port-au-Prince: Imprimerie Henri Deschamps, 1985), 28–29, who add another forty thousand for sailors and other support personnel.

[31] Geggus, *Haitian Revolutionary Studies,* 207–20.

[32] See David Geggus, ed., *The Impact of the Haitian Revolution in the Atlantic World* (Columbia: University of South Carolina Press, 2001); on deaths in Saint-Domingue, see Auguste and Auguste, *L'Expédition Leclerc,* 316.

Major Revolutionary Figures and Groups

Individuals

Jean-Baptiste Belley   An African-born former slave freed in the 1760s who represented Saint-Domingue in the National Convention in Paris in 1793 and 1796.

Georges Biassou   One of the two most important leaders of the rebel slave armies.

Napoléon Bonaparte   A talented artillery officer who came to power in France in November 1799 and later had himself crowned emperor of France.

Boukman   An important early leader of the slave insurrection who is said to have been the central celebrant at the slave meeting at Bois-Caïman.

Jacques-Pierre Brissot   Founded the Society of the Friends of the Blacks in 1788 and was elected to the Legislative Assembly in 1791. He was guillotined as a counterrevolutionary in October 1793.

Étienne-Louis-Hector Dejoly   Parisian lawyer and member of the Society of the Friends of the Blacks who worked to obtain political representation for free people of color.

Louis Delgrès   A Martinique-born free man of mixed ancestry who later became a prominent officer on Guadeloupe. He led the resistance to French officers who attempted to deny citizenship to ex-slaves and free people of color.

Jean-François   The most powerful rebel general to emerge in Saint-Domingue after the August 1791 slave uprising.

Jean-Jacques Dessalines   A former slave who became Toussaint Louverture's top general. After Toussaint's surrender, he joined Leclerc's army but later took command of the anti-French forces and defeated Rochambeau. He declared Haitian independence in 1804 and proclaimed himself emperor the following year, but was assassinated in 1806.

Abbé Grégoire   A priest from eastern France who was a member of the Estates General and the Society of Friends of the Blacks.

Victor Hugues   Served as the French Revolution's civil commissioner to Guadeloupe from 1794 to 1798 and was charged with emancipating the slaves. In 1802, he reestablished slavery in French Guiana.

Étienne Laveaux   A French revolutionary army officer who led Saint-Domingue's struggle against Spanish and British invaders from 1794 to 1796.

Charles-Victor-Emmanuel Leclerc   Napoléon's brother-in-law and leader of the expedition to Saint-Domingue. In November 1802, after only eight months in the colony, he died of yellow fever.

Louis XVI   King of France from 1774 until revolutionaries executed him in January 1793.

[François-Dominique] Toussaint Louverture   A free man of color and ex-slave who eventually became a leader of the Saint-Domingue revolt. After emancipation was declared, he joined the French army and became Saint-Domingue's highest ranking military officer. In 1801, he picked a committee to write a constitution for Saint-Domingue, which named him governor-in-chief for life. After being removed from power and arrested in 1802, he died in a prison in France in 1803.

Vincent Ogé   A wealthy free colored merchant from Cap Français who, during a trip to France, became involved with the free men of color meeting there. He was executed in 1791 for leading an insurrection in Saint-Domingue.

Étienne Polverel   A member of the Jacobin club from 1791 and one of three members of Saint-Domingue's Second Civil Commission in 1792–1794.

Julien Raimond   A wealthy indigo planter of one-quarter African descent who moved to France in 1784 and made racism, not slavery, the top colonial issue in revolutionary Paris. Fearing that Bonaparte would restore slavery, he allied with Toussaint and helped write the 1801 constitution.

André Rigaud   The leader of free people of color in the south province in 1790. He established an autonomous government there in 1794, ruling independently of the rest of the colony until Toussaint Louverture overthrew him in 1800.

Donatien-Marie-Joseph de Vimeur, Comte de Rochambeau   Took command of Napoleon's Saint-Domingue expedition after Leclerc's death; his brutal treatment of people of color incited rebellion. He surrendered to Dessalines in November 1803.

Léger Félicité Sonthonax   The leader of the Second Civil Commission to Saint-Domingue from 1792 to 1794. In 1797, he was elected to represent the colony in France.

Groups

Club Massiac   A group of conservative colonists who met in the Hotel Massiac in Paris in 1789 to monitor revolutionary events, which they felt posed a danger to their Caribbean properties.

Creoles   People of European or African ancestry born in the New World. In the French Caribbean, the term applied to both blacks and whites.

Estates General   An ancient assembly of the different "estates" or feudal groups in the kingdom of France, called by the bankrupt Louis XVI and convened in 1789. As the French Revolution began, the Estates General became the National Assembly.

Free People of Color   People of African or mixed European and African ancestry who had attained freedom. By 1789, they made up approximately half of the free population of Saint-Domingue, and several hundred were wealthy planters, merchants, or artisans.

Jacobins   A political club in revolutionary Paris that held meetings in an old monastery called the Jacobins and had a radical vision of what the French Revolution could accomplish, including using the power of the central government to erase social distinctions. Members of the Jacobin club led the political campaign to reform colonial racism and controlled the National Assembly when it approved the emancipation of all slaves in the French Empire.

Legislative Assembly   France's second legislature, elected in early fall 1791 to work with the king in governing France. Disbanded when France became a republic in September 1792.

National Assembly/Constituent Assembly   Formed in July 1789 by members of the Estates General to write a constitution for France. The assembly sat for two years, until September 29, 1791, when the constitution was finished and approved.

National Convention   A legislature created to write a new republican constitution for France, which it completed in August 1795. It disbanded in September to make way for the new institutions.

Patriots   Colonists who resented the colony's military government and were strongly opposed to the equality of free colored people with whites.

Society of the Friends of the Blacks   An antislavery society founded in Paris by Jacques-Pierre Brissot in 1788 that worked to abolish colonial race laws, the slave trade, and slavery itself.

PART TWO

The Documents

1

The French Caribbean
in the Eighteenth Century

1

The Code Noir

1685

Since at least the 1630s, French Caribbean colonists had held enslaved Africans. However, it was only after sugar planting became the islands' main crop in the middle of the century that enslaved people came to out-number colonists. In 1685, the French monarchy issued a comprehensive slave code to replace the piecemeal local laws written by colonial admin-istrators and judges. Drafted by European legal scholars who knew far more about ancient Roman jurisprudence than about New World planta-tions, The Code Noir *contained many provisions that colonists ignored or deliberately violated. Nevertheless, although it was reissued and sup-plemented by local legislation throughout the eighteenth century,* The Code Noir *remained the foundation for the legal framework of French Caribbean slavery through the early years of the Haitian Revolution.*

Le Code Noir ou recueil des reglements rendus jusqu'à présent (Paris: Prault, 1767).

Edict of the King

Concerning the enforcement of order in the French American islands from the month of March 1685

Louis, by the grace of God, King of France and Navarre: to all present and to come, Greetings. Since we owe equally our attention to all the peoples that Divine Providence has put under our obedience, we have had examined in our presence the memoranda that have been sent to us by our officers in our American islands, who have informed us that they need our authority and our justice to maintain the discipline of the Catholic, Apostolic and Roman Church[1] there and to regulate the status and condition of the slaves in our said islands. And we desire to provide for this and to have them know that although they live in regions infinitely removed from our normal residence, we are always present to them, not only by the range of our power but also by the promptness of our attempts to assist them in their needs. For these reasons, by the advice of our Council and by our certain knowledge, full power, and royal authority, we say, rule, and order, wish and are pleased by that which follows.

I. . . . we charge all our officers to evict from our islands all the Jews who have established their residence there, who we order, as to the declared enemies of the Christian religion, to leave within three months of the publication date of these present [edicts], or face confiscation of body and property.

II. All the slaves in our Islands will be baptized and instructed in the Catholic, Apostolic and Roman religion. . . .

III. We forbid any public exercise of any religion other than the Catholic, Apostolic and Roman; we wish that the offenders be punished as rebels and disobedient to our orders. . . . We prohibit all such [religious] assemblies, which we declare illicit and seditious, subject to the same penalty that will be levied even against masters who allow or tolerate them among their slaves.

VI. We charge all our subjects, whatever their status and condition, to observe Sundays and holidays that are kept by our subjects of the Catholic, Apostolic and Roman religion. We forbid them to work or to make their slaves work on these days from the hour of midnight until the next midnight, either in agriculture, the manufacture of sugar, or

---

[1]This was the official name commonly used to describe the Roman Catholic Church at the time. It was meant to emphasize the connection to the early Apostles of Christ.

all other works, on pain of fine and discretionary punishment of the masters and confiscation of the sugar and of the said slaves. . . .

VII. We also forbid the holding of *nègre*[2] markets and all other markets on such days under similar penalties. . . .

IX. Free men who will have one or several children from concubinage with their slaves, as well as the masters who permitted this, will each be condemned to a fine of two thousand pounds of sugar. And if they are the masters of the slave by whom they have had such children, we wish that beyond the fine they be deprived of the slave and the children, and that she and they be confiscated for the profit of the [royal] hospital, without ever being manumitted. Nevertheless, we do not intend for this article to be enforced if the man . . . would marry this slave in the church, which will free her and make the children free and legitimate. . . .

X. The marriage ceremonies prescribed by the Ordinance of Blois[3] . . . will be observed both for free persons and for slaves; nevertheless, for the slave the consent of the father and the mother is not necessary, only that of the master.

XI. We forbid priests to officiate at the marriages of slaves unless they can show the consent of their masters. We also forbid masters to make their slaves marry against their will.

XII. The children born of marriages between slaves will be slaves and will belong to the master of the female slaves, and not to those of their husbands, if the husband and the wife have different masters.

XIII. We wish that if a slave husband has married a free woman, the children, both male and girls, will follow the condition of their mother and be free like her, in spite of the servitude of their father; and that if the father is free and the mother enslaved, the children will be slaves for the same reason.

XIV. Masters are to be put into Holy Ground in cemeteries so designated; their baptized slaves and those who die without having received baptism will be buried at night in some field near the place where they died.

---

[2]Throughout the documents, we have sometimes left racial terms, particularly *nègre,* untranslated because no English term precisely captures its connotations. It could be translated as either *negro* or *black,* but in writings and legislation, especially during the French Revolution, the decision to use the term *nègre* rather than the more respectful *noir* (black) carried important implications.

[3]This ordinance governed the practice of marriage throughout the French kingdom.

XV. We forbid slaves to carry any weapon, or large sticks, on pain of whipping and confiscation of the weapon, with the sole exception of those who are sent hunting by their master and who carry their note or known mark.[4]

XVI. In the same way we forbid slaves belonging to different masters to gather in the day or night, whether for a wedding or otherwise, whether on their master's property or elsewhere, and still less in the main roads or faraway places, on pain of corporal punishment, which will not be less than the whip and [branding with] the fleur-de-lis;[5] frequent violations and other aggravating circumstances can be punished with death, which we leave to the decision of judges. We charge all our subjects, even those who are not officers, to approach the offenders, to arrest them and take them to prison, even if there is not yet any warrant against them.

XVII. Masters who are convicted of having permitted or tolerated such assemblies of slaves other than those belonging to them will be condemned in their own and private name to pay for all the damages done to their neighbors by these said assemblies and a fine . . . for the first time and double for repeat offenses.

XVIII. We forbid slaves to sell sugar cane for whatever reason or occasion, even with the permission of their master, on pain of whipping for the slaves and . . . [a fine] . . . for their masters who permitted it, and a similar fine against the buyer.

XIX. We also forbid them to sell any kind of foodstuffs in the market or by carrying them to private houses, including fruits, vegetables, firewood, animal fodder, or handicrafts, without the express permission of their masters by a note or by known marks on pain of confiscation of the goods thus sold. . . .

XXII. Each week masters will have to provide their slaves ten years and older, for their nourishment, two-and-a-half Parisian quarts of cassava[6] flour or three cassavas weighing at least two and a half pounds each or equivalent items, with two pounds of salted beef or three pounds of fish or other things in proportion, and to children, after they are weaned to the age of ten years, half of the above supplies.

XXIII. We forbid masters to give the slaves rum or taffia[7] in place of the subsistence mentioned in the previous article.

---

[4]Known mark refers to the mark (often an x) made by masters who could not write or sign their names.

[5]The fleur-de-lis was the symbol of the king.

[6]Cassava, also known as manioc or yucca, is a starchy root vegetable often used in the Caribbean to make flour.

[7]Like rum, taffia was an alcohol produced from molasses, but it was of lower quality.

XXIV. We similarly forbid them to relieve themselves of providing food and subsistence to their slaves by permitting them to work a certain day of the week for their own ends.

XXV. Each year masters will have to furnish each slave with two outfits of canvas or four yards of canvas, at the master's discretion.

XXVI. Slaves who are not fed, clothed, and supported by their master as we command in these articles will notify the royal attorney and give him their statements. Based on this, even if the information comes from elsewhere, the master will be prosecuted at no cost to the plaintiff, which we desire because of masters' crimes and barbarous and inhumane treatment of their slaves. . . .

XXX. Slaves may not be given offices or commissions with any public function, nor be named agents by anyone other than their masters to act or estimate losses or testify, either in civil or criminal matters. And in cases where they will be heard as witnesses, their depositions will only serve as memoranda to aid the judges in the investigation, without being the source of any presumption, conjecture, or proof.

XXXI. Slaves cannot be party to either judgments or civil proceedings, nor can they be plaintiffs or defendants in civil or criminal proceedings. . . .

XXXIII. The slave who will have struck his master or the wife of his master, his mistress, or their children and drawn blood, or in the face, will be punished with death. . . .

LV. Masters twenty years old will be able to manumit their slaves by [legal] deed or by cause of death, without being required to provide the reason for this manumission. Provided that they are minors twenty-five years of age, they will not need the permission of parents.

LVI. Any slave whose master leaves him all his property or who names him executor of his testament or tutor of his children will be regarded as manumitted.

LVII. We declare that manumissions enacted in our islands will be considered as birth in our islands and manumitted slaves will not need our letters of naturalization in order to enjoy the advantages of our natural subjects in our kingdom, lands, and countries under our obedience, although they be born in foreign lands.

LVIII. We command manumitted slaves to retain a particular respect for their former masters, their widows, and their children; and any insult that they make against them will be punished more severely than if it had been done to another person. However, we declare them free and absolved of any other burdens, services, and rights that their former masters would like to claim, as much on their persons as on their possessions and estates as patrons.

LIX. We grant to manumitted slaves the same rights, privileges, and liberties enjoyed by persons born free; desiring that they merit this acquired liberty and that it produce in them, both for their persons and for their property, the same effects that the good fortune of natural liberty causes in our other subjects.

2

Prophesies of Slave Revolution
1771 and 1780

In his L'An deux mille quatre cent quarante (The Year 2440), *first published in 1771, Louis-Sébastien Mercier critiqued the society he lived in by imagining waking up from a very long nap to find the world perfected and the tyranny and oppression of the past erased. As he wanders in this new world, he comes upon a monument representing a remarkable man who had brought liberty to slaves and redemption to Europeans.*

[T]o the right I saw on a magnificent pedestal a *nègre,* his head bare, his arm outstretched, with pride in his eyes and a noble and imposing demeanor. Around him was the debris of twenty scepters.[8] At his feet were the words "To the Avenger of the New World!"

I shouted with surprise and joy. Yes, I was told with an energy equal to my exclamations, nature had finally created this surprising and immortal man who had delivered a world from the most atrocious, longest, and most insulting tyranny of all. His genius, his audacity, his virtuous vengeance were rewarded; he broke the chains of his compatriots. So many slaves oppressed by the most odious slavery seemed to be awaiting only his signal to become as many heroes. The torrent that breaks dikes and lightning that strikes have a less immediate and violent effect. In the same instant they spilled the blood of their tyrants. French, Spanish, English, Dutch, Portuguese all fell prey to

[8]A scepter is a symbol of royalty.

Source: Louis-Sébastien Mercier, From *L'An deux mille quatre cent quarante: Rêve s'il en fût jamais* (Paris: Lepetit jeune et Gerard, An X [1802]), 180–84.

iron, poison, and flame. The soil of America avidly drank the blood that it has been awaiting for so long, and the bones of their ancestors, murdered by cowards, seemed to stand up and shake with joy. . . . This heroic avenger freed a world of which he is the god, while the other [the Old World] has rendered him homage and granted him crowns. He came like a storm spreading across a city of criminals that is about to be destroyed by lightning. He was the exterminating angel to which God and Justice had handed its double-edged sword: He demonstrated that sooner or later cruelty will be punished and that Providence stores away souls that she unleashes on the earth to reestablish the balance that the iniquity of ferocious ambition has destroyed.*

This passage from a history of European colonialism, the publication of which was overseen by Abbé Raynal, followed a common eighteenth-century practice by directly incorporating some of Mercier's language. But the author of the passage, Denis Diderot, also included details not in Mercier, notably referring to events in Jamaica and Suriname, where colonial governments had made treaties with maroon communities, assuring them of their freedom. In this version, which followed a description of the slave trade, Diderot appealed to the sense of justice of European monarchs, urging them to end their own participation in the slave trade and declare war against any leaders who continued participating in the traffic. Then, however, he suggested that a violent revolution among the slaves themselves might ultimately be required to overturn slavery.

Refuse the seal of your authority to this infamous and criminal traffic of men who are turned into herds of cattle, and this commerce will disappear. Unite, for once, in pursuit of good, those forces that are so often gathered together for its destruction. If one among you dares to base hope for his richness and grandeur on the generosity of all others, he becomes an enemy of the human race that must be destroyed. Carry fire and iron against him. Your armies will be filled with the

---

*This hero, no doubt, will spare the generous Quakers who have just granted liberty to their *nègres* in a touching and memorable moment that made me spill tears of joy and makes me hate those Christians who do not imitate them.

Guillaume Thomas François Raynal, *Histoire philosophique et politique des établissements et du commerce des Européens dans les Deux Indies* (Genève: Pellet, 1780), vol. 3, book 11, chap. 24.

saintly enthusiasm of humanity. You will see what a difference virtue makes between men who are saving the oppressed and mercenaries who serve tyrants.

But what am I saying? Let us no longer seek to make the useless voice of humanity heard by people and their masters; it has perhaps never been consulted in public decisions. Your slaves do not need your generosity or your advice to shatter the sacrilegious yoke that oppresses them. Nature speaks louder than philosophy or interest. Already there have been established two colonies of fugitive Negroes who are safe from your attacks thanks to treaties and force. These bolts of lightning announce the thunder, and all that the Negroes lack is a leader courageous enough to carry them to vengeance and carnage.

Where is he, this great man that Nature owes to its vexed, oppressed, tormented children? Where is he? He will appear. . . . He will show himself and will raise the sacred banner of liberty. This venerable leader will gather around him his comrades in misfortune. More impetuous than torrents, they will leave everywhere ineffaceable traces of their just anger. The American fields will be intoxicated by the blood that they have been awaiting for so long, and the bones of so many unfortunates, piled up for three centuries, will shake with joy. The Old World will join its applause to that of the New. Everywhere people will bless the name of the hero who reestablished the rights of the human species; everywhere monuments will be erected to his glory. Then *The Code Noir* will disappear, and *The Code Blanc* will be terrible if the victors consult only the law of revenge!

3

MÉDÉRIC-LOUIS-ÉLIE MOREAU DE SAINT-MÉRY

Description . . . of the French Part
of the Island of Saint-Domingue
1797

In the introduction to his encyclopedic Description, *written before the French Revolution but first published in Philadelphia in 1796, the Martinican-born lawyer Moreau de Saint-Méry portrayed the different kinds of people living in Saint-Domingue at the end of the eighteenth century. He drew on the latest scientific theories as well as on his personal observations and historical research. In this selection, he depicts the free people of color, who were culturally, physically, and legally distinct from, yet intimately connected to, the colony's white and black populations. Though Moreau de Saint-Méry never mentioned it in his writings, he, like nearly all white colonists, appears to have had a free colored mistress and perhaps a daughter with her.*[9]

Of the Freedmen

The freedmen are universally known as "people of color" or "mixed bloods," although this name, taken exactly, could also refer to enslaved *nègres*. As soon as the colony had slaves, it had freedmen, and several causes seem to have coincided to form this intermediary class between master and slave. In Saint-Domingue, slaves were not only *nègres* but also Indians and savages only distinguished from *nègres* by their color. The scarcity of women, the ways of the freebooters and

---

[9]See "Une fille naturelle de Moreau de Saint-Méry à Saint-Domingue," *Revue de la société haïtienne d'histoire et de la géographie* (March 1989): 51.

Médéric-Louis-Élie Moreau de Saint-Méry, *Description topographique, physique, civile, politique et historique de la partie française de l'Isle Saint-Domingue* (Philadelphia, 1797), vol. 1, pp. 45–51 and 90–99.

buccaneers, and the lure of the submissive *négresses*[10] produced mulattos whose skin color put them in a class with Indians and savages, as
is seen in the census of 1681, where all 480 of them were mixed
together. But at that time, only whites were free.

The men who unscrupulously enslaved savages and Indians, colored like mulattos, nevertheless had particular feelings for these
[mulattos]; and by a kind of agreement, which must have come from
paternal affection and pride, it became established that mulattos
would leave slavery when they reached their twenty-first year. Nevertheless, more than once personal greed broke this unofficial custom,
and mulattos lost this advantage when *The Code Noir* established
rules about the role of slaves in colonial inheritances. Only those
[slaves] whose masters had formally given up their rights in writing
were recognized as freedmen. . . . The censuses of the beginning of
the present century show about five hundred free people [of color] of
all ages and all sexes. . . .

I have already said that the [mulattos] were well formed, of an
agreeable shape, and quite intelligent. But they push laziness and love
of rest as far as the *nègres* do. These men are capable of succeeding in
all the mechanical and liberal arts, and some have proved this in a way
that should have excited them all, if it wasn't that their greatest pleasure is to do nothing. . . . The mulatto loves pleasure; it is his only master, but it is a tyrannical master. Dancing, riding horses, abandoning
himself in sensuality, these are his three passions. He equals the white
Creole in the first and far surpasses him in the third of these. . . .

The *mulâtress*[11] has even more of the advantages that nature has
given the mulatto. My description of the white Creole women fits her
perfectly, as far as the elegance of shape, the ease of movement; but she
carries much farther that nonchalance that would suggest weakness, if
this were not contradicted by the language of her eyes. You will recognize by her slow and graceful walk, accompanied by the movements of
her hips and the swaying of her head, by that arm that moves along her
body holding a scarf, by that small piece of root turned into a kind of
brush that often cleans the most beautiful teeth, one of these priest-
esses of Venus[12] who would eclipse the fame of Lais[13] and Phriné.[14]

---

[10]Black women.
[11]Female mulatto.
[12]The ancient Roman goddess of love.
[13]Famous prostitute of ancient Greece.
[14]An ancient Greek prostitute said to have been so beautiful that judges dropped all
charges against her when they accidentally glimpsed her breasts.

The entire being of a *mulâtresse* is dedicated to sensual pleasure, and the fire of that goddess burns in her heart until she dies. . . . There is nothing that most passionate imagination can conceive that she has not already sensed, foreseen, or experienced. Her single focus is to charm all the senses, to expose them to the most delicious ecstasies, to suspend them in the most seductive raptures. In addition, nature, pleasure's accomplice, has given her charm, appeal, sensitivity, and, what is far more dangerous, the ability to experience more keenly than her partner sensual pleasures whose secrets surpass those of Paphos.[15]

In the following passage, Moreau de Saint-Méry describes a ritual dance called "vaudoux" that was practiced by the slaves of Saint-Domingue. Vaudoux was undoubtedly only one piece of a larger set of practices with which Moreau de Saint-Méry was likely unfamiliar, and which would coalesce into the contemporary religion known as Haitian Vodou. Though this is one of the few contemporary descriptions of such rituals, the extent to which Moreau de Saint-Méry based his description on personal observation is not clear. Whites do seem to have seen and participated in such events in Le Cap, however.

According to the Arada[16] *nègres*, who are the true practitioners of *Vaudoux* in the colony and who maintain its principles and rules, *Vaudoux* signifies an all-powerful and supernatural being who controls all the events that take place on this globe. And this being is the nonvenomous snake, a kind of grass snake, and all those who profess the same doctrine gather together under its patronage. The knowledge of the past, the science of the present, the prescience of the future all belong to this snake, which nevertheless only communicates its power and prescribes its will through a high priest that the practitioners choose, and even more through that of the *négresse,* whose devotion to it has elevated her to the rank of high priestess.

These two ministers who declare themselves inspired by the god, or in whom the followers have seen the gift of this inspiration, carry the pompous names of king and queen, the despotic ones of master and mistress, or finally the sentimental ones of father and mother. They are, throughout their lives, the leaders of the great family of

---

[15]The legendary birthplace of Aphrodite, the ancient Greek goddess of love.

[16]This term was used to identify Africans brought from France's West African slave trading ports.

Vaudoux and have the right to the unlimited respect of its members. It is they who determine whether the snake will accept the admission of a candidate in the society, who prescribe the obligations and duties they must fulfill; it is they who receive the donations and gifts that the god expects as a just homage. To disobey or resist them is to resist god himself, and to expose oneself to the greatest misfortune.

With this well-established system of domination on one side and blind submission on the other, they hold assemblies at certain predetermined times, presided over by the *Vaudoux* king and queen according to customs they may have borrowed from Africa, to which Creole customs have added several variations. Some details also reveal the influence of European ideas, for example the scarf or the luxurious belt that the queen wears in these assemblies and that she changes from time to time.

The meeting for the true *Vaudoux,* that which remains closest to its primitive purity, takes place only in secret, once the night has spread its shadow, in a place that is closed off and safe from all worldly eyes. There, its initiate puts on a pair of sandals and places around his or her body a more or less considerable number of red kerchiefs, or kerchiefs where this color is very dominant. The *Vaudoux* king has kerchiefs that are more beautiful and numerous, and one that is all red and is tied around his forehead is his crown. A cord, usually blue, emphasizes his brilliant dignity.

The queen, dressed with a simple luxury, also shows a predilection for the color red, which is most often that of her cord or her belt.

The king and the queen place themselves at one end of the room, next to a kind of altar on which is a case in which the serpent is kept and in which each member can see it through bars.

Once it has been established that no curious person has penetrated the enclosure, the ceremony begins with the adoration of the snake and with proclamations of loyalty to its cult and submission to all it prescribes. The king and queen administer the oath of secrecy, which is the basis of the association, and add to it the most horrible things lunacy can devise to make it more fearsome.

Once the practitioners of *Vaudoux* are ready to receive communications from the king and the queen, these two adopt the affectionate tone of a sensitive mother and father and boast of the happiness that is the right of any *Vaudoux* devotee. They exhort them to have confidence in the god and to prove this by taking his advice on how to behave in important circumstances.

Then the crowd makes way, and each person comes to implore the *Vaudoux* according to his or her needs and following the order of their seniority in the sect. The majority ask for the ability to control the spirit of their masters, but that is not enough: One asks for more money, another for the ability to please an uninterested woman, this one to bring back an unfaithful mistress; another wants to heal quickly or to live a long life. . . . There is no passion that does not produce a wish. Even those planning crimes do not always disguise their prayers for success.

At each of these invocations, the *Vaudoux* king meditates; the spirit moves within him. Suddenly he takes the box with the snake in it, places it on the ground, and has the *Vaudoux* queen stand on it. As soon as the sacred sanctuary is underneath her, she becomes a new python, penetrated by god. She moves; her entire body is in a convulsive state, and the oracle speaks through her mouth. Sometimes she flatters and promises happiness; sometimes she thunders and explodes with reproaches. According to her own desires or interests, she dictates what she pleases as laws from the snake to the idiotic troop, which never doubts the most monstrous absurdities and only obeys what is despotically prescribed to it.

After all questions have received some response from the oracle, which is also sometimes ambiguous, a circle is formed, and the snake is placed back on the altar. It is the moment when each person brings an offering, which they have sought to make worthy of her and which is placed in a covered hat so that jealous curiosity will not embarrass anyone. The king and the queen promise to make her accept them. Plans are proposed, steps decided on, actions prescribed, which the *Vaudoux* queen supports as the god's will and which are not always in the interest of good order and public tranquility. A new oath, as repulsive as the first, commits everyone to be silent about what has happened and to participate in what has been decided on. Sometimes all those present drink from a pot containing fresh hot goat's blood, which seals their promise to suffer death rather than reveal anything and even to kill anyone who might forget that he had solemnly taken the same oath.

After this, the *Vaudoux* dance begins. . . .

What is very true and quite remarkable in *Vaudoux* is the kind of magnetism that is carried by those who gather together and dance until they are senseless. The impulse in this direction is so strong that whites found spying on the mysteries of this sect, and touched by one of its members who had discovered them, have sometimes started to dance and have consented to pay the *Vaudoux* queen to end this punishment. Still, I must note that no man who is part of the police troop, which has declared war against *Vaudoux,* has ever felt forced to dance by this power. . . .

Probably in order to weaken the alarm that this mysterious cult of *Vaudoux* has caused in the colony, its members pretend to dance it in public to the sound of drums and with the clapping of hands; it is even followed by a meal, where only poultry is eaten. But this is only another strategy to escape the authorities' vigilance and to ensure the success of these shadowy meetings, which are not a place of amusement and pleasure, but rather a school where weak souls surrender themselves to a dangerous kind of domination.

It is hard to believe the power of the *Vaudoux* leaders. The other members of the sect would prefer anything to the miseries with which they are threatened if they do not faithfully attend the assemblies and blindly do everything that the *Vaudoux* demands of them. Some have been so frightened that they have lost the capacity of reason. Nothing is more dangerous than this cult of *Vaudoux.* The ridiculous idea that the ministers of this being know and can do everything could be transformed into a terrible weapon.

2

The Revolution Begins, 1789–1791

4

Letters from the Slave Revolt in Martinique
August–September 1789

*In late August 1789, slaves in Martinique began spreading the rumor
that the king of France had decided to abolish slavery, but that local
administrators had decided not to apply the decree. The exact origin of
this false rumor is difficult to pin down: The taking of the Bastille on
July 14, 1789, was not yet known on the island, although the meeting of
the Estates General, a body of elected representatives called to advise the
king, and the presence of abolitionist sentiment in France were. Whatever the source, the rumor provided a potent mobilizing force in Martinique, leading to a series of meetings and a revolt that was quickly
suppressed. The following letter from the governor of the island described
the revolt.*

Governor Vioménil to the Minister of the Marine and the Colonies, September 14, 1789

Monseigneur:

For a relatively long time, there has been a great deal of worry, agita-
tion, and insubordination among the Negro slaves of this colony. The
principal origin of this has been the seditious insinuations that have
been made to them by a man named Father Jean-Baptiste, Capuchin
[a priest], the former Director of the *nègres* of the parish du Fort in
Saint-Pierre, who has taken refuge in Dominica and who, according to

---

Centre des Archives d'Outre-Mer, Aix-en-Provence, C⁸ᴬ 89, p. 57.

a few clues that I hope to verify, continues even today to keep up a guilty correspondence with several whites. You can judge this, *Monseigneur,* by the copies of two anonymous letters that I have the honor of sending to you.

The threats that these writings contain have just been realized in part, but thanks to the precautions that I felt forced to take, the effect has happily been reduced to an uprising among the slave gangs of two relatively large plantations next to Saint-Pierre, whose *nègres,* armed with the tools that they use to cut sugarcane, refused to work, saying loudly that they were free, and then retreated into the heights above Saint-Pierre.

I hastened to break up these gatherings and most of all to prevent these rebels from joining the old *nègres marrons* in the underpopulated mountains of the interior of this island by sending out the colonial militia supported by detachments from the Martinique regiment and, at the same time, stopping all communication with the domestic slaves in Saint-Pierre, whose numbers are considerable. . . .

The day after their desertion, the two escaped work gangs came back on their own, and everything was back in order where the revolt had appeared; detachments successively brought in suspect *nègres* and maroons, among which were found the two principle instigators of this revolt, named Fouta and Honoré, who, having been convicted and judged, were condemned, one to be broken on the wheel and the other hung, and were executed in Saint-Pierre on the third of this month. . . . These prompt acts of justice and severity against the guilty will suffice to immediately reestablish order and tranquility, and there is no need, *Monseigneur,* for you to worry any longer about this.

In the meantime, in order to leave nothing undone in a matter that is of essential importance for public security, I have ordered the general assembly of the militia. Having left all at once and at the same time from all the different districts of the island, they headed toward the same point while searching even the most inaccessible areas; in so doing they were able to surround and arrest many of the old *nègres marrons*[1] who have been brought back to their masters. I will continue to have frequent special hunts carried out that I hope will totally destroy this troublesome sort . . . until now I do not think there is an organized plot or chiefs who have decided to revolt. If we do not remedy the problem promptly, this small band of *nègres marrons* will be

---

[1] Maroons.

the nucleus that will produce the miseries that this colony fears so. Until now, everything has made it easy for the *nègres* to desert and escape . . . the *nègres marrons* come in large numbers and mix freely with the slaves in the markets and the public squares, which never happens without inciting in the latter the desire for independence and liberty.

Although the governor suggested the identity of the author of the following letters, it is in fact unclear who wrote them. The evocation of the power of the king against local enemies was part of a long tradition within slave political action in the Americas. But these letters also represent a powerful early example of how rebels agitating against slavery connected their cause with the revolutionary conflicts that were beginning in France.

Copy of an Anonymous Letter Addressed to M. Mollérat, Saint-Pierre, August 28, 1789

Dear Sirs:

General, Intendant, the Government, Advisers, and other individuals, we know that we are free and that you are aware that rebellious people are resisting the orders of the king. Well, remember that we *nègres* are numerous, and we want to die for this liberty; for we want it and plan to get it at whatever price, even with the use of mortars, cannons, and rifles. Why, for how many hundreds of years, have our fathers been subjected to this fate that still falls on us? Did God create anyone as a slave? The sky and the earth belong to the lord God, along with everything they contain; you have corrupted our ancestors, not only them, but also their descendants. Isn't this horrible, sirs? It must be believed in truth that you are very inhumane not to be touched with compassion for the suffering that we endure. Even the most barbarous of nations would melt into tears if it knew our misery. I will let you think for a while about how quickly it would seek to abolish such an odious law. But in the end, it is in vain that we seek to convince you by invoking sentiments and humanity, for you have none; but by using blows we will have it, for we see that this is the only way to get anywhere. It will start soon if this prejudice is not entirely anni-

Source: Centre des Archives d'Outre-Mer, C8A 89, p. 68.

hilated . . . there will be torrents of blood flowing as powerful as the gutters that flow along our streets.

> Sirs,
> We have the honor of being
> Signed by us, Nègres

Copy of a Letter from the Slaves of Martinique, August 29, 1789

Great General:
The entire Nation of the Black Slaves very humbly begs your august person to accept its respectful homage and to cast a humanitarian eye on the reflections it takes the liberty of presenting to you.

We are not unaware, Great General, of all the negative things that have been presented to you about us; we are painted in such a foul way that even the most solidly virtuous person would have reason to turn against us; but God, who sooner or later always stops the proud plans of men, this God who is so just knows what is deep inside us; he knows that we have never had any project but to patiently accept the oppression of our persecutors. This eternal God, who could no longer suffer so much persecution, must have given Louis XVI, the greatest of monarchs, the charge of delivering all the miserable Christians oppressed by their unjust fellow men. . . .

We have just learned with extreme desperation that the mulattos, far from taking care of their enslaved mothers, brothers, and sisters, have dared claim that we do not deserve to enjoy, as they do, the benefits that come from peace and liberty and are incapable of continuing the hard work that supports the merchants of the white nation and cannot provide any service to the state. This is a great absurdity, and this vile action must demonstrate to you the baseness of spirit of this proud nation and make you see the hate, the jealousy, and all the horror of the disdain this nation has for us. . . . It is not jealousy that forces us to complain about the mulattos, but the harshness they have shown in creating a plan for liberty for only themselves, when we are all of the same family. We do not know, Great General, if you have received the request of the mulattos, but you will receive it soon, and we are happy if we have the good fortune to have reached you before it. . . .

We end our reflections by declaring to you that the entire Nation of

---

Source: Archives Nationales, C[8A] 89, p. 69.

Black Slaves united together has a single wish, a single desire for independence, and all the slaves with a unanimous voice send out only one cry, one clamor to reclaim the liberty they have gained through centuries of suffering and ignominious servitude.

This is no longer a Nation that is blinded by ignorance and that trembles at the threat of the lightest punishments; its suffering has enlightened it and has determined it to spill to its last drop of blood rather than support the yoke of slavery, a horrible yoke attacked by the laws, by humanity, and by all of nature, by the Divinity and by our good King Louis XVI. We hope it will be condemned by the illustrious [Governor] Vioménil. Your response, Great General, will decide our destiny and that of the colony. Please send it to the parish priests who will inform us about it at the announcements at the end of mass. We await it with the greatest impatience, but without leaving behind the respect that is due to your dignity, and the Nation asks you to believe it to be, [Great] Grand General, your most humble and obedient servant.

> Signed,
> The Entire Nation
> Saint-Pierre, August 29, 1789

5

THE FREE CITIZENS OF COLOR

Address to the National Assembly
October 22, 1789

Summer 1789 had been a tumultuous time in Paris. Within three months, the Estates General had become the National Assembly and had voted the Declaration of Rights of Man and Citizen as the preamble to a new French constitution. Inspired by these events, more than a dozen of the hundreds of people of color living in the capital city began to hold meetings in late August. Gathering in the offices of Étienne-Louis-Hector Dejoly, a white lawyer who became their spokesman, they drew up a formal

From "Discours de M. Joly au nom d'une députation des hommes de couleur," 22 October 1789, in *Archives parlementaires,* première série (Paris: P. Dupont, 1877), IX: 476–78.

collection of grievances, as most of France had done earlier in the pre-ceding year. They then approached a group of wealthy absentee planters who were meeting in Paris to discuss how the emerging revolution might affect the colonies. When the planters rejected their proposed reforms in early September, the Parisian free coloreds appealed to the National Assembly.

Address to the National Assembly, To Our Lords, the Representatives of the Nation.

Our lords, the free citizens and landowners of color of the French islands and colonies are honored to inform you that there still exists in one of the lands of this empire a species of men scorned and de-graded, a class of citizens doomed to rejection, to all the humiliations of slavery: in a word, Frenchmen who groan under the yoke of op-pression.

Such is the fate of the unfortunate American colonists known in the islands under the name of mulattos, quadroons,[2] etc.

Born citizens and free, they live as foreigners in their own father-land. Excluded from all positions, from honors and professions, they are even forbidden to practice some of the mechanical trades. Set apart in the most degrading fashion, they find themselves enslaved even in their liberty.

The Estates General has been summoned.

All France has hastened to support the king's benevolent plans; citi-zens of all classes have been called to the great work of public regen-eration; all have contributed to writing complaints and nominating deputies to defending their rights and set forth their interests.

The call of liberty has echoed in the other hemisphere.

It should certainly have erased even the memory of these outra-geous distinctions between citizens of the same land; instead, it has brought forth even more appalling ones.

For an ambitious aristocracy, liberty means only the right to rule other men, without sharing power.

The white colonists have acted according to this principle, which even today consistently guides their behavior.

They have taken upon themselves the right to elect colonial repre-sentatives.

[2]Individuals of one-quarter African ancestry.

Excluded from these meetings, the citizens of color have been deprived of the ability to look after their own interests, to discuss things that affect them too, and to carry their wishes, complaints, and demands to the National Assembly.

In this strange system, the citizens of color find themselves represented by the white colonists' deputies, although they have still never been included in their partial assemblies and they have not entrusted any power to these deputies. Their opposing interests, which sadly are only too obvious, make such representation absurd and contradictory.

You, our lords, must weigh these considerations; you must return to these oppressed citizens the rights that have been unjustly stripped from them; you must gloriously complete your work, by ensuring the liberty of French citizens in both hemispheres.

The Declaration of the Rights of Man and Citizen has awakened the colonists of color to their past condition; they have shown themselves worthy of the dignity that you have assigned to them; they have learned their rights and they have used them. . . .

The citizens of color are clearly as qualified as the whites to demand this representation.

Like them they are all citizens, free and French; the edict of March 1685 accords them all such rights and guarantees them all such privileges. It states "that the freedmen (and all the more so their descendants) have earned their liberty; let this liberty produce in them, as much in their persons as for their property, the same effects as the fortune of liberty that is natural to all Frenchmen."[3] Like them they are property owners and farmers; like them they contribute to the relief of the state by paying the levies and bearing all expenses that they and the whites share. Like them they have already shed their blood and are prepared to spill it again for the defense of the fatherland. Like them, finally, though with less encouragement and means, they have proven their patriotism again and again. . . .

They beseech you, our lords, not to forget them, and to act strictly on principle.

They ask for no favors.

They claim the rights of man and of citizen, those inalienable rights based on nature and the social contract, those rights that you have so solemnly recognized and so faithfully established when you established as the foundation of the constitution "that all men are born and remain free and equal in rights.

---

[3]From Article 59 of *The Code Noir.* Note that this is a paraphrase, not an exact quote.

"That the law is the expression of the general will; that all citizens have the right to participate personally, or through their representatives, in its formation;

"That each citizen has the right to certify the necessity of public contribution, and to freely consent to it, either personally or through his representatives."

Is it your intent to reject these fundamental principles, setting the interests of the whites against those of the colonies? Do we want to muffle nature's voice with the calculations of sordid profit?

Can we not recognize the language of ambition and greed, whose speakers do not value the prosperity of the state unless they profit personally?

But this is not the place to conduct such serious discussions about basics of the rights of the citizens of color.

After you have agreed to their preliminary claims: when they have descended into the arena to fight their adversaries, they will easily show that the legitimate interests of the whites themselves, like those of the colonies, lie in guaranteeing the status and the liberty of the citizens of color. For a state's good fortune consists in the peace and harmony of its constituent members, and there can be no true peace or strong union between a strong group that oppresses and a weak one that yields; between a commanding master and an obedient slave.

6

THE NATIONAL ASSEMBLY

Decree of March 8 and *Instructions of March 28*

1790

On March 8, 1790, the French National Assembly passed a brief decree describing how elections should be organized in the colonies. Despite the arguments of the free men of color and their Parisian supporters that they were qualified to be citizens, neither the March 8 decree nor the Assembly's "Instructions," passed twenty days later, specifically mentioned

R. P. Adolphe Cabon, *Histoire d'Haïti. Cours professé au Petit Séminaire, Collège Saint Martial*, vol. 3 (Port-au-Prince: Édition de la Petite Revue, 1920–1937).

whether free people of color would be allowed to vote. These documents were based on the recommendations of the assembly's Colonial Committee, which free colored advocates described as controlled by planter interests.

Decree of the National Assembly, Monday March 8, 1790

First Article—Each colony has the right to express its wishes regarding the constitution, laws, and administration appropriate to its prosperity and the good fortunes of its inhabitants, as long as it conforms to the general principles that connect the colonies to the metropole[4] and guarantee the protection of their respective interests.

Article II—In colonies that have Colonial Assemblies, freely elected and acknowledged by the citizens, these assemblies will be allowed to express the wishes of the colony. Those colonies without such assemblies will immediately create them in order to perform these same functions. . . .

Article IV—The plans prepared by these Colonial Assemblies will be submitted to the National Assembly, which will examine them, issue a decree, and present them for royal acceptance and approval.

Article V—The National Assembly's decrees on the organization of municipal governments and administrative assemblies will be sent to these Colonial Assemblies, which will be authorized to execute those parts of the said decrees that can be adapted to local customs, pending the final decision of the National Assembly and the king on any modifications, and with the governor's provisional approval of measures voted by the administrative bodies.

Instructions Addressed by the National Assembly to the Colony of Saint-Domingue

On March 28, 1790

First Article—As soon as the Saint-Domingue's governor receives the king's dispatch containing these Instructions and the National Assembly's March 8 colonial decree, he will immediately communicate them to the Colonial Assembly if one is already formed, notify the provincial assemblies, and inform the residents of the colony legally

---

[4]The term *metropole* was used to refer to the part of the French nation located on the European continent, in contrast to its overseas colonies.

and authentically by having them proclaimed and posted in all parishes.

Article II—If a Colonial Assembly exists, it may declare that it would be better for the colony to form a new assembly rather than continue its own activity, and in this case new elections will be held immediately.

Article III—If, on the other hand, it believes that its continuation would be more advantageous to the colony, it may begin to work following the directions of the National Assembly. But it will not execute certain decrees until the colony's intentions about this continuation have been made clear in the forms described below.

Article IV—Immediately after the proclamation and the posting of the decree and the Instructions in each parish, all persons having attained twenty-five years of age and owning property or, failing this, resident in the parish for two years and paying taxes will gather to form a parish assembly. . . .

Article XVII—Examining the forms that will guide how legislative power is to be exercised over the colonies, they will recognize that, though they may discuss and prepare their own laws, those laws do not fully and definitively exist until the National Assembly has ratified them and the king approved them. And while purely internal laws may be provisionally executed with the governor's approval, awaiting the definitive approval of the king and the French legislature, laws that affect external affairs, and that might in any way modify or change the relations between the colonies and the metropole, cannot be even provisionally executed until they are established by the national will. This does not include the momentary exceptions accorded to imports of food because of pressing needs and with the governor's approval.

7

ABBÉ GRÉGOIRE

Letter to Those Who Love Mankind

*about the Hardships, Rights, and Demands of
the Free People of Color in Saint-Domingue
and the Other French Islands in America*

October 1790

*On October 12, 1790, responding to the insistence of Saint-Domingue's
whites that Parisian legislators could never understand how important
racism was to colonial security, the National Assembly voted to put all
power to reform racial laws in the hands of the Colonial Assemblies.
Planters warned that, even when French lawmakers openly debated
racial discrimination, they endangered the Caribbean colonies. The Abbé
Grégoire, one of the strongest allies of the Parisian men of color, was not
allowed to speak in the assembly, but he published a pamphlet that foresaw
dire consequences if qualified free men of color were not given civil rights.*

October 12, 1790, is a date forever sorrowful in the annals of history.
Every year Liberty, Humanity, and Justice will mourn its passing,
while our descendants will remember with shock or indignation that
on this day one part of the nation was sacrificed to the prejudices and
greed of another. This was no Saint Bartholomew's Day Massacre.[5]
But is it more humane to rob a man of his life and its sorrows in an
instant, or to prolong his existence while stripping him of everything
that might make it more bearable?

. . . We have decided (something unheard of in any nation!) that there
will be no change in the status of the people in our islands, except at
the colonists' request. That is, the National Assembly will not stamp out
injustice except at the request of those who feed on the situation and
want to prolong it! In other words, the eternal rights of men are less

---

[5]The Saint Bartholomew's Day Massacre, beginning on August 24, 1572, was a notorious event in France's wars of religion in which thousands of Protestants were attacked and killed by their neighbors.

Abbé Grégoire, *Lettre aux philanthropes, sur les malheurs, les droits et les réclamations des gens
de couleur de Saint-Domingue, et des autres îles françoises d'Amérique* (Paris, October 1790).

important than pride and avarice! Put another way, these men will be the victims of oppression until their tyrants agree to lighten their fate.

The representatives of the French people voted this strange decree almost unanimously, at the very moment in which they were congratulating themselves for having struck down tyranny and reconquered liberty. Moreover, as if they were afraid of gaining some insight on an issue of such great importance, they had already voted to prohibit any discussion of this one. . . .

The political world is certainly going to look different. The volcano of liberty that has been lit in France will soon bring about a general explosion and change the fate of the human species in the two hemispheres. The interests of the colony and of the metropole, their internal and external security, require that all forces work together, like the bundle of sticks that, according to the story, a dying father offered his family as an emblem. But our islands harbor the seeds of their own destruction, which are sending out roots. It is always a despicable policy to degrade one group of people instead of involving them in maintaining order. Did not the oppression of soldiers cause regimental uprisings [in France] that almost dissolved the army? It would be a great mistake to imagine that the colonies could remain in this unnatural repressed state very long; to believe this, one would have to know very little about human affairs. And the following considerations reinforce this opinion.

Everywhere the people of mixed race see this cockade, which, according to the prediction, will be known around the world; they see the revolutionary flag paraded with honor. How can one believe that the cries of liberty ringing endlessly in their ears will not awaken in their hearts a longing for their rights? Add to this a consideration of their strength, whose steady growth is extraordinary. I will cite just one fact. In 1779, there were 7,055 people of color in Saint-Domingue; in 1787, 19,632 were counted. Therefore, in the period of eight years, the population more than doubled; while France's population barely grew by one-ninth over a period of seventy-two years.

How can you limit that population when the unrestrained lechery of so many whites guarantees its future growth? The mulattos' industriousness and its results will follow the same pattern. Will you disarm all the free colored militias and patrols in fear of an uprising? They would have to be replaced and restrained by multiple expeditions of French soldiers, who would have to carry out all duties in a burning climate that devours effeminate Europeans and overworked *nègres.*

Who can say whether this degraded caste, pushed to despair, will not use its strength to rescue justice, if the mulattos will not ally with the *nègres* against those whites who might have easily claimed them, thanks to filial love or the habit of respect? The easiest path for them would be to emigrate to the neighboring Spanish territory, where a diversity of skin colors has not produced legal distinctions. Already several have taken this step, and I can assure you, for I have proof, that if the injustices of the whites do not end soon, many people of mixed race plan to abandon a country where the sun shines only on their sorrows, and take their productivity and wealth elsewhere.

Moreover, do you not fear a coalition between the people of mixed race, those whites who aim at independence, and others who would greedily seize an opportunity to free themselves from paying the enormous sums they owe to France? Might not bitterness, ambition, and disloyalty stir up trouble and cause secession, with incalculable consequences? . . .

Oh, that I were a false prophet! But if events prove my fears correct, at least I will not have to reproach myself for saying nothing about these important matters. Is it not obvious that, if pride could be set aside, there would be more citizens and they would have less to fear from the slaves? If people of mixed race and whites could be brought together by their common interests and advantages, the size of their combined forces would more efficiently ensure the colonies' tranquility. There can be no doubt that sooner or later the repressed energy of the mulattos will rise up with an unstoppable violence. The oppressed can be forced into inactivity now only because they are temporarily weak. Such dangerous apathy! Evil's frightening silence is usually broken only by a tumultuous dash for liberty.

8

Letters from the Uprising of Vincent Ogé
October 1790

The light-skinned son of a French merchant in the main colonial city of Cap Français, Vincent Ogé was one of the wealthiest men of color in Saint-Domingue, dealing in sugar, coffee, and real estate with French and colonial merchants alike. He had come to Paris on business in the late 1780s and had offered his own version of racial reform to absentee planters before joining the Paris free colored group and soon becoming one of its leaders. After the National Assembly voted to send its ambiguous March 28 Instruction

Archives Nationales, Section Outre-Mer, DXXV 65, dossier 658, piece 11.

to Saint-Domingue, Ogé left France secretly, traveling first to England and then Charleston, South Carolina, before returning to Saint-Domingue in October 1790. On arrival, he sent a letter to Saint-Domingue's governor, the Count de Peinier, in an attempt to get the royal government to apply the reforms he believed had been legislated in Paris. He intimated that, if the governor did not take action, he might soon be facing an insurrection.

Ogé to the Count de Peinier

October 21, 1790
Monsieur Count,

We had the honor of writing you collectively from Paris last April 18, under the seal of M. Bisonar, treasurer, to provide you with an excerpt of the National Assembly's decree of March 28 concerning the colonies, and copies of all our demands.

I was indeed surprised, *Monsieur,* to see when I arrived that you had not published the decree and that you undoubtedly intended to ignore it as your predecessors did the Edict of 1685.

No, no, *Monsieur* Count, we will not remain under the yoke as we have for two centuries. The iron rod that has beaten us down is broken. We call for the enacting of this decree; be prudent, therefore, and avoid a crisis that you would not be able to subdue.

I have sworn to see the execution of the decree that I worked to obtain, to rebut force with force, and, finally, to put an end to a prejudice that is as unjust as it is barbaric.

I am, with respect, etc.,
Signed Ogé the Younger

Peinier rebuffed Ogé, who began gathering armed supporters in order to put additional pressure on the government. He also appealed to leaders of color in other parts of the colony to join him, but they were more cautious, as this letter shows.

The Free-Colored Leaders of the West to Ogé

Port-au-Prince
October 29, 1790

Monsieur,
You must be aware of all our gratitude for the services you ren-

Archives Nationales, F³ 196, f⁰ 114.

dered in France to the entire free colored class; at this time, we are unable to communicate our sentiments to you. We will have to be satisfied with telling you that, while admiring your patriotic zeal, we cannot join the steps you want to take with the governor. We believe that the present circumstances are not favorable to such a request. We also observed that the letters that Monsieur your brother brought us are written in imprudent terms and may have a bad effect, especially at a time when many persons appear to be disposed in our favor. We believe that you should come to Mirebalais with all the documents that show the National Assembly's recognition of our rights. Some of us will also travel to Mirebalais to discuss with you what measures we should take to get what we legitimately request. We hope you will not attribute our refusal to join the steps you are planning to a lack of enthusiasm or energy on our part. On the contrary, please understand that, rather than give up the pursuit of our rights, we are more committed than ever to uphold them with the last drop of our blood. But we believe that waiting several days will allow us a better means of success. We hope that you will not misunderstand the observations that we make here, and that you will indeed be persuaded of the sincerity of the sentiments with which we have the honor, etc.

Signed P. Pinchinat, Beauvais, La Bastille, Borno Jeune, La Bastille fils, Drouillard fils.

Ogé wrote the following letter to the Provincial Assembly of the North when he was under attack by the white colonial militia, which aimed to capture him and disperse his band of supporters. Although his troops initially defeated the white militia, they were soon routed, and Ogé fled to the Spanish colony of Santo Domingo. Extradited back to the French colony a few weeks later, he was publicly tortured and executed.

Ogé to the Provincial Assembly of the North

Hear ye, hear ye, the worthiness of a man whose intentions are pure. When I asked the National Assembly for a decree that I received on behalf of the American colonists formerly known under the insulting epithet "mixed-blood," my claims included nothing about the fate of the *nègres* who live in slavery. You and all our adversaries have distorted my efforts so that respectable landowners will have no regard for me. No, no, Monsieur, we have only made claims on behalf of the class of free men who have been oppressed for two centuries. We

Archives Nationales, DXXV 65, dossier 658, pièce 9.

want the execution of the March 28 decree; we continue to work for its adoption, and we will never stop repeating to our friends that our adversaries are unjust and that they cannot conceive of reconciling their interests with our own.

I have the honor to be, etc. your very humble and very obedient servant.

Signed, Ogé the Younger

9

JULIEN RAIMOND

Observations on the Origin and Progression of the White Colonists' Prejudice against Men of Color

1791

Born in 1744 in Saint-Domingue's southern peninsula to a French immigrant and a free woman of color, Julien Raimond was a successful indigo planter who owned more than a hundred slaves by the 1780s. In 1785, he moved to France, where his speeches and pamphlets helped convince the National Assembly to dismantle colonial racism. He stepped up his efforts during the early years of the French Revolution and in 1791 penned this essay in support of granting political rights to free coloreds. At the core of his argument was a history and description of the free people of color of Saint-Domingue that differed sharply from the way they were often portrayed by other writers, such as Moreau de Saint-Méry (Document 3), by emphasizing their sexual virtue and loyalty to France.

For a long time, we have been debating a great question regarding our colonies: whether the free people of color will be given the status of active citizen [i.e., given full political rights] in the colonies.

Julien Raimond, *Observations sur l'origine et les progrés [sic] du préjugé des colons blancs contre les hommes de couleur; sur les inconvéniens de le perpétuer; la nécessité, la facilité de le détruire; par M. Raymond, homme de couleur de Saint-Domingue* (Paris, 1791).

The white planters, who are the aristocrats, the nobles of the colonies, want to take these priceless rights from the free mulattos they detest and want to disgrace. To do this, they have deliberately confused the free colored cause with that of the slaves. This carefully planned misunderstanding has so scrambled ideas about the true status of the free people of color that up to now a large part of the National Assembly still has no clear understanding of this free and property-owning class of color.

It is therefore essential to clarify things and state here: (1) how the free population of color started; (2) how it survived over time, and, finally, what it is today.

A mulatto is the offspring of a white man with a black woman. The terms *people of color* or *people of mixed race* refer to the product of two mulattos or of mulattos with whites, and to their different offspring.

When the colonies were founded and at the moment when Africans began to be brought in to cultivate them, there were no or almost no European women present. Only single men burning with a desire to succeed dared cross the seas and expose themselves to a climate that was all the more dangerous because they had none of the measures that exist today.

Transported to this foreign and still uncultivated land, weakened by the hot climate, often sick and without the assistance that wives of their own color might have provided, these Europeans became attached to African women, who cared for them all the more attentively because they hoped liberty would be their reward.

These first whites lived with these women as in the state of marriage; they had children with them. Some, touched by their affection and care and swept away by paternal love, married their slaves. This not only freed them from slavery; it also legitimized the fruit of their love or habits.

When they died, they usually left these children the property they had acquired. Other men, less sensitive than this, perhaps more proud, perhaps already committed [to another woman] by indissoluble bonds, simply manumitted the children and the woman who brought them into the world and gave these children lands and some slaves.

Such, in the colony's first age, was the free population of color. Then they married among themselves, and the daughters married whites who came from France.

When the colony was a little more developed and the government began to pay more attention to it, a number of white women were sent there to increase the white population. The whites preferred girls of color over these women, and those who did not share this preference chose women among their slaves to care for them and their households. Though they called them housekeepers, they made them into wives. As soon as these women had children with their masters, they became free, as did their children, who were always raised like free children. There was still so much uncultivated land available then that they could give some to each of their children.

Such was the status of the free people of color in the colony's second age.

Until this point, there was no prejudice against this class of free men. There was no dishonor in knowing them, spending time with them, living with them, forming relationships with their daughters; and men of color were commissioned as officers in the militia.

Prejudice started around the middle of the colony's third age, and here is its origin. Just before the 1744 war [War of Austrian Succession], the colonies were so profitable that France paid more attention to them than ever before. Many Europeans crossed the sea, including large numbers of poor women who came to seek their fortunes. Mothers brought their daughters to marry them to rich colonists. They were frequently disappointed. Since these immigrant women brought no resources, many of the young men who came to the colony to get rich preferred to marry girls of color, whose dowries included land and slaves they could use profitably. Such preferences began to inspire jealousy in white women. *Inde irae.*[6]

Jealousy changed into hate in the colony's third age. By that time, there were many young folk from good families. Many younger sons of nobility came to the colony to marry girls of color whose parents had become rich,* establishing themselves comfortably this way and even increasing their fortunes.

This was the situation at the end of the colony's third age, in 1749. . . .

The peace of 1749 attracted to the islands a great many white families who quickly adopted the resentments and prejudice that the earlier whites began to manifest against the people of color, whose growing fortunes only increased these feelings.

The peace of 1763 strengthened these sentiments. All those young people of color who had received a good education [in France], includ-

---

[6]Latin for "Hence this resentment."
*In 1763, more than three hundred whites, including several gentlemen, had married girls of color. See the *Considerations of Saint-Domingue* by H.D.

ing several who had held honored positions at court or served as officers in different regiments, returned to the colony at that time.

Their talent, character, sophistication, and knowledge only drew attention to the vices and ignorance of the islands' whites, who therefore scorned them. Just as tyrants cannot forgive virtue, the dim-witted resent intelligence. In addition to the humiliations whites heaped upon these young people of color, they tried to create harsh laws that would reinforce these insults and stifle all the talents and industry of this class. . . .

It was during the reestablishment of the militia [in 1769] that white jealousy against the people of color was wielded with a furor that had never been seen before. It was not enough to strip men of color of their officers' commissions despite their outstanding service. This injustice was followed by a host of laws that outdid each other in tyranny and absurdity. One forbade people of color to use a carriage; another forbade them to dress like whites or wear the same fabrics or jewels; this was in fact the most ill-advised law, since it attacked a branch of French industry, but jealousy knows no bounds and cuts its own throat. The colonial ministry refused to acknowledge the noble status of whites who had married women of color. It sent letters forbidding people of color from coming to France or sending their children for education. Others stripped all honors from whites marrying women of color, or required notaries and priests to insert the word "free" on all official documents drafted for people of color to remind them, so it was said, of their origins [in slavery], no matter how distant it was. Other orders required them to drop the European name they had and adopt one in an African language. Finally, this frenzy was pushed so far that Hilliard d'Auberteuil[7] dared recommend that whites take justice into their own hands with people of color without ever informing the judicial system. . . .

The basic idea of everything that you have just read is that the majority of the free colored class was born free, of free parents, and in legitimate marriage, and that those who are illegitimate were born of free mothers. Out of this entire class there are not two hundred who were truly enslaved and manumitted.

As for the free blacks who are also included in the free colored class, there are no more than fifteen hundred in all, and more than two-thirds of them were born free and the others manumitted. These

---

[7]An eighteenth-century author who penned a famous book about Saint-Domingue.

facts and calculations can be easily verified using militia rolls and parish registers.[8]

[8]Although much of Raimond's account rings true, the claims in these last two paragraphs are misleading. Depending on the region of the colony, approximately one-third to one-half of all free people of color in Saint-Domingue were ex-slaves. Similarly, the colony was home to thousands of free blacks, most of whom would have been ex-slaves.

10

The Debate of May 15, 1791

This cartoon was published the day that the National Assembly voted to give citizenship to a small group of legitimately born free men of color. The image reveals that the cartoonist saw the controversy as exotic, yet connected to the deepest values of the French Revolution. The cartoon depicts the various forces pressuring Antoine Barnave (2), chair of the Colonial Committee, who is being offered bribes by a colonist (1) and ideas by a conservative writer (3). As the tiny figures of the rest of the Committee (#24) climb Barnave's legs, the decrepit and deaf Gerard (8) exclaims, "I agree with Mr. Barnave. What did he say?" His companion, Médéric-Louis-Élie Moreau de Saint-Méry (Document 3), replies, "Ask my mulatto mistress [she lives at] Clergy Street, No. 22." In the center of the image, Barnave turns his back on the child labeled "the Little Mulatto" (11), who cries out to "Gouy d'Arcy" (Louis-Marthe Gouy d'Arcy), the leader of the conservative planters, "Father, father, for God's sake, speak on our behalf." The white man answers, "Alas, my son, I would do it, if it would only earn me 42 percent."

Behind the child is Julien Raimond (16; see Document 9), described as a "citizen of color," holding part of the Declaration of the Rights of Man and Citizen. He says, "By wrenching this immortal declaration from my hands, cruel sir, do you believe you are tearing it from all the hearts in which it is written?" A colonist of color (15) asks, "Are we not free, property owners, and taxpayers; why in God's name are we treated like slaves?"

Hovering over these men are the allegorical figures (12) of Humanity, Justice, and Reason, identified respectively as Maximilien Robespierre, a prominent member of the National Assembly, "Pethion" (Jérôme Pétion de Villeneuve), President of the Friends of the Blacks, and the Abbé Henri Grégoire (see Document 7). The artist describes them as having "come to the rescue of the men of color that Barnave holds in chains and wants to deliver to the white colonists."

Bibliothèque Nationale.

11

THE NATIONAL ASSEMBLY

Law on the Colonies,

*with an Explanation of the Reasons That Have
Determined Its Content*

1791

---

*By spring 1791, a number of events had loosened the French National
Assembly's position on free colored citizenship, including the execution of
Vincent Ogé and increasing Jacobin support of the antislavery position of
the Friends of the Blacks. At the same time, the National Assembly voted
to send more troops to deal with colonial unrest and asked the Colonial
Committee to draw up instructions for these forces. When the committee
presented its work to the assembly on May 9, 1791, Grégoire and other
pro-free colored deputies again raised the issue of race and citizenship.
The result was the decree of May 15, 1791.*

Decree of the National Assembly of May 13, 1791

The National Assembly decrees as an article of the constitution that
the legislature shall make no law on the status of unfree persons
in the colonies except at the specific and unprompted request of the
colonial assemblies.

Decree of the National Assembly of May 15, 1791

The National Assembly decrees that the legislature will never deliber-
ate on the political status of people of color who were not born of free
fathers and mothers without the previous, free, and unprompted
request of the colonies; that the presently existing Colonial Assemblies will remain in place, but that the Parish Assemblies and future
Colonial Assemblies will admit the people of color born of free fathers
and mothers if they otherwise have the required status.

Loi relative aux Colonies, avec l'exposition des motifs qui en ont détérminés les dispositions
(Paris, 1791).

From Explanation of the Reasons for the Decrees of May 13 and 15 Above and Elsewhere on the Status of Persons in the Colonies, Decreed May 29, 1791

The National Assembly, attentive to all means of assuring prosperity in the colonies, to ensure that the citizens living there enjoy the advantages of the constitution..., recognizes that local circumstances and the kind of agriculture that brings colonial prosperity appear to require introducing into the colonial constitution several exceptions to the [French Revolution's] general principles.

... [On March 28, 1790] The National Assembly declared that the legislature would discuss the status of nonfree persons only on the unprompted request of the Colonial Assemblies.

The National Assembly was able to make this commitment because it only involved individuals of a foreign land[9] who, by their profound ignorance, the misfortune of their exile, the consideration of their own interest, and the urgent law of necessity, can only hope that in time the progress of public opinion and enlightenment will produce a change of conditions that, in the present state of things, would be contrary to the general good and might become equally dangerous for them.

... where property is guaranteed, where agriculture and trade can prosper, one finds all the sources of wealth and all the means of happiness. The National Assembly believed it necessary to guarantee these to the colonies, using the clearest and unequivocal expressions.... Even under the Old Regime[10] and under the most despotic of governments, the edict of 1685 had given the freedmen all the rights that the other citizens enjoyed. A new law would be necessary to exclude them from the new rights of citizens under the revolution. Any uncertainty was resolved by the decree of March 28, which says specifically and without exception: "That all free persons, property-owning or established for two years and paying taxes, will enjoy the voting rights that constitute active citizenship."

The National Assembly could not refuse to render this March 28 decree; it is not up to it to restrict its meaning, damaging the essential rights of the citizens; it cannot grant one part of the empire the ability to exclude men from active citizenship when the constitutional laws guarantee those rights in the entire empire. The rights of citizens exist before society; they serve as its base. The National Assembly can only recognize and declare them; fortunately, it is powerless to infringe upon them.

[9]This paragraph refers to slaves.
[10]The term *Old Regime* was used to describe the order that had prevailed before the French Revolution of 1789.

3

From Slave Revolution to Emancipation, 1791–1794

12

HÉRARD DUMESLE

Voyage to the North of Haiti

1824

In the early 1820s, a Haitian politician named Hérard Dumesle, whose free colored ancestors had owned slaves in the southern province before the revolution, traveled to the northern part of Haiti, visiting historical sites in the region. In his account of the journey, he included the following description of a meeting and religious ceremony, now referred to as the Bois-Caïman ceremony, during which the 1791 slave insurrection was planned. Unfortunately, Dumesle did not indicate the source for his account of the ceremony, although during his trip he could have spoken to individuals who had lived in the area during the early 1790s, and perhaps even to some who had participated in the ceremony itself. Whatever its source, Dumesle's account was also clearly shaped and embellished by his fascination with classic Roman and Greek civilization. Presented in verse, it included a short speech he claimed was delivered by someone present at the ceremony. Dumesle did not identify the speaker, but later authors have attributed the speech to the slave and religious leader Boukman.

Hérard Dumesle, *Voyage dans le nord d'Hayti, ou, Révélation des lieux et des monuments historiques* (Cayes: Imprimerie du Gouvernement, 1824), 85–90.

Toward the middle of the month of August 1791, the cultivators,[1] [sugar] manufacturers, and artisans from several work gangs gathered during the night, in the midst of a violent storm in a thick forest that covers the summit of the *morne rouge*,[2] and there formed a plan for a vast insurrection, which they sanctified through a religious ceremony. . . .

> Through the furrows traced by the lightning
> Where the light of a hundred eclipsed fires is shining
> Groups of the oppressed assemble in silence
> They prostrate themselves invoking the assistance
> Of the God who awakened amongst a people brilliant
> The illustrious Spartacus,[3] this slave valiant
> Victim of destiny, but through the centuries an example
> Whose name, whose virtues deserve a temple . . .
>
> Nature stirred . . .
> Three centuries of slavery outraged her clemency,
> Dirtied her august presence with its crimes . . .
> Vengeance awakens and shines the double-edged sword . . .
> Excites that extraordinary thirst, the surprise of the senses,
> The guide of desperation, and precursor of crime,
> That by necessity has become legitimate.
>
> A bull appeared, and this black color . . .
> [Was] offered by innocence as a sacrifice
> To that deity adored by Hope.
> Among the participants a speaker rises up
> He has the august job of making the sacrifice
> Holding a sacred blade, his arm brings to the victim
> The fatal blow . . . He immediately consults its flank . . .
> Prophetic delirium! . . . Holocaust of blood! . . .
> You unveil the fate of the noble enterprise
> That forms heroes and renders them immortal! . . .
>
> He speaks; and this language loved by our ancestors
> That ingenious language that seemed made for them,

[margin annotations: poetic verses; hymn; doubtful; priest; spoke in rhyming prose]

[1] Plantation laborers.
[2] A hill near Le Cap.
[3] Spartacus led a famous slave revolt in ancient Rome.

Whose naive accents, the portrait of their souls,
Give more eloquence to this burning speech. . . .[4]
"This God who made the sun, who brings us light from above,
Who raises the sea, and who makes the storm rumble,
That God is there, do you understand? Hiding in a cloud,
He watches us, he sees all that the whites do!
The God of the whites pushes them to crime, but he wants us to do
  good deeds.[5]
But that God who is so good orders us to vengeance;
He will direct our hands, and give us help,
Throw away the image of the God of the whites who thirsts for our
  tears,
Listen to the liberty that speaks in all our hearts."
The oracle had spoken. . . .

The next day it was almost midnight when the bell gave the signal
for the disaster. The insurrection exploded with such furor that it created the most sad of spectacles. The conjured gathered on the plain,
dispersed themselves into groups, and carried the spirit that animated
them everywhere: Horror preceded them, destruction followed them
and left behind them the disastrous traces of their passage. "Liberty,
vengeance," these were their rallying cries; they were the divinities to
which they sacrificed.

[4]Dumesle provided two versions of this speech, one in Creole and one in French. We
have translated primarily from the Creole version, though with some consultation of the
French version he supplied.
   [5]There are two possible interpretations of this very famous line. Dumesle's French
version suggests that there are two different gods: "The God of the whites pushes them
to crime, but our God wants us to do good deeds." But the Creole he provides could be
read, as in the translation above, as suggesting that the same God pushes the whites
and the slaves to different ends.

13

ANTOINE DALMAS

History of the Revolution of Saint-Domingue
1814

Dalmas was a colonist who emigrated from Saint-Domingue to the United States in 1793. Once there, he wrote an account of the uprising in the colony based in part on his own experiences, which was eventually published in 1814. Along with Dumesle's work, Dalmas's work provides us with one of the most detailed descriptions of the meetings and other organizational work that preceded the slave uprising of August 1791 as well as of the ceremony that accompanied these meetings.

It was on August 20, 1791, that the revolt of the blacks broke out on one of the plantations of M. de Galliffet [*sic*] known as *La Gossette,* with the [attempted] murder[6] of M. Mossut, who was its manager. The following details are the core of the testimony of several *nègres* who testified the following day before the judge of Cap Français, who went to these places to investigate the guilty parties. They said that an old *nègre* called Ignace—who, it is interesting to note, was different from all the others in being exempt from any kind of work [and] by the individual care he received—kept for a long time the secret of the conspiracy. In a long meeting that he had had the very eve of the revolt with a free black of Grande-Rivière (one of those tried in absentia in the Ogé affair), this free black told him this: "The moment of revenge is coming; tomorrow night, all the whites must be killed. We are counting on your promises and your influence. M. Mossut will be one of the first victims, and you must convince Blaise[7] to strike him down. No more delays, no more worries; the plot is too widespread to leave any refuge or security for the whites. They will all share the

---

[6]Although Dalmas uses the term *assassinat* (murder) here, he seems to have known that Mossut was wounded but not killed by the insurgents, as the remainder of the document makes clear. On Mossut's experience, see Document 14.
[7]The plantation's head slave or *commandeur.*

Antoine Dalmas, *Histoire de la révolution de Saint-Domingue* (Paris, 1814), 116–27.

same fate, and if some of them avoid our daggers they will not escape the fires that will reduce the plain to cinders."

The specifics of this plan had been decreed several days before between the principal leaders on Le Normand plantation in Morne Rouge. Before carrying it out, they had a kind of celebration or sacrifice in the middle of an uncultivated woods on the Choiseul plantation, known as Caïman, where the *nègres* gathered in great numbers. A black pig, surrounded by objects they believe have magical power, each carrying the most bizarre offering, was offered as a sacrifice to the all-powerful spirit of the black race. The religious ceremony in which the *nègres* slit its throat, the greed with which they drank its blood, the importance they attached to owning some of its bristles which they believed would make them invincible reveal the characteristics of the Africans. It is natural that a caste this ignorant and stupid would begin the most horrible attacks with the superstitious rites of an absurd and bloodthirsty religion.

M. Mossut, who had been in Cap Français on business, returned that evening with one of his friends. As soon as the slaves thought they were both asleep, they went first to Mossut's bedroom, whose door was always left open. Awakened by the noise, he asked who was there. They responded: "We are here to talk to you." He tried to raise the mosquito netting around his bed. At that very moment, two machete blows cut it into shreds; a third struck M. Mossut in the shoulder and on the hand. He only had time to yell out and throw himself in the space between his bed and the wall. The height and size of his bed sheltered him from the blows they tried to strike. Thanks to the dim light, he was able to grab the spear of a slave who was waiting for him to come out and, with a kick, knocked him out into the veranda. Astonished by all this resistance, the others fled in fright. Then M. Mossut called his house slaves, ran to his friend's room, where he found him sleeping deeply, woke him up, and sent him to the large Galliffet plantation. Then, arming himself with a sword and a pistol, he swore to kill anyone who came near without having been called.

There were normally six whites on the large Galliffet plantation. M. Odelucq, who had managed all that family's property for fifteen years, went to the La Gossette estate, taking three whites. The *nègres'* cowardice, then as always, allowed three men, poorly armed but well-informed and determined to die fighting, to pass through one hundred fifty rebels who had decided to kill them, without any of them daring to make the slightest movement. Returning to the large plantation,

M. Odelucq and his companions found the gate open and the lock broken. This was the work of the rebel leader, who, seeing the failure at La Gossette, ran at top speed to hold back the other plotters. Despite his efforts, he could not prevent several fires that broke out in the neighborhood. The alarm bell rang several times. But instead of running to the fire, as one would normally do, M. Odelucq, fearing the worst, would not let the two slave crews go out and ordered the drivers to watch them scrupulously.

At daybreak he went back to La Gossette. There, before the assembled work crews, he arrested three slaves, relatives and friends of the driver, whose absence since the disturbances of the previous night raised justifiable suspicions about them. Then he left for Cap Français and returned with the local judge. Right away, they examined the evidence and interrogated the arrested slaves. Three hours elapsed before they knew the truth; it might have been a long time before they realized the extent of the conspiracy had it not been for a young house slave who admitted some specifics that put them on the right track. However, at six in the evening, one of the three prisoners, astonished by what the judge knew and believing that the two others, held separately, had betrayed him, confessed the specifics described above and moreover told them that Blaise, the driver at La Gossette, had guided the two assassins, and confirmed the plan of all the slaves: to fight to the death against the whites.

If the strong measures taken on the Galliffet plantations had been more widespread, it is likely that the revolt would have ended there. But in the time it took to extinguish the fires at the Petite Anse, another more powerful one broke out at Acul. A band led by Boukman[8] spread like a flood throughout this parish. With a torch in one hand and a dagger in the other, this *nègre* pitilessly massacred all the whites who escaped the flames. His own master was murdered in the arms of his weeping and dying wife.

The number of victims would have been even greater if Boukman had been able to be in more places. In spite of his orders and his example, several *nègres* spared their masters, even saved them. Others, flushed by the fire out of the cane fields where they were hidden, fell into the hands of the rebels; the most fortunate made it to Cap Français. Since the previous night, the townspeople had suspected the plot. The fugitives' reports of the horrors they had witnessed spread

---

[8]The insurgent leader Boukman is believed to have been one of the priests officiating at the Bois-Caïman ceremony described in Document 12.

panic throughout the city. Three cannon shots summoned a special
session of the Provincial Assembly. Stores closed and house slaves
were closely watched. People came and went, passing each other
unrecognized, posing a thousand questions without waiting for an
answer. Soon the call to arms was heard, echoed by everyone's voice.
Eventually two or three hundred national guards, reinforced by a
detachment of the Cap regiment and by three small artillery pieces,
were dispatched to the Haut du Cap.* There they encountered the
whites fleeing from Acul and neighboring parishes. The roads were
filled with carriages, carts, women, children, the sick and the
dying. . . .

During the night of Tuesday to Wednesday August 23, the rebels
left the parish of the North Plain behind them and attacked Petite
Anse. Their furor was exerted against the Choiseul plantation. Enraged at not finding the manager, they took his domestic slave, who
they accused of helping him escape, and threw him into the burning
plantation house alive, despite the prayers, sobs, and despair of his
mother. From here they went to the plantation of the Fathers of Char-
ity; some lit the bagasse houses† on fire while others pitilessly took
the under-manager and killed him. The Bongars and Clericy plantations experienced the same horrors. The bodies of their manager and
under-manager were displayed at the gate. Pushed away from the
Quartier Morin by the resistance of the slave crews, the brigands
retraced their steps and arrived as a group at La Gossette. M. Odelucq
was there with all the whites. There were even fifteen or twenty
national guardsmen who had arrived the previous day, but they were
so poorly armed, so little accustomed to war that as the rebels
approached, hearing the sound of their ferocious cries, they threw
down their weapons and fled through the cane fields to the camp at
the Cap Français Heights. M. Odelucq remained, almost alone, believing he could face down the brigands. He appeared before them; the
most savage of all, named Mathurin, came up to him and plunged his
knife into his chest. M. Daveiroult, the representative of Gros Morne
to the new Colonial Assembly, was cut down at his side, as well as two
men from the detachment that had arrived the previous day.

The *nègres,* emboldened by their success and rendered even more
violent by their overindulgence in wine and strong spirits, advanced

*A small town one league from the city.
†These are vast barns used to store the sugarcanes after they have passed through
the mill. They are kept to burn for heating [in the refinery].

toward the Haut du Cap. The cannon here stopped them. But the Denort, Decourt, and Vergennes plantations went up in flames, and before ten o'clock the three parishes of Acul, the North Plain, and Petite Anse were only a heap of cinders. . . .

The size and the number of establishments consumed by the flames created a spectacle that witnesses will never forget. The thick cloud of black smoke, which during daylight hung above the Cap Français horizon, after sunset took on the appearance of an aurora borealis situated above about twenty plantations changed into so many volcanoes. At midnight, fire appeared at the wharf of Limonade, announcing the appearance of the rebels in this district. And the next day, the two richest and most important parishes of the northern province were nothing more than a pile of ashes and ruin.

This was just the fourth day of the revolt, and already the whites of six parishes were either refugees, prisoners, or corpses. Flames had consumed one hundred sugar works; and twenty thousand slaves, once peaceful and submissive, were now so many cannibals, threatening Cap Français with the same fate.

14

PIERRE MOSSUT

Letter to the Marquis de Gallifet
September 19, 1791

In this letter, plantation manager Pierre Mossut described the slave uprising to his absentee employer, the Marquis de Gallifet. Mossut blamed the circulation of abolitionist writings and the indiscreet conversations of planters for the revolt, but he also wrote that there was something driving the insurgents that he could not understand.

The varied writings produced in your capital [Paris] in favor of the Negroes, the unbelievable discussions that led to the May 15 decree,

Mossut to Gallifet, September 19, 1791, Archives Nationales, 107 AP 128.

writings that have long circulated in the colony and that the negroes knew about, the very indiscretion of the planters who show no restraint in their actions or their statements, all these causes united have finally led the class of the slaves to revolt. . . .

We were attacked by a horde of assassins and could only offer meager resistance. After the first volley, we took refuge in flight. M. Odelucq, weakened by his age, by a wound he had already received, and weighed down by the boots he was wearing at the time, had the misfortune to fall under the daggers of these brigands. I owe my safety to a domestic servant who presented me with a horse at the moment when our resistance was becoming impossible. But, Monsieur, I saved myself wounded, with only the shirt on my back, having lost in an instant the fruit of nine years of work on your plantations; the other people employed on your properties are all more or less in the same situation. . . .

There is a motor that powers them and that keeps powering them and that we cannot come to know. All experienced planters know that this class of men have neither the energy nor the combination of ideas necessary for the execution of this project, whose realization they nevertheless are marching toward with perseverance. . . . we have executed many slaves, among them ten from your plantation; all have observed their obstinate silence when questioned about who armed them and incited this odious conspiracy,[9] though they admit to being guilty and having participated in it. . . .

Despite my wounds, I climbed up the highest hill bordering Le Cap, and from there with a telescope I could see your plantations perfectly well. All the bagasse houses have been destroyed, along with all the cane that was to be crushed between now and the end of the year. The main houses, the buildings, the sugar refineries are intact . . . but it is to be feared, and in fact it is probable and almost certain, that when these fanatics are attacked in their retrenchments, they will set fire to all the remaining buildings before retreating to the hills. If we are able to defeat them, we will have to resolve ourselves to the sacrifice of a large portion of the work gangs and establish the most severe discipline to control those people, who more than ever will be difficult to command.

treat/look at blacks as beasts

[9]This word is unclear in the letter; it could be either *transe* (trance) or *trame* (conspiracy), but the context of the document makes it probable that it is the latter.

15

PHILADELPHIA GENERAL ADVERTISER

Reports from the Insurrection

October–November 1791

The following reports from the Philadelphia General Advertiser *provide interesting fragments of information about the insurrection, notably regarding the presence of some whites among the insurgents, the various roles played by free people of color in both supporting and resisting the insurrection, and the military tactics of the rebels. Newspapers captured only a small portion of information about the insurrection that spread to North America by word of mouth, including among communities of slaves to whom the news of insurrection was of particular interest. We have maintained the sometimes awkward punctuation of the original reports here. The first report is in the form of a journal, with the numbers at the beginning of each entry corresponding to the date of the month.*

PHILADELPHIA GENERAL ADVERTISER, NO. 322, TUESDAY, OCTOBER 11

The following concise and connected account of the late disturbances at St. Domingo, from their origin down to the latest intelligence received from that island, is taken from a Journal kept there, handed to us by an obliging Correspondent, and translated for the GENERAL ADVERTISER. . . .

Sept. 1. There has been an engagement in the upper part of the Cape. About 60 negroes were killed. A mulatto and two negroes, after the engagement, advanced, and asked to parley with the General,— He came forward, and they were asked what they wanted. They answered that they required perfect liberty for all the negroes;—the two negroes were killed, and the mulatto was suffered to escape.

A free negro, named Cappe, made his appearance on the plantation *Lambert* near the city, to encourage the negroes to revolt. He has been seized, and it is expected much will be learned from him.

2. Two whites have been stopped, together with a Spanish mulatto. Their names were given up by Cappe; who has given an account of the

intended plot. He says that in the night of the 25ᵗʰ ult.[10] all the negroes in the plain were to attack the city in different parts; to be seconded by the negroes of the city, who were to set fire to it in several parts at once. Guards and vigilance has been doubled, and nothing has yet happened. . . . Cappe has declared that in every workshop in the city there were negroes concerned in the plot. For these two days past we have been engaged in making barricades for every possible entrance to the city. This will effectually prevent any attacks from the exterior proving successful.

3. At five in the evening the mulattoes of the army asked for permission to go against the negroes; they obtained leave, set off 100 strong, accompanied by 20 dragoons of the whites. They killed 100 negroes, took a small cannon, one white, and two negro chiefs.

4. Cappe has been broke on the wheel. He was possessed of an income of 30,000 livres,—all in town houses.

5. The negro army at *L'Acul* have taken a fort. In it there are six 24 pounders. They can have but little annunition. Yesterday, being Sunday, the negroes celebrated two marriages in the church at *L'Acul.* On the occasion they assumed titles, and the titled blacks were treated with the greatest respect, and the ceremony was performed with great pomp. A Capuchin,[11] retained among them, has been obliged to officiate. Their colours were consecrated, and a King was elected. They have chosen one for each quarter. Cappe was King of *Limbé* and *Port-Margot.*

8. A detachment of 120 men of the army returned from *Mornet,* 5 leagues from the Cape. They brought with them several carts full of women and goods. On the way they had several engagements with negroes, in which they were generally successful. On the 7ᵗʰ they killed several negroes and a white chief, and also took a white man, who was said to be a deserter from the regiment of Port-au-Prince, and the son of a former President of Parliament[12] in France.

10. In the night the negroes set fire to an outhouse in the plantations *Breda.* They attacked the camp in three different places; they were with difficulty driven back—three whites were wounded. Ten of their number were killed, and fifteen taken prisoners. Two whites taken yesterday among the negroes at *Pont Margot* have been brought to town.

---

[10] August 25.
[11] A priest of the Capuchin order.
[12] This refers to the French *"Parlements,"* or courts, of the Old Regime.

11. A negro taken yesterday in the heights of the Cape, has declared that the rebels in that quarter, have eight pieces of artillery.

The armed boat sent to dislodge the negroes who had taken possession of a battery on a seashore, returned today. She fired 250 times without effect, because her pieces were not of heavy metal enough. The negroes made use of the bullets fired at them—they fired them back from their 24 pounders, with effect, struck the armed boat, which was obliged to retire, in a very leaky condition. No lives were lost.

12. . . . M. de Rouvray writes that in an engagement he has killed a number of negroes, and among the rest one of their first leaders. He had him buried; but the negroes took him up and buried him again with great pomp. They were mourning. He thinks he will soon be able to overcome them entirely, in the place where he commands.

13. The General on the heights of the Cape has just written that his spies had informed him, that the chief of the insurgents in his quarter was determined to abandon them; but that he was detained among them, by main force. This gives hope that we shall be able to master them.

At this time, there have been about 150 sugar-houses entirely consumed, and 3000 negroes killed. These losses amount to about 6000.000 livres; but it will yet be necessary to destroy 1000 or 1200 negroes more.

The negro belonging to M. Lambert, who caused Cappe to be seized, has obtained his freedom from the Assembly, with a medal and an annuity of 500 livres. He refuses to quit his former master, convinced that he could not better his condition by a change.

PHILADELPHIA GENERAL ADVERTISER, No. 322, TUESDAY, OCTOBER 11

Boston, Nov. 3
St. Domingo Disturbances

Captain Bickford is arrived at Salem, from Cape-Francois. A Mr. Harrington, of this town, who resided there several years past, came as a passenger. He was one of their militia, and in several engagements. He came away at the risk of his life, as no resident is permitted to depart. He informs, on the 20th of September, 500 troops from Haut du Cap, and another 400 from Petite Ance, he saw attack a fortified camp of negroes on Galifaut's [*sic*; Gallifet's] estate, defended by 9 cannons. It began at 5 in the morning, and they gained possession at

9: the free mulattoes and negroes, chiefly mounted, first entered: a horrid carnage ensued, as they had orders to give no quarter to men, women or children; the slaughter finished at two, and the troops began then to plunder; they burnt everything they could not carry, and men could not be spared to retain the place: retook five white women, whose lives the negroes spared for wives. There were previous to the attack, about 6000 negroes in the place; but they secretly retreated, and carried off their effects to Red Bank,[13] and only 2000 remained when attacked. The main body of the negroes to that quarter, then established themselves at the Red Bank, a mountain steep and difficult of access, 30 miles from the Cape. Here they are 8 or 10,000 in number; including many whites, and a large proportion of mulattoes, of good property and information, who in revenge for the equality denied them, have inspired the negroes with ideas of liberty.

Besides Red Bank, the insurgents have possession of Limbe, consisting of 10,000, a strong fort, with heavy artillery, and amply provided with ammunition: they had also possession of D'Acul, and of Port-Francois. There is also a body at the mouth of Salt-river and the Bridge.

They are supposed to consist of about 80,000. They are masters of the country for 30 leagues, from Dimbe to Carricole, and also the country back of Port au Prince. . . .

In the beginning of the insurrection, the negroes made their attacks with much irregularity and confusion, and their weapons were mostly their implements of labor, but as they pay much attention to discipline, being daily exercised by their leaders (who now show themselves as white men and mulattoes) they now come on in regular bodies, and a considerable part of them are well armed with the muskets, swords, &c. which they have taken and purchased. They fight under a bloody flag, having on it a motto, denouncing death to all whites! They march by the music peculiar to the negroes, and begin an engagement with a considerable degree of order and firmness, crying out Victory! They are however soon broken, through want of discipline, and are never able to rally.—They throw obstructions of one kind and another in the roads, to impede the progress of the whites, and it was said had poisoned the water.

It is supposed the negroes are supplied with arms from the Spaniards, and the cannon and fusils[14] taken from them are Spanish,

[13]English translation of *Morne Rouge*.
[14]Muskets.

and in this respect, as well as in discipline, they were growing more formidable.

Mr. Harrington relates, that a flag [of peace] was sent in to the assembly from a body [of insurgents] near Haut-du-Cap, offering to return to their services upon the plantations, if they were assured of pardon, and be allowed three days in the week besides Sunday, for themselves; the assembly sent back seven men with answer of refusal, which on the leaders [of the insurgents] reading, they rushed upon the gentlemen with the flag[15] and killed six of them, the seventh (formerly of Philadelphia) made his escape with a wound.

According to all accounts, there is less prospect of peace and security than at the first moment of the insurrection. They have received no succor, except about 1500 stand of arms sent from Jamaica. . . . The country is filled with dead bodies, which lie unburied. The negroes have left the whites, with stakes, &c. drove through them into the ground; and the white troops, who now take no prisoners, but kill everything black or yellow, leave the negroes dead upon the field.

[15]Those sent with the assembly's message.

16

JEAN-FRANÇOIS AND BIASSOU

Letters to the Commissioners
December 1791

In late 1791, a new group of commissioners arrived in the colony, carrying a decree of general amnesty issued by the king meant to forgive political acts committed during the revolutionary turmoil of the previous years. Taking advantage of the decree, the rebel leaders Jean-François and Georges Biassou approached the commissioners with a set of proposals for ending the insurrection. If the French granted liberty to several hundred of the insurgent leaders, they promised, those who were liberated would oversee the return of their followers to the plantations. The negotiations ultimately fell through, in part because of the intransigence of

Archives Nationales de France, Paris, DXXV 1, Folder 4, #6.

whites in the Colonial Assembly. But, as these letters suggest, many of the rebels themselves were wary of returning to the plantations without clear changes in the way they were treated.

Jean-François and Biassou to the Commissioners, December 12, 1791

Dear Sirs:

Infinitely flattered and thankful for the kindness and care you showed our envoys, we take the liberty to express our gratitude, and at the same time address to you some observations that we feel are indispensable for the reestablishment of order in such critical circumstances. Since our proposals have the general welfare as their only goal, we dare flatter ourselves that, by virtue of your own principles laid out in the end of the third paragraph of the proclamation that you kindly sent us, you will welcome them and weigh them with your wisdom.

When you arrived in Saint-Domingue, you doubtless were shocked by the disasters, whose existence you did not suspect, but you will not succeed in reestablishing the disturbed equilibrium by searching for the authors[16] or in deploying troops that the nation has placed under your command. When we learned of your arrival, we rushed to tell you of our satisfaction, but we feel obliged to send you, before you announce to us your final intentions, our reflections on experience and a perfect knowledge of the area. We could justly be blamed for causing great misfortunes if we kept silent. We therefore owe you these important details.

We are inspired by your proclamation and admire its moderation and wisdom, but we must tell you that you do not understand our position and that you have inaccurate ideas about the nature of the revolution that has made us, along with the whites, its sad victims. In ordering us each to return to our own homes, you are demanding something both impossible and dangerous. A hundred thousand men are in arms; we make up 80 percent of this population, which is a lot. Most of us are fathers, and you must understand that because of this we depend entirely upon the general will. And whose will is it? That of a multitude of *nègres* from Africa, most of whom can barely say two

---

[16] Of the revolt.

words in French but who, at the same time, were accustomed to fighting wars in their own countries, and how? You are undoubtedly familiar with accounts of this. We must therefore, as much for ourselves as for you, convince you to grant liberty to the number of chiefs that we suggest. We have carefully examined the situation. The [rebel] generals are well-intentioned and are eagerly waiting for you. Aided by a certain number of the principal chiefs, they are the only ones who can accomplish what would otherwise require a long time with many troops and great difficulty, in a process that would complete the ruin of the property owners.

Nevertheless, we cannot hide from you that this undertaking has its dangers. False rumors will make the slaves obstinate, for example, the idea that the king has granted them three days per week. They will say they have been tricked, and the consequences can be deadly if we do not approach this operation with the greatest caution. Because of this, sirs, we think it would be useful to grant liberty to all the commanders, leaving the choice to the generals because they know which of them have influence over the *nègres* either because of the fear they inspire in them or for other known reasons. Then it would be politic and would make the approach more effective for you yourselves to write to the generals, saying that all the higher-level chiefs who behave well, and who use all their power to return their followers to order, can and must expect benevolence from the king. . . . The task will not be finished. We will need help from the king's forces who, without fighting, will simply show themselves in the countryside at a prearranged time. As long as you, sirs, are leading them, everything will proceed in good will, and those of us who can join forces at that moment will carry out the rest. We must tell you that we will have to be camped and spread through the parishes for a long time. Many *nègres* will hide in the woods; it will be necessary to pursue them diligently and to brave dangers and fatigue. But the generals and chiefs that we are begging you to emancipate for this important purpose will join us in this task, and the public fortunes will be reborn out of their ashes.

Your most humble and obedient servants,
Jean-François, General, and Biassou, General

Jean-François and Biassou to the Commissioners, December 21, 1791

Dear Sirs:

Permit us to take the liberty to share with you our reflections on the statements made to us by the *nègre* slaves. You must know that in our role as chiefs we have a great deal of power over them. Since the first time you did us the honor of sharing your intentions with our representatives, we have worked constantly to calm the minds [of our followers], which have been excited to the highest degree. We have been able to unite most, if not all of them. Reassured by the king's general pardon, we still believe that with all the firmness with which we are pursuing this we will be able to avoid bloodshed by using the voice of kindness. But there are many things that still hold them back: (1) The fear of being treated like those involved in the Ogé affair who, after having surrendered voluntarily and thinking themselves in complete safety on the word of the leaders of Le Cap, were partially sacrificed! You would not believe, sirs, how they are struck by what they call this treason. (2) The bad treatment of their masters, most of whom torture their slaves by mistreating them in all sorts of ways, taking away their two hours,[17] their holidays, and Sundays, leaving them naked, without any help even when they are sick, and letting them die of misery. Yes, sirs, how many barbarous masters there are who enjoy being cruel to these miserable slaves, or else managers or administrators who, to stay in their employers' good graces, inflict a thousand of the same cruelties on the slaves as they pretend to carry out their responsibilities.

Oh, sirs, in the name of humanity, deign to look favorably on these unfortunates by clearly outlawing such harsh mistreatment, abolishing the terrible plantation prisons, where the stays are miserable, and trying to improve the condition of this class of men so necessary to the colony, and we dare assure you that they will take up their work once again and will return to order. We beg you to be willing to provide us with your reflections.

We have the honor of being, with respect, sirs
Your most humble and obedient servants,
Biassou, Jean-François

---

[17] Of midday rest.

Archives Nationales, DXXV 1, Folder 4, #14.

17

GROS

In the Camps of the Insurgents
1791

Late in October 1791, slave insurgents captured a group of men fighting them, including a local official named Gros. (His first name is unknown.) Gros spent several weeks in the insurgents' camps and eventually served as a secretary to Jean-François in negotiations with the colonial government. After he was freed, he wrote an account of his time in the camps. It provides a rare glimpse into disagreements among the rebels over tactics, treatment of white prisoners, and the ultimate goals of the insurrection.

After our defeat, we were chained two by two, and placed in the center of the strongest escort of *nègres* and mulattos to be led to the brigands' main camp. As we left our home in this sorrowful state, we saw fire devour our greatest possessions; in an instant, these barbarians had burned the area, and we marched with only the light of flames to guide us. These villains amused themselves by forcing us to see our brothers' mutilated corpses and by painting a picture of the tortures they were going to inflict on us when we reached Grande-Rivière, as we did that same day, after traveling ten leagues,[18] with our heads and feet bare and wearing only shirts.

On the road, the old *nègres* and *négresses,* assembled before all the fences, humiliated us with their words and celebrated the exploits of their warriors, who constantly mistreated us, beating us with sticks.

When we arrived at the Cardinaux plantation, where the *nègres* had a sizable camp, we were brought under the porch of the great house for a short while, where we were given, with a thousand insults, a few drops of rum. We recognized that a kind of decency reigned in this

---

[18]More than twenty-four miles.

Gros, *Isle de St. Domingue, Province du Nord. Précis Historique* (Paris, 1793).

camp and that an absolute silence was required. The commander, a *nègre* slave named Sans-Souci (a very bad seed), told us, walking around the house, "You all will see the priest after you sleep." We were then taken to the stocks and fell asleep; and the next morning we saw a priest on the porch: He came to us, and made us hear these shocking words: *"My children, you must know how to die, our savior Jesus Christ died for us on the cross."* Dismayed by this exhortation, which we certainly did not expect, we asked him if his verdict was final and if he could not do anything to change it; he responded, walking away, *"You must die."*

Since then, we frequently saw the same priest in all the camps of Grande-Rivière. He was the priest of this parish. . . .

The commander of the central camp was named Michaud, a *nègre* slave of the Armand plantation; he came to us, and on his face I thought I discovered a deep well of sensitivity. I was not wrong: He softened our miseries when he could, and it was to him that we owed the liberty we finally obtained two months later. Nevertheless, he was obliged to put us in chains, waiting for the implacable Jeannot,[19] who had not yet returned from his expedition; but he gave us some glimpses of hope and promised to take care of us. . . .

Jeannot . . . came to visit us . . . and, having reproached us for the death of Ogé and having raged at length against the revolution, . . . chose, among the prisoners, the first victims of his rage, and ordered that two of them be brought to the seat of the government;[20] he had already announced that we would be sacrificed two by two, and every twenty-four hours, in order to stretch out the enjoyment of it. A plantation driver and executioner . . . took my unfortunate companion, named Antoine: He was stretched out on a ladder where he was given four hundred lashes of the whip at least, in my presence. . . .

Our prison was constantly full: They came from all sides to examine us. Some, but a small number, seemed pained by our situation; the others, in contrast, rejoiced; but it was principally during the night that our terror increased because of the speeches that we heard; and the mournful songs, accompanied by instruments, seemed to be a prelude to new tortures. . . .

But a very different event took place. Jean-François, known for his greater humanity, and general in chief, irritated by the cruelties of

[19]A higher-ranking insurgent leader.
[20]The central command of the insurgents.

Jeannot, had him arrested and brought to Dondon, where he was killed by a firing squad the same day.

Jean-François came to visit us and told us about Jeannot's punishment; he promised us safety and all the help that we needed.

We were indeed freed after his departure; but, despite the fact that his intentions and his orders were for us to be left free, we were put back in chains, and we would have stayed there for a long time if a mulatto named Aubert, who was surprised to see us in this state, had not complained to Michaud, who restored our liberty and granted us permission to walk in the pasture, though under the escort of two *nègres.* . . .

We arrived at the [insurgent] headquarters just as they were serving dinner and were kindly welcomed by Jean-Louis, nicknamed the Parisian, a *nègre* owned by M. de la Combe, the commander of Grande-Rivière, who had been killed in the battle at Cadouche. This *nègre* was a lieutenant of the king in the Dondon quarter. He was proud of his civility, talked constantly of France, where he had spent several years, and pushed the other chiefs toward peace, threatening them with all the weight of his power if they did not put an end to so many atrocities.

Jean-Louis invited us to eat, which was not much of a favor . . . it was announced to us that it was time to rest: An excellent mattress was immediately brought to us . . . We must be fair to the leaders of the Dondon camp; we never had to complain about them; they left us in the greatest liberty, but it was not the same with the other *nègres,* who abused us at every occasion. The *négresses* were far more rude, harsher, and less willing to return to work than the *nègres.*

During the first two days of our arrival at Dondon, I realized that I was right about the true causes of our miseries. There, as elsewhere, I heard a uniform language among all the *nègres;* everywhere they believed that the king had been imprisoned and that they had been ordered to arm themselves and restore his liberty; they were aware of the destruction of the clergy and the nobility; and swearing on what is most sacred, we can assure you that to this evidence we could add a thousand others that will confirm that the slave revolt is a counter-revolution. . . .

On the fourteenth, we learned of the death of Bouqueman [Boukman]; it would be impossible to tell you the effect this death had on the *nègres.* The leaders went into mourning and ordered a solemn service: as onlookers, suffering from everything that was happening, we were dismayed by this accident . . . Already we heard the speeches of the *nègres;* their criminal conspiracies frightened us, for these canni- bals proposed nothing less than assassinating us to avenge their chief, dead for the most just of causes, the defense of his king. Though these statements were a bit hard to hear, luckily they had no effect; they avenged themselves in a less barbarous and even amusing man- ner; they imagined the death of M. Touzard,[21] and to commemorate this great exploit, started a *calinda*[22] that lasted three days, during which they presented their feats of battle and criticized us for our cow- ardliness; to hear them it was as if they had filled wagons with our heads and had lost only a few people. We had to listen, responding only with silence or applause. . . .

Jean-François, who had a small court, enjoyed giving parties. There was a large gathering on the seventeenth at the headquarters . . . I heard part of the conversation. Here we are, they said, at the end of November. The forces that are to arrive from France will not be long, and it would be to our advantage to settle with the whites in order to avoid great setbacks; for we have to worry that they will reduce us to dust. . . .

Jean-François approved everything that was proposed to him: He even spoke to us in a language that was rare among the *nègres;* his re- flections showed common sense, humanity, and an intelligence greater than that of his kind: for, having freed me, even to the point that I could ask him the real goal of the war he was fighting against us, he responded honestly . . . Here are his own words: "I did not make myself general of the *nègres.* Those who had the power to do so gave me this title: in taking up arms, it was never my intention to fight for general liberty, which I believe is a delusion, as much because of France's need for its colonies as because of the danger of granting uncivilized hordes a right that would become infinitely dangerous to them and would inevitably lead to the destruction of the colony; and if the property owners had all been on their plantations, the revolution might not have happened." Then he lashed out against the managers and drivers; he wanted to insert, as a basic article in the conventions[23] that they would no longer exist in Saint-Domingue. . . .

The well-known character of Biassou made me worry. I was happily mistaken when I found him far more disposed toward peace. He

[21]A colonial officer.
[22]Ceremonial dance.
[23]To be negotiated with the whites.

accused [Jean-François] of going too slowly ... and explained why he wanted peace ... but when we had to discuss the number of liberties,[24] I ran into obstacles that were almost insurmountable; and without the *nègre* Toussaint, of Breda ... the talks would have ended without success. He[25] first asked for three hundred liberties, not including those he wanted to grant his family; and it was only after long and dangerous discussion that I convinced him to reduce them to fifty. ...

The delegation sent to Le Cap returned the same day[26] ... for some reason I was completely taken over by a terrible premonition: Events justified my worries. ... Biassou, in the throes of a violent rage, ordered all of us assembled and, picking up his weapons, had us lined up to be shot ... In this terrifying situation Toussaint, of Breda, Biassou's aide, braved all dangers to try to save us, even though he himself was likely to be the victim of this monster's rage. He explained that we should not be sacrificed in this way, that we should be put in the stocks and judged by the Council of War. ...

That was where we were when they came to tell us that Biassou had pardoned us and that we were free. Sure enough, we were set loose and brought to the headquarters. ... Jean-François, as the *generalissimo,* was in control. This supreme chief of the African army was always well-dressed ... he wore the cross of Saint Louis[27] and a red cord: He had ten body guards, who wore a bandolier covered with fleur-de-lys.[28] He was loved by all of those who were free and by the best of the slaves; his command was respected, and his army was well disciplined. ...

... [W]e left [for Le Cap] at ten o'clock, escorted by fifty dragoons, nearly all men of color and free blacks, and commanders in the camp. Imagine our surprise when ... [on the way to Le Cap], we saw the *nègres* assembled and rushing toward us with sabers in their hands, threatening to send only our heads to Le Cap, cursing the peace and their generals. We owed our survival in this situation only to the firmness of our escort. We were ... convinced of a great truth, that the *nègres* will never return to work without repression and partial destruction.

---

[24]*Number of liberties*: the number of their followers who would be granted liberty in the deal they were trying to make with the French.

[25]Biassou.

[26]Bringing news of the rejection of the insurgent leader's offer.

[27]The symbol of a royal military order.

[28]The symbol of French royalty.

18

OLYMPE DE GOUGES

Preface to The Slavery of the Blacks

1792

Best known today for her 1791 Declaration of the Rights of Woman and Citizen, Olympe de Gouges had already established herself as a playwright and irrepressible intellectual force before the French Revolution. In December 1789, her play, The Slavery of the Blacks, or the Lucky Shipwreck, *ran for three performances before being shut down as a result of heckling by hostile planters. De Gouges continued her political activities during the next years and in 1793 was executed for her criticism of the violent repression carried out by the regime then in power. For all her abolitionism, de Gouges was a determined opponent of violence, as she emphasized in this preface to a 1792 edition of* The Slavery of the Blacks.

During centuries of ignorance men fought each other; in the most enlightened century they want to destroy each other. What kind of knowledge, regime, period, or age do men need to live in peace? Such metaphysical questions confound and confuse learned men. But I have studied only nature's good principles; I no longer try to define mankind, and my primitive understanding has taught me to use only my soul to make judgments. Therefore my works have no color other than that of humanity.

Here it is then, this play banned by greed and ambition and approved by righteous men. Of these various opinions, which should be mine? As author, I am entitled to approve of this humanitarian production, but having heard horrible tales of the evils afflicting the Americas, I might hate what I had written if an invisible hand had not brought about that revolution. My only involvement was to have prophesied it. Yet I am blamed and accused by those who do not even

---

Olympe de Gouges, *L'esclavage des noirs, ou l'heureux naufrage* (Paris, 1792).

know *The Slavery of the Blacks,* which was received at the Comédie Française in 1783, printed in 1786, and performed in December 1789. The colonists, who spare no expense to satisfy their cruel ambitions, bought off the actors. I have been assured that the play's profits were not harmed when it was shut down; but I am not here to indict either the actors or the colonists, but myself.

I publicly denounce myself; I place myself under arrest; I go myself to plead my case before this distinguished and frivolous but formidable tribunal. Conscience is the jury that will hear my arguments; according to its votes, I will either lose or win my case.

The author who is the friend of truth, who has no other goal than to remind men of nature's beneficial laws, who nevertheless still respects the laws and social customs, is always an admirable stimulus, and if his writings do not produce all the benefits he intended, he is more to be pitied than blamed.

It is therefore important that I convince the public and my detractors of the purity of my philosophy. This play might have lacked talent but not moral purpose. It is because of that moral purpose that public opinion must rebound in my favor. . . .

Now I will speak to you, slaves and men of color. I have perhaps indisputable rights to rebuke your savagery; by imitating the cruelty of tyrants, you vindicate them. The majority of your masters were humane and well intentioned, and in your blind rage you do not distinguish innocent victims from your persecutors. Men were not born to be in chains, yet you prove that they are necessary. If you are stronger, why resort to all the fierceness of your fiery countries? They say that it is easy for you to use poisons, irons, and daggers and invent the most barbaric and appalling tortures. What cruelty! What inhumanity! Ah! What suffering you inflict on those moderates who wanted to soften your fate. Would that not have been better than the unrealistic pleasures with which the instigators of disasters in France and the Americas have misled you? Just as crime has become associated with these perverse men, so will tyranny dog your footsteps. Nothing will bring you together. Fear my prediction; you know that it is based on true and solid foundations. Reason and divine justice inspire my prophecy. I will not back down. I detest your tyrants; I am horrified by your cruelties. Ah! If my words reach you, if you recognize all their advantages, I dare to believe that they will calm your untamed spirits and bring you to a peace that is necessary for the welfare of the colony and for your own interests. Those interests reside in the social order, your rights under the wisdom of the law, which recognizes that all men are brothers, that august law, which greed plunged into chaos, has finally emerged from the shadows. If the savage, ferocious man does not recognize it, he is made to be loaded with chains and broken like a beast.

Slaves, men of color, you who live closer to nature than the Europeans, may your tyrants therefore recognize its gentle laws and prove that an enlightened nation did not err in treating you like men and giving you rights you never before enjoyed in the Americas. To take the side of justice and humanity, you must remember and never forget that it was in your fatherland that you were condemned to this awful servitude and that it was your own parents who led you to the slave market; that in your horrible latitudes men are hunted the way that animals are hunted in other countries. The true philosophy of an enlightened man leads him to pull his fellow from the midst of a horrible primitive situation where men not only sell each other but where they still eat each other. The true man only thinks of mankind. These are my principles, quite different from those so-called defenders of liberty, those firebrands, those inflammatory spirits who preach equality and liberty with despotic authority and ferocity. The Americas, France, and perhaps the universe owe their fall to a handful of maniacs produced by France, as well as to the weakening of empires and the loss of the arts and sciences.

. . . Even the most ignorant person can easily create a revolution in a few paper notebooks; but, alas, the experience of all peoples and the experiments of the French have taught me that the wisest and most knowledgeable [individuals] cannot establish their doctrines without producing all kinds of evils. The history of all countries teaches us this. I have strayed from the goal of my Preface, and time does not allow me to give free reign to philosophical reason. I wanted to defend *The Slavery of the Blacks,* which the hateful colonists had censured and described as an incendiary work. Let the public be the judge; I await its verdict to exonerate me.

19

JEAN-PAUL MARAT

From *The Friend of the People*

1792

Jean-Paul Marat was one of the most influential journalists and orators of the French Revolution. As a young man, he had worked in Bordeaux, a leading slave port, tutoring the children of a wealthy merchant. In 1774, he published a book entitled The Chains of Slavery, *which was an attack on the French royal government, not an abolitionist tract. He threw himself into the cause of the French Revolution in 1789 and acquired a reputation as one of its most principled and unyielding advocates through his revolutionary newspaper,* The Friend of the People. *This article was published in the weeks after news of the slave uprising in Saint-Domingue reached continental France.*

The session of the tenth was almost solely devoted to hearing Sr. Roustan, a member of Saint-Domingue's General Assembly, defend himself against the accusations of my lord Dupont, the author of a journal entitled *Patriotic Correspondence*. This journalist accused the white colonists of having rebelled against the metropole, of planning to invite the English to rule them after having tried to establish their own republic. But in my opinion this accusation that has been pressed so hard is frivolous, either unfounded or barely worth raising. This is because the residents of the colonies are a completely separate people from the residents of France, who can have not even the slightest rights over them. This truth is so obvious when simple good sense is applied, and it is indeed strange that someone who accepts the legitimacy of the French constitution should cast doubt upon it. The basis of all free government is that no people can be legally subject to another people, that a people should have no laws other than those it has given itself, that it is the supreme authority in its own territory,

Ami du Peuple ou le Publiciste Parisien, Journal Politique et Impartial, Par M. P. Marat, auteur de l'Offrande à la patrie, du Moniteur, du Plan de constitution, &c. Vitam impendere vero Monday, December 12, 1791, no. 624.

self-ruling and independent of all human powers. At the same time, simple good sense, accepting these principles, adds that it is absurd and crazy that a people be governed by laws coming from a lawmaker two thousand leagues away. The inhabitants of our colonies have committed one folly, which is to have agreed to send representatives to the French National Assembly. But this foolishness was the work of the white colonists alone. And yet in fact everyone has the right to free themselves from the yoke of the metropole, to choose another ruler for themselves, or to establish themselves as a republic; and why not? Since the supremacy that France claimed over them was wrongfully taken, based on tyrannical principles and only exercised by virtue of France's superior strength. To go farther, what if the residents of our colonies had declared their independence, how would we dare disapprove that they followed the example of the English colonies? By what bizarre inconsistency would we criticize in them what we approved so strongly among the [North American] rebels? From the complete right of our colonies to free themselves from the metropole, do not conclude that I am trying to support the cause of the white colonists: In my opinion they cannot be forgiven for trying to set themselves up as the despotic masters of the mulattos and the tyrannical masters of the blacks. If the laws of nature precede those of society and if the rights of man are inalienable, then whatever complaints the white colonists have against the French nation, the mulattos and the blacks have against the white colonists. To bring down the cruel and shameful yoke that oppresses them, they have the right to use all possible means, even death, should they be forced to massacre their oppressors to the last man.

These are the principles that would guide an equitable lawmaker in the question of Saint-Domingue: This is to say that the recent decree about the [free] men of color is fair and that on the *nègres* is appalling. But how would we be able to treat men with black skins as free beings, when in fact [in France] we have not treated men paying less than a crown in taxes as citizens? We boast of our philosophy and our liberty; but today we are as enslaved by our prejudices and our elected officials as we were ten centuries ago.

20

THOMAS CLARKSON

The True State of the Case, Respecting the Insurrection at St. Domingo

1792

Many commentators, particularly Saint-Domingue planters, claimed that the slave insurrection in the colony had been incited, either directly or indirectly, by abolitionists. Some actually claimed that the emissaries from antislavery groups were working with the insurgents, but more common was the assertion that attacks on slavery in Europe had convinced slaves that they had allies who would support them if they rebelled. In this 1792 pamphlet, the leading British abolitionist, Thomas Clarkson, who had extensive contacts with abolitionists and activist free people of color in Paris, sought to refute this idea. It was the barbarity of slavery itself, he asserted, that was the cause of the insurrection.

It is impossible for any one to have read the history of Greece and Rome with attention, without knowing that there were many and bloody insurrections of slaves in the countries which their Histories respectively comprehend.—Now it is impossible to attribute these with any propriety to persons associated either for the Abolition of the Slave Trade, or personal slavery; because, it does not appear from History, that there ever were associations in those days for so laudable a purpose.

Whoever, again, has read the History of the West India Islands from their first establishment to the year 1786, must have read it very superficially, not to know, that there have been various insurrections of slaves there, within this period. There was formerly a bloody one at St. Domingo, besides that which has lately happened. There have been several in Jamaica, and other Islands have had their share of them also.

Thomas Clarkson, *The true state of the case, respecting the insurrection at St. Domingo* (London, 1792).

Now, it is impossible that any of these could have had their origin in the efforts of the Gentlemen associated for the Abolition; because it was not till 1787, that the first Committee was formed, which was in London, for the Abolition of this execrable Trade.

To what cause then may we attribute the insurrections in the Islands? Undoubtedly to the Slave Trade, in consequence of which thousands are annually poured into the Islands, who have been fraudulently and forcibly deprived of the Rights of Men. All these come into them, of course, with dissatisfied and exasperated minds; and this discontent and feeling of resentment must be farther heightened by the treatment which people coming into them under such a situation must unavoidably receive; for we cannot keep people in a state of subjection to us, who acknowledge no obligation whatever to serve us, but by breaking their spirits and treating them as creatures of another species. Now, that this is the cause is evident from Mr. Long, the celebrated champion of the Planters themselves, who states in his *History of Jamaica,* that all the Insurrections of the Slaves that he could ever trace in the Islands, were begun by the imported Africans, and never by the Creole, or island-born, Slaves. . . .

As, however, the present insurrection in St. Domingo is somewhat connected with the late Revolution in France, it may be necessary to say a few words upon it as relative to that event. . . . Here then we see no less then three factions prevalent at the same moment in St. Domingo. The Whites divided into two parties; and the White and People of Colour burning with a fury hardly satiable by the extirpation of one another. What then did the negroes do at this interesting moment? Seeing their Lords and Masters not able to agree among themselves, but at daggers drawn with one another, they determined to take advantage of the divisions among them, and to assert their violated rights by force of arms.—Such is the true state of the case respecting the Insurrection at St. Domingo, and what do we learn from it but the following truth? "That the slave trade, and the oppression naturally resulting from it, was the real and only cause of this Insurrection," as it ever has been, and ever will be, of similar events; but that the Revolution of France, by causing the three divisions before mentioned, did afford the Negroes an opportunity which they would otherwise not so easily have found, of endeavoring to vindicate for themselves the unalterable Rights of Man.

The above accounts then lead us to three separate conclusions: First, That the Slave Trade is the real cause of all West Indian Insurrections.—Secondly, that as long as it exists, so long may these Insurrections be expected.—And Thirdly, That the St. Domingo Insurrection, in particular, so far from affording us a just argument (as the Planters say) to discontinue our exertions at the present moment, calls upon us to redouble them, if we have any value for our own islands, or any wish that the present Proprietors of them may preserve their estates to themselves, and perpetuate them to their posterity.

21

THE NATIONAL ASSEMBLY

Law of April 4

1792

In fall 1791, French voters selected a new legislature, which by law contained no members of the first National Assembly. Horrified by news of the slave uprising of August 1791, the outgoing Assembly had rescinded its controversial May 15, 1791, decree. But on March 28, 1792, the new legislators passed the following decree, which was signed by the king on April 4, 1792, and thereafter was known as the Law of April 4.

The National Assembly, in view of the fact that the enemies of the public have used the minor disagreements that have developed in the colonies to maintain their own power by raising the slaves in revolt, disrupting the forces of order, and dividing the citizens, whose unified effort is the only thing that can save their property from the horrors of fire and pillage;

That this odious plot appears to be part of conspiracies that have been hatched against the French nation and that have occurred simultaneously in the both hemispheres;

In view of the Assembly's hope that the love all colonists have for their fatherland will allow them forget the causes of their conflicts and the various wrongs done to all sides as a consequence, and that they

R. P. Adolphe Cabon, *Histoire d'Haïti. Cours professé au Petit Séminaire, Collège Saint Martial* (Port-au-Prince: Édition de la Petite Revue, 1920–1937), 3: 134–35.

will unreservedly devote themselves to reuniting openly and sincerely, which is the only thing that can stop the troubles that have affected them all and would allow them to enjoy the advantages of a solid and lasting peace; it decrees that this is a matter of great urgency.

The National Assembly recognizes and proclaims that the free blacks and men of color, as well as the white colonists, should enjoy equality in political rights. And, after having proclaimed the urgency of this situation, decrees the following:

... Art. 2. The free blacks and men of color will be admitted as voters in all the parish assemblies and will be eligible for all offices, as long as they meet the conditions prescribed by Article IV of the March 28 [1790] Instruction.[29]

[29]These conditions were that they be twenty-five years old and either own property or have lived in the parish for two years and pay taxes.

22

JOURNAL RÉPUBLICAIN DE LA GUADELOUPE

Account of the Slave Revolt

April 24, 1793

On the night of April 20, 1793, in the town of Trois-Rivières, Guadeloupe, hundreds of slaves rose up in revolt. The uprising was much smaller than that in Saint-Domingue two years earlier, but it took a remarkable course. Rather than punishing the insurgents, local white republicans, who were in open conflict with royalists on the island, welcomed and celebrated what the slaves had done. The Journal Républicain de la Guadeloupe, *a short-lived Jacobin newspaper published on the island, provided this account of the uprising.*

Rumors of war with the English and the appearance of a few pirates along our shores had reanimated the hope of the enemies of the

Journal Républicain de la Guadeloupe, April 24, 1793, in Centre des Archives d'Outre-Mer, C⁷ᴬ, 46, 124.

nation. The most horrible of plots was hatched in the shadows, and in one night all of the friends of equality were to fall under the blades of hired assassins. To these bloody men, any means is acceptable in the pursuit of their goal, and they have recently used the most dangerous means imaginable. It is by inciting the slaves against the patriots and by distributing money and arms to the slaves that they hoped to execute their vile project. But, by some effect of providence, the daggers that they sharpened were turned against them.

On Saturday night, the second-in-command of the Saint-François battalion, while making his rounds with two soldiers, encountered *nègres* armed with guns and pistols below the Godet plantation. The watchword was demanded of them, and they immediately fled. As they ran, they punched the patrolling officer and the two soldiers . . . the second-in-command . . . went to the municipal building and requested a detachment of infantry and cavalry to surround this armed troop. But just as the citizens were leaving for this expedition, [it was] announced that a large assembly of *nègres* was taking place at Trois-Rivières. A general alarm was sounded; all the citizens gathered their weapons, and in a few minutes the thirteen companies of the town were ready to march. In the absence of the governor, citizen Aubert, the *adjudant général*,[30] gave the order to a few companies to march immediately to the site of the assembly of the slaves. At Valcanard, we learned that the *nègres* were marching toward Basse-Terre; we sent forward a detachment to scout out the situation; they soon spied the rebels and warned the captain of their approach. The company took up their battle position near a cannon that was loaded with buckshot. Soon afterwards, we saw a column of about two hundred men armed with rifles, pistols, sabers, and axes. This column advanced in silence and in fairly good order; their movements did not seem hostile; they were allowed to approach to within rifle range. Then the advance sentinel called out, "Who goes there?" The *nègres* responded, "Citizens and friends!" They were told to stop. Six men from the company separated themselves and moved forward to investigate; they approached with rifles ready and bayonets chest-high. One of the slaves began to speak and asked if we were citizens, patriots; the response came that yes, we were. In that case, he said, we are friends; we have come to save you, and hate only those aristocrats who want to kill you. We have no bad intentions; we want to fight for the republic, the law, the nation, order. (These are their actual words.) We asked if they had as

---

[30]A military officer.

leaders some free men of color or whites. They responded no, that they acted on their own. On our invitation, four of their leaders separated themselves from the group to come speak to the captain; they told the others to await their return peacefully. . . . [T]hey told them the story of the massacre that had happened in Trois-Rivières.

As these *nègres* told us about these horrible scenes, the captain had sent an envoy to Basse-Terre to report what was going on. The slaves had been told that, in order to avoid alarm, it was necessary to announce their desire to enter into the town. They consented to everything, [and] waited peacefully for the arrival of the general warrant officer, who arrived accompanied by several soldiers and the Belvue company, which, through a well-coordinated maneuver, placed itself behind the two hundred slaves, while Charlvet's company was in front. On the way, cries of "Long live the Republic" were repeated many times by the slaves. When they arrived in front of the arsenal, the *adjudant général* had the doors opened, and the entire troop entered into the courtyard. The *gardes citoyennes*[31] immediately took control of the streets, with orders to keep all slaves from coming or going. All of the insurgents were disarmed not long afterwards, with no words or resistance on their part.

The commission had named four commissioners to interrogate the chiefs. On the basis of the depositions and the answers to the various questions we have asked of them ourselves, it is certain that there was a large conspiracy formed to hand the colony over to the English, and that one of the main chiefs was Brindeau. On his plantation, the slaves had found six barrels of powder, twenty-six sabers, a number of rifles, and boxes full of bullets . . .

The conduct of the slaves in this insurrection is surprising and almost unbelievable. After having used their weapons against those who had armed them in order to sacrifice the patriots, they committed no additional thefts; they barricaded the doors they had kicked in, posted sentinels, and outlawed everyone from touching anything in the houses, under penalty of death. It is true, nonetheless, that they took three trunks and one bag full of money; but on their arrival they put these in the hands of the commissioners who, at this moment, are working around the clock to stop the movements that have been incited throughout the entire colony.

---

[31] Local militia.

23

LAURENT JOLICOEUR

Petition

1793

In the midst of the ongoing slave uprising in Saint-Domingue, a man named Laurent Jolicoeur wrote to officials in the town of Saint Marc requesting freedom for a woman, Zaïre, that he owned as a slave. The Code Noir gave masters the right to free their own slaves; but for several decades before the revolution, the colonial administrations required them to pay liberty taxes for each slave they manumitted. Jolicoeur may have written this petition hoping to avoid the tax, as well to get an official document securing Zaïre's free status. The petition, which expresses a powerful vision of racial loyalty and sexual morality, provides a glimpse of the changing ideological and social landscape of Saint-Domingue during this period.

Citizens:

Citizen Laurent Jolicoeur, a merchant in Saint Marc and a leading personality in that town, previously described as a citizen of color, although he is as black as the white is white, is honored to inform you that he owns a *négresse* named Zaïre, of the Ibo nation, about forty years old, who has rendered him great service since he has owned her. Zaïre is not an ordinary individual; and if she were not enslaved, she would rival any female citizen in terms of her elevation of her sentiments; therefore her situation makes her suffer constantly; and several times the petitioner has said to her, "Oh, dear! Zaïre, you are crying," words from a tragedy that he has seen more than once.[32]

Yes, citizens, Zaïre is grief-stricken especially since the revolution began; and the petitioner requests your benevolence, or rather your

---

[32]Jolicoeur is referring to, and quoting from, *Zaïre,* a very popular play by the Enlightenment philosopher and playwright Voltaire. First performed in 1732, it was a romantic tragedy about a woman named Zaïre who was a slave in Jerusalem, and whose master wished to free her and marry her.

Moniteur Général de Saint-Domingue, No. 81, vol. III, 5 Février 1793, p. 322.

119

justice, to help her escape a bondage that he has relaxed as much as he can. She is the mother of three children who have her color, which proves her wisdom and even her virtue. What female citizen could claim, like her, to have experienced only the caresses of those who ressemble him? ... Zaïre is therefore a model of virtue, and if she reaches her goal, she will be able to claim to be the foremost of all female citizens. Zaïre's beautiful soul would not be satisfied if she had to enjoy the new existence she desires alone; she also requests it for her children.

It is therefore up to you, citizens, to bring happiness to four people, in granting to Zaïre and to Jean-Laurent, Jean-Paul, and Jean-Marie, her sons, a state worthy of society.

24

LÉGER FÉLICITÉ SONTHONAX

Decree of General Liberty
August 29, 1793

Two members of a team of commissioners sent to Saint-Domingue to enforce the Law of April 4, Léger Sonthonax and Étienne Polverel worked closely with the free men of color who were newly made citizens, promoting them in the armies that were fighting the slave rebels and their Spanish allies. In May 1793, angry white colonists in Cap Français rallied around a new governor, Thomas François Galbaud, who was sympathetic to their complaints. When the commissioners placed Galbaud under house arrest, his supporters revolted. To regain control of the city, Sonthonax offered freedom to the rebel slave bands camped outside the city in exchange for a military alliance, and he prevailed over Galbaud's forces. He deported the governor, many of whose supporters fled to the United States. In the other regions of Saint-Domingue, counterrevolutionaries invited a British invasion from Jamaica, putting yet more pressure on Sonthonax and Polverel to extend their emancipation decrees to

H. Pauléus Sannon, *Histoire de Toussaint Louverture* (Port-au-Prince: Imprimerie Aug. A. Heraux, 1938), 1:146ff.

the rest of the colony, culminating in a decree of general liberty on August 29.

By declaring emancipation in the rapid way they did, Sonthonax and Polverel had taken an extremely radical step. Most antislavery writers and activists in Europe agreed that an enslaved population should be introduced to freedom only gradually. A rapid transition to liberty, they predicted, would make it difficult to "civilize" the former slaves. They were also concerned that the plantation economy would collapse if freedom arrived too suddenly. Although he did not provide for a transition period from slavery to freedom, Sonthonax did integrate such concerns into his decree.

Men are born and remain free and equal in rights; citizens, this is France's gospel. It is high time that it be proclaimed in all areas of the republic.

Sent by the nation to Saint-Domingue as civil commissioners, our mission was to enforce the law of April 4, to see it applied in all its force, and gradually, smoothly, without rupture, to prepare the general emancipation of the slaves.

Upon our arrival, we found a horrible division among the whites who, separated by interest and opinion, agreed only on a single point: to maintain the slavery of the *nègres* forever and therefore to prohibit any system of liberty or even improvement of their fate.

In order to foil malicious persons and to reassure everyone, since they all feared any sudden action, we declared that we believed slavery was necessary for agriculture.

What we said was true, citizens; at that time slavery was as essential to the continuation of work as it was to keeping the colonists faithful to France. A group of ferocious tyrants still ruled Saint-Domingue, men who publicly preached that one's skin color should be a sign of power or condemnation. These were men like those who condemned the unfortunate Ogé or the creators and members of those notorious military tribunals who filled the towns with gallows and torture racks in order to sacrifice Africans and men of color to their own foul pretensions. The colony was still full of these bloodthirsty men. If by some great foolhardiness, we had then broken the chains that bound slaves to their masters, undoubtedly their first reaction would have been to throw themselves upon their persecutors, and, in their justifiable rage, they might easily have confounded innocent with guilty people. At that time, we did not have the legal authority to decide the status of the Africans; we would have been disloyal and in violation of the law had we done so.

Today the situation is quite different. The slave traders and cannibals are gone. Some of them have died, victims of their impotent rage, while others have sought safety by fleeing to foreign countries. Those whites who remain believe in France's laws and values.

The men of April 4[33] make up the majority of the [remaining] population; these are men to whom you owe your freedom, the first to show you what it is to have the courage to fight for natural and human rights. These men were so proud of their independence that they chose to lose their property rather than suffer the shame of putting on their old shackles. Never forget, citizens, that they gave you the weapons that conquered your liberty; never forget that you fought for the French Republic, that of all the whites in the universe, the only ones that are your friends are the Frenchmen of Europe.

The French Republic wants all men to be free and equal with no color distinctions. Kings can only be content when they are surrounded by slaves; they are the ones who sold you to the whites on the African coast; they are the tyrants in Europe who want this vile trade to continue. The republic adopts you among its children; these kings wanted only to load you down with chains or eliminate you.

The representatives of this very republic were the ones who rescued you by untying the hands of the civil commissioners and giving them authority to make provisional changes in the slave regime.

This regime is going to be changed; a new order of things will be born, and the old slavery will disappear. Yet do not think that the liberty that you will enjoy means laziness and inactivity. In France, everyone is free and everyone works; in Saint-Domingue under these same laws, you will follow the same model. After returning to your old work crews or your former owners, you will be paid for your work; you will no longer suffer the humiliating punishments previously inflicted upon you; you will no longer be property, as before. You will be your own master and live contented.

Since you have chosen to become citizens of the French nation, you must also be the zealous defender of its laws; you will undoubtedly defend the interests of the republic against kings, more out of gratitude for the benefits she has heaped upon you than to preserve your

---

[33]The men of color given political rights by the April 4, 1792, decree.

own independence. Liberty has brought you from nothingness into existence; show that you are worthy of her. Renounce laziness forever as if it were a crime. Have the courage to want to be a people, and soon you will be equal to the nations of Europe. Your detractors and your tyrants maintain that an African who is set free will never work again. Prove them wrong. Work twice as hard to win the prize that awaits you. Let your activity prove to France that, by including you on her side, she has truly increased her capacities and resources.

And you, citizens misled by the vile royalists, you who took up the flags and uniforms of the cowardly Spanish to fight blindly against your own interests, against the freedom of your women and children, open your eyes at last to the enormous advantages that the republic offers you. The kings promise you liberty, but do you see them giving this to their subjects? Do the Spanish free their own slaves? No, surely not. To the contrary, they are likely to weigh you down with chains as soon as they no longer need your services. Aren't they the ones who turned Ogé over to his killers? What misfortune you suffer! If France returned to its kings, the [royalist] *émigrés* would turn on you. They flatter you today, but they would be the first to torture you.

Given this situation, the civil commissioner, reflecting on the petition signed by individuals assembled in a meeting, exercising the powers given him by Article 3 of the law passed by the National Convention last March 5:

Orders the following, to be carried out in the northern province [of Saint-Domingue].

First Article: The Declaration of the Rights of Man and Citizen will be printed, published, and displayed everywhere it is needed.

2. All the *nègres* and mixed blood people currently in slavery are declared free to enjoy all the rights of French citizens; they are nevertheless subject to the regime described in the following articles. . . .

5. Servants of either sex can be hired by their masters and mistresses only for three months, and this for a salary that they will fix according to the wishes of each.

6. Former house slaves working for persons who are older than sixty, or sick, or for nursing infants less than ten years old, are not free to leave them. Their salary is set at 1 *portuguaise* (8 *gourdes*)[34] per

---

[34]The *portugaise* and the *gourde* were, respectively, Portuguese and Spanish coins that circulated widely in the Caribbean in the eighteenth century. Just before the revolution, one gourde, equal to 8½ colonial livres, would buy a medium-size table or rent a coastal trading boat for two days.

month for wet nurses and 6 *portuguaise* for the others, for men and women alike. . . .

9. The *nègres* currently working on the plantations of their former masters are required to remain there. They will work in agriculture.

10. The enlisted fighters who are serving in army units or in forts will be allowed to establish themselves on plantations for agricultural work by first obtaining a furlough from their leader or an order from us, to be delivered if they find a willing man to replace them.

11. The former field hands will be obliged to work for a year, during which time they can change plantations only by permission of a justice of the peace.

12. The profits of each plantation will be divided into three equal portions after taxes are deducted from the whole amount. One-third will remain with the owner of the land. He will have access to another third to cover the costs of planting. The remaining third will be divided between the field workers in a manner to be set . . .

In addition, the field workers will have their own provision grounds; they will be divided equally between each family, according to the quality of the land and the amount needed. . . .

27. Punishment by the whip is absolutely forbidden; for violations of discipline it will be replaced by the stocks for one, two, or three days, according to the severity of the case. The most severe punishments will be fines, up to complete loss of salary.

28. For civil crimes, the former slaves will be judged like other French citizens.

29. Field hands cannot be forced to work on Sunday. . . .

31. Women who are seven months pregnant will not work and will only return to the fields two months after their deliveries.

32. Field hands can change plantations for health reasons or for an incompatible personality at the request of the crew in which they work. These affairs will be subject to the decision of a justice of the peace and his counselors.

33. On the fifteenth day after the publication of this proclamation, all men who do not own property and are neither in the military, nor working in agriculture, nor employed in someone's home, within the time limits set above, or are found to be vagrants, will be arrested and put in prison.

34. Women who do not have an obvious source of income, who are not working in agriculture or employed in someone's home, within the time limits set above, or are found to be vagrants, will be arrested and put in prison.

35. The men and women imprisoned in these cases for the first

time will be held for a month. The second time they will be held for three months, and the third time they will be sentenced to a public work detail for one year.

36. Persons working in agriculture and household workers will not leave their employment for any reason without permission of the city or town government where they live. . . .

38. *The Code Noir* is provisionally repealed.

25

Insurgent Responses to Emancipation
1793

After Sonthonax decreed general liberty in August 1793, some insurgents joined the French side. But many, including such leading generals as Jean-François and Georges Biassou, as well as Toussaint Louverture, decided to continue fighting with the Spanish. In this letter, Bramante Lazzary, one of the rebel leaders who had joined the French side, pleaded with Louverture to abandon the Spanish king and join the republic. It is not clear whether Lazzary was a slave or had, like Louverture, been freed before 1793, although the invocation of Ogé's killing suggests that he may have been a free man of color. Like many contemporary French writers, Lazzary equated royal tyranny with slavery. In Saint-Domingue, this equation was much more than a convenient form of symbolism: the French Republic, in Lazzary's opinion, represented liberty for all, while the royal government Louverture was fighting for would ultimately defend the brutal system of chattel slavery.

Bramante Lazzary, Commander-in-Chief of the forces of the Tannerie, made up of brave French citizens of all colors without distinction

To: Citizen Toussaint Louverture, supposed General of the Armies of His Most Catholic Majesty today, yesterday supposed General of the King . . . the chief disturber of the order and the tranquility of our brothers.

Bramante Lazzary to Toussaint Louverture, Archives Nationales, DXXV 23, 231, letter 96.

Citizen:

The vengeful god whose name you profane will, you say, extermi-
nate me. But it is you who should tremble, my brother. It is against
you he will act for plunging our other brothers, who seek only happiness, into error. The cause of my co-citizens and myself is the same; it
is that willed by twenty-five million Europeans who have annihilated
tyranny and persecution. Without the error that Spanish barbarism
and slavery has thrown you into, Saint-Domingue would already be
peaceful and would enjoy the same happiness. The proof is the proclamation of our good father Sonthonax, the civil commissioner and the
representative of the will of France in its entirety, which I sent you
yesterday. . . . There are no more slaves in Saint-Domingue; all men of
all colors are free and equal in their rights and believe that this is the
greatest of gifts. What have you received from the time of kings for
centuries for your work and your natural virtues? Shame and disdain.
You have lived, I say, under the cane[35] of fire and cruelty. Is it possible
that today you are not grateful for the good the motherland has done
for us? I swear that you will have to answer for this, that you will be
the victim of your crazy pretensions. Remember above all that all good
Frenchmen shudder at the word *king,* who you must know were never
happy unless they were surrounded by slaves, and that since the
twenty-first of January our motherland no longer has one and enjoys
perfect happiness. We are her children and of the same opinion and
will all die rather than recognize tyrants and their ferocious imitators.
We all have as our motto "to live free or die" and will prove it to you
when you give us the chance.

From me to you, my brother Toussaint, I have nothing to be
ashamed of; I explained to you in friendship the indignation I felt at
your Old Regime attitudes, because all my brothers and I shudder at
the memory of our tyrants. You know as I do how much we suffered.
And you know the disgraceful way the Spanish villains treated our
brave brother Ogé, who they handed over to supporters of the former
king so they could sacrifice him on the wheel. They succeeded in
their treacherous project, and all of France, composed as I said of
twenty-five million of our brothers, cried out for vengeance. . . . They
wanted happiness for all of us. How can you still resist such generous sentiments? No! I cannot believe it. You will open your eyes and

---

[35]Under the threat.

come back to your best friends who seek nothing but our common happiness.

At the same time, Lazzary issued a general call to local insurgents to join the French. In it, he celebrated republican emancipation by describing the flag flown in his insurgent camp: a tri-color flag superimposed with figures of a white, a mulatto, and a black man.

Bramante Lazzary, Commander of the Camps of the Tannerie and Lacombe

August 30, 1793, year 2 of the Republic[36]
To my brothers and friends in rebellion in the northern province
Can there be any greater happiness for us than to see ourselves all united together and enjoying a good and sweet natural liberty that France has given us?

At last, my friends, general liberty has been proclaimed on the island; it has given us our well-being and made us all children of the law. It is to them, the civil commissioners, to whom France gave its power, it is to them, my brothers, that we owe our legitimate happiness; it is to them and only to them that France had confided it to grant it to us. As soon as you receive my letter, you must gather together and present yourself to the representatives of the nation, and swear to be loyal to the nation and to die for the safety of our country, to march under the national flag, which is the sign of our union, which finally announces the reunion of the three colors.

Our flag makes it clear that our liberty depends on these three colors; white, mulatto, black. We are fighting for these three colors. The nobility and the Spaniards want us to have only the white in order to bring us back to the old order. But no, we are French; we are fighting for our freedom; we want to live free or die, that is the motto of all good French republicans.

You fought for something that now has been legitimately granted

---

[36]Lazzary is combining the Gregorian calendar, which he uses for the day and month, with the Republican calendar, which he uses for the year. The calendar began with "Year 1" in September 1792, with the establishment of the French Republic, and subsequent calendar years began on the same date.

Bramante Lazzary to Toussaint Louverture, Archives Nationales, DXXV 23, 231, letter 98.

to us, so let us unite as your brothers from Limbé and Morne Rouge have, to form a single and same family, to march against those who wish to attack our liberty. Spain has joined a conflict that it made you think it would support. But remember, my brothers, that they will not do so for as long as they tell you. They will bite their thumbs, like the aristocrats of Le Cap who have gone to their side. France is more powerful than you think and has already made itself respected by several crowns, and Spain will be pinched in its turn. And France will also punish those to whom it has offered happiness but who pretend they do not know the law. . . .

Such appeals, however, left many insurgents fighting on the Spanish side unmoved. Indeed, one rebel who had joined Sonthonax and Polverel, the Kongo-born Macaya, deserted them soon afterwards. Sent as an emissary to Jean-François and Biassou by the commissioners, he instead stayed with his former comrades. In response to one entreaty to come back to the service of the republic, Macaya—who seems to have been Catholic, like many of those brought to the Americas from the Kongo region, where many communities had practiced Catholicism since the sixteenth century—responded by evoking a complex mix of allegiances.

Response of Macaya

I am the subject of three kings: of the King of Congo, master of all the blacks; of the King of France who represents my father; of the King of Spain who represents my mother. These three Kings are the descendants of those who, led by a star, came to adore God made man. If I went over to the Republic, I might be forced to make war against my brothers, the subjects of these three kings to whom I have promised loyalty.

Pamphile de Lacroix, *Mémoires pour servir à l'histoire de la révolution de Saint-Domingue* (Paris, 1819) vol. 1, p. 253.

26

THE NATIONAL CONVENTION

The Abolition of Slavery

February 4, 1794

In an atmosphere of military, economic, and social upheaval, the French Revolution entered a period known as the Terror, characterized by radical measures like an intensified search for internal enemies and increasing use of public executions. Despite its much-criticized violence, this period was also marked by an extraordinary optimism about what the French Republic could accomplish in the cause of human rights.

It was in this context that three representatives from Saint-Domingue, elected in August 1793 at an electoral assembly overseen by Sonthonax, arrived in Paris: a man of color, Jean-Baptiste Mills; an African-born former slave, Jean-Baptiste Belley; and a white man named Louis Dufay. They brought news of the emancipation decrees that Sonthonax and Polverel had issued in Saint-Domingue, and in so doing led the National Convention to abolish slavery throughout the French empire. While some representatives were probably convinced that they had no choice but to ratify the fait accompli that was already in force in the colonies, others proclaimed the end of slavery as an opportunity to spread the revolution's humanitarian benefits far beyond Europe.

[An unnamed deputy announces]: Citizens, your Committee on Decrees has verified the papers of the deputies Saint-Domingue has sent as its national representatives; it finds that they are in order. I move that you admit them as members of the Convention.

Camboulas: Since 1789, a great transformation remained incomplete; the nobilities of the sword and the Church were eliminated, but an aristocracy of the skin still ruled; it has just breathed its last. Equality is established; a black man, a yellow man, and a white man will sit among you representing the free citizens of Saint-Domingue. (The deputies applaud.)

Réimpression de L'Ancien Moniteur, depuis la réunion des états-généraux jusqu'au consulat (mai 1789–novembre 1799). (Paris: Bureau Central, 1841) 19: 385–87.

Danton: Yes, equality is established, but tyranny must stop; I move that the Colonial Committee report on the persecutions inflicted on black people in France since 1787.

The Convention approves this motion.

[Other business is heard. Then]:

The three deputies from Saint-Domingue enter the hall.

Repeated waves of applause welcome them.

Lacroix (representing the Eure-et-Loire): For a long time this assembly wanted to include in its ranks men of color, who had been oppressed for so many years. Today we have two of them; I move that the president [of the Convention] mark their introduction with a fraternal kiss.

This motion passed amid cheering.

The three deputies from Saint-Domingue approach the president, and receive the fraternal kiss from him. (The hall rang with new cheers) . . .

[The Convention heard a series of other reports and adjourned at 4 o'clock. The following day]:

One of the three deputies newly arrived from Saint-Domingue presents a report summarizing the events that have occurred there. He describes the cause of its misfortunes; he sees in them the odious policies and intrigues of England and Spain, who, attempting to strip this valuable colony from the Republic, found a way to foment a civil war there. But the courage of the *nègres* armed for the French cause foiled these treacherous projects. In exchange for their services, they demanded liberty, which was granted to them.

The speaker beseeched the Convention to ratify that promise and to allow the colonies to fully enjoy the benefits of liberty and equality.

Levasseur (of the Sarthe): I move that the Convention, motivated not by a temporary enthusiasm but by the principles of justice, faithful to the Declaration of the Rights of Man, rule that from this moment slavery is abolished in all the Republic's territory. Saint-Domingue is part of that territory, yet we have slaves in Saint-Domingue. I move that these men be free, with no color distinctions.

Lacroix (of the Eure-and-Loire): In writing the constitution of the French people, we did not consider the unfortunate men of color. Posterity will blame us greatly for this; but we must repair this wrong. Was it irrational for us to decree that no feudal dues be collected in the French Republic? You just heard one of our colleagues say that there are still slaves in our colonies. It is time that we rise to the height of the principles of liberty and equality. For though we say that there are no slaves in France, isn't it true that men of color are slaves in our colonies? Let us proclaim the liberty of the men of color. With this act of justice you will give a great example to the men of color enslaved in the English and Spanish colonies. Like us, the men of color wanted to break their chains; we have broken ours, we have refused to submit to the yoke of any master; let us grant them the same benefit.

Levasseur: If it was possible to show the Convention the heartbreaking picture of slavery's evils, I would make it tremble at the aristocracy that some whites still practice in our colonies.

Lacroix: President, don't allow the Convention to dishonor itself by a longer discussion.

The entire assembly stands, in agreement.

The president proclaims the abolition of slavery, amid applause and thousands of repeated cries of Long live the Republic! Long live the Convention! Long live the Mountain!

The two deputies of color stand at the rostrum; they kiss each other. (Applause.)

Lacroix leads them to the president, who gives them the fraternal kiss. They are successively embraced by all the deputies.

Cambon: A female citizen of color, who regularly attends the Convention's meetings, and who has taken part in all the revolution's phases, felt such great joy in seeing us grant liberty to all her brothers, that she fainted dead away. (Applause.) I move that this fact be included in the minutes; that this citizen be admitted to the session to receive at least this recognition of her civic virtue.

This motion passes.

This citizen could be seen to the left of the president, on the front bench of the auditorium, drying the tears that this moving scene had brought to her eyes. (Applause.)

[Unknown deputy]: I move that the naval ministry have dispatch boats leave immediately to inform the colonies of the happy news of their freedom.

Danton: Representatives of the French people, until now our decrees of liberty have been selfish, and only for ourselves. But today we proclaim it to the universe, and generations to come will glory in this decree; we are proclaiming universal liberty. Yesterday, when the [Convention's] president kissed the deputies of color as brothers, I saw the moment in which the Convention must decree the liberty of our brothers. The session was too poorly attended. The Convention just did its duty. But, after having granted the benefit of freedom, we must play a moderating role, so to speak. Let us ask the Colonial Committee and the Committee of Public Safety to devise ways to make the decree useful for humanity but not dangerous to it.

By not carrying our work far enough, we disgraced our reputation. We ignored the great principles developed by the virtuous Las Casas.[37] We are working for future generations; let us launch liberty into the colonies; the English are dead, today. (Applause.) We are hurling liberty into the New World; she will bring abundant fruits and establish deep roots there. In vain Pitt[38] and his accomplices will apply political pressure to try to repeal the effects of this good deed; they will be dragged into the void. France will regain the rank and influence that its energy, its soil, and its population merit. We ourselves will benefit from our generosity, but we will not extend it farther than prudence dictates. We will fell the tyrants just as we have crushed those treacherous men who wanted to push back the revolution. Let us not lose our momentum. Let us launch our frigates, confident of the blessings of the universe and posterity, and let us rule that these measures be referred to the attention of the committees.

The Convention approves this referral.

Lacroix makes a proposal that is adopted in these terms:

"The National Convention declares that slavery of the *nègres* is abolished in all the colonies; consequently, it decrees that all men living in the colonies, without distinction of color, are French citizens and enjoy all the rights guaranteed by the constitution."

---

[37]The speaker was referring to Bartolomé de Las Casas, a sixteenth-century critic of the brutality of the Spanish conquest and defender of indigenous rights.

[38]William Pitt, the British prime minister.

4

Defining Emancipation, 1794–1798

27

VICTOR HUGUES

Proclamations

1794

In June 1794, a small mission of French troops invaded Guadeloupe, which had been occupied by the British a few months earlier, carrying the decree of emancipation passed in Paris in February. Facing a much larger force, the French freed slaves on the plantations and recruited many to help rid the island of the British, and therefore of slavery. Within a few months, the entire island was back in French hands.

The mission was led by three commissioners appointed by the National Convention to bring emancipation to Guadeloupe. One of them, Victor Hugues, would quickly emerge as the central leader in the colony. The following documents are proclamations issued by Hugues and another commissioner, Pierre Lebas, during their first months on the island. They represent the complicated balancing act of Hugues's regime in Guadeloupe, which brought liberation to the slaves but simultaneously sought, like the parallel regimes in Saint-Domingue, to maintain the colonial economy by forcing them to keep working on the plantations.

The first document was attached to posters that proclaimed the emancipation decree in Guadeloupe.

"Extrait du procès-verbal de la Convention Nationale" 19 Prairial 1794 (June 7, 1794), Centre des Archives d'Outre-Mer, C7A 47, 8.

CITIZENS,

A republican government accepts neither chains nor slavery, and therefore the National Convention has just solemnly proclaimed the liberty of the Negroes and confided the execution of this law to the commissioners it has delegated for the colonies; the result of this natural redress and its civic organization must be (1) the beneficial equality without which the political machine is like a clock whose pendulum loses its equilibrium and its perpetual action; (2) an administration both generally and individually committed to guaranteeing the property already held by some, and the product of the work and industry of others.

CITIZENS of all colors, your happiness depends on this law . . . but the white citizens must kindly offer, in fraternity, and with reasonable wages, work to their black and colored brothers; and the latter must also learn and never forget that those who have no property must provide, through their work, for their own subsistence and that of their family, as well as to the support of their nation. CITIZENS, you have become equal in order to enjoy happiness and to share it with all others; the person who oppresses his co-citizen is a monster who must be banished from the social world.

Six days later, the commissioners issued another proclamation that made clear they were unhappy with the way the former slaves had responded to freedom.

The National Convention, through its decree of February 4, has granted you the highest of blessings: LIBERTY. She has confided the application of this law to us; her intention in smashing your chains was to grant you greater happiness by allowing you to enjoy your rights: We will be responsible to the nation and humanity if we do not prevent the disorders that the enemies of the public interest hope to make you the victims of.

We have been pained to learn that depredations have been committed in the countryside, that manioc[1] plants have been cut and bananas removed, for no reason, with the simple intention of hurting the owners. It is hard for us to believe these accusations; but in the circum-

---

[1]A root vegetable commonly used in the Caribbean to make flour.

"Les Commissaires délégués . . . aux habitants des campagnes de toutes les couleurs," 25 Prairial an 2 (June 13, 1794), Centre des Archives d'Outre-Mer, C7A 47, 10.

stance that the colony finds itself in, it is vital to provide for the conservation of the property of each individual, and especially of the provisions of all kinds. Therefore we expressly forbid all citizens of whatever color to touch the provisions of the habitations, such as maniocs, bananas, corn, etc., without the express permission of the owner. Those who contravene this order will be pursued to the full extent of the law; and in those cases where they take the said provisions with malevolence, they will be declared outlaws and punished with death as traitors who have consorted with the enemies of the republic.

In the next proclamation, addressed to the "Black Citizens" and written soon afterwards, the commissioners took an even harsher tone towards the former slaves.

The republic, in recognizing the rights that nature gave you, did not intend to release you from the obligation of working for what you need to live.

He who does not work deserves only disdain and must not profit from the blessings of our regeneration; we must assume, with good reason, that the lazy survive only through pillaging.

Since all citizens cannot be employed in the defense of the colony, it is indispensable that those who are not incorporated into the armed forces go to work cultivating the land and planting food as quickly as possible.

In fact, Citizens, he who sacrifices his pain and his sweat to provide food to his co-citizens deserves just as much a reward as he who sacrifices to defend them. In consequence, citizens, we invite and require those of you who are not incorporated into the army to return to the plantations where you previously lived, and to work there without respite planting potatoes, yams, and other edible roots. We promise to protect you and to pay you for your work; but if, against our will, some of you refuse to respond to our invitation, we will declare you traitors, in the name of the republic, and punish you to the full extent of the law.

We order the municipality to use the armed forces to break up the mobs and force the black citizens to return to their respective plantations to plant provisions.

"Proclamation: Le Commissaire délégué . . . aux citoyens noirs," 2 Messidor an 2 (June 20, 1794), Centre des Archives d'Outre-Mer, C7A 47, 14.

28

Geneviève Labothière Secures
Her Brother's Freedom
1796–1801

While Hugues brought liberty to Guadeloupe, the British held on to Martinique, and as a result slavery was maintained there. In this document, drawn up in front of a notary in Basse-Terre, Guadeloupe, a woman explained how she was able to secure freedom for her brother, who was still enslaved in Martinique. Many ex-slaves like Labothière used their new right to create legal documents to document and solidify their access to liberty and property. This document is relatively unique, however, because in the process of confronting the fact that her actions were technically illegal—the slave trade was abolished in France—Labothière related her individual actions to the broader policies of republican emancipation. It also shows how networks that tied together families, as well as blacks and whites such as Jacques Dupuy (who assisted Labothière), crossed geographic and imperial boundaries during this period.

Today, the morning of September 28, Year 10 [1801], of the French Republic, united and indivisible, before the notary public of the aforementioned republic, established for the region of the island of Guadeloupe and its dependencies, at the Basse-Terre residence of the undersigned, appeared the citizen Geneviève Labothière, called Mayoute, shopkeeper, and the citizen Joseph Labothière, tailor, her natural brother, in the neighborhood of Saint-François, region of Guadeloupe, district and commune of Basse-Terre.

These two have declared that at the time when slavery was abolished in the colony, Citizen[2] Joseph Labothière, who then belonged to

---

[2]During the French Revolution, the terms *citizen* and *citizenness* replaced *sir* and *madam* as forms of official address as a way of emphasizing equality.

"Declaration of Citizen and Citizenness Labothière, Brother and Sister, Certifying the Free Status of the Said Citizen Labothière," Archives Departmentales de la Guadeloupe, Notaires, Dupuch 2E2/27, 6 Vendemiaire, an 10 (September 28, 1801). The editors would like to thank Sue Peabody for providing us with her translation of this document, which is the basis for the translation we present here.

Lauzeau of Saint-Pierre, island of Martinique, fell under the power of the English, [and] was deprived of benefiting from the general emancipation established by the laws of the French Republic. In order to improve the [text illegible] of his manumission, he brought together the means that he had already procured himself through his savings, those provided to him successively by active work and the resources of honest industry. When he found himself in possession of the necessary sum for the realization of his plan, he had a letter written to Citizenness Labothière, his sister, who is present and who will stay involved in the present process at his request, . . . [they have] judged it appropriate to make the present declaration to certify the truth, which is that Citizen Joseph Labothière, although he was taken out of slavery by the laws of the republic, was forced by circumstances to reclaim his liberty with his own money, being in a colony that had been usurped by the enemies of France. And that on this occasion, Citizenness Geneviève Labothière, his sister, has* carried out an act of† fraternity, founded on the laws of nature, without hurting the laws of the republic, since her brother had paid the price of his freedom himself and was not sold to her. Consequently, Citizenness Labothière never had any sort of right over her brother's person, nor over the use of his time and services.

And, in order to avoid all future difficulties that could challenge her brother, as a result of the three privately signed [documents] attached to this deed, Citizenness Labothière declares that she surrenders completely to Citizen Joseph Labothière, her brother, all the rights the aforementioned private deeds might give her over the use of his time and of his services. . . . And she consents that her aforementioned brother use and dispose of his time and his services, of his talents and his industry, for his personal profit, as he has done until now, since the period previously cited, without having to answer to anyone, and without his ever being disturbed, troubled, or sought out in this regard by the present party,³ nor by her heirs or other representatives. Which has been accepted by the Citizen Labothière, her brother.

The parties requested a deed of all of this, which was given to them by the undersigned notary, to serve them and to verify for whatever reason.

---

*Original: purely and simply.
†Original: of benevolence and.
³Geneviève Labothière.

Attached to the document above were the following private deeds mentioned in the text, which documented how the money that was used to buy Joseph changed hands over the course of several years in several different locations.

I received from Mister Jacques Dupuis [Dupuy] the sum of two thousand livres for the mulatto Joseph, tailor, who I sold and delivered to him in Saint Pierre, October 13, 1796.

   Signed, Gourrige Lazeau, representative of Mary

I recognize having received from Geneviève Mayoute the sum of two thousand livres for the price of the mulatto Joseph, tailor by profession, who I sold and delivered to her in St. Thomas,[4] April 14, 1798.

   Signed, Jacques Dupuy

I recognize having received from my brother Joseph the sum of two thousand livres which I reimbursed to Sir Jacques Dupuy for the acquisition he made of the said Joseph from the hands of the Dame Gourrige Lauzeau, representation of the citizen Mary, the said receipt dated April 14, 1798. Saint Thomas, July 6, 1798.

   X (Mark of Geneviève Mayoute)

   [4]This island, one of the Virgin Islands, was then under Danish control. It was a busy port and neutral territory in the war between France and Britain.

29

The Plantation Policies of Étienne Polverel

1794

Though Sonthonax's declaration of general liberty made him the most famous of Saint-Domingue's revolutionary commissioners, the efforts of his colleague Étienne Polverel, who proclaimed emancipation in the southern and western provinces, were just as important. Polverel decreed emancipation more slowly than Sonthonax; once it was in place, he also

"Documents aux origines de l'abolition de l'esclavage: Proclamations de Polverel et de Sonthonax, 1793–1794," *Revue d'histoire des colonies,* 36 (1949), 391ff.

issued numerous decrees that sought to lay out and control exactly how it would be implemented. In the regions under Polverel's control, many plantations had been abandoned by their owners and, following French revolutionary law, had been sequestered and taken over by the state, which meant that the administration often had direct control over them and those who worked there.

In the following document, Polverel explains to field workers some of the finer points of his plan in a way that suggests he was responding to attempts by the freed people to take advantage of and expand the limits of their new liberty. He insisted, for instance, that it was acceptable for women to receive less pay than men, something many women on the plantations had contested in the intervening months.

Regulations on the proportion of work and compensation and on the sharing of agricultural revenues between the landowners and the field workers. Plaine de l'Île à Vache, February 7, 1794. . . .

The enemies of liberty had predicted that no one would ever get any work out of the Africans once they were free, that they would pillage and destroy, that they would burn everything, and that they would murder those who were free before: whites and people of color. Some letters being passed around in the various parishes even claimed that this was what the civil commissioners had planned and hoped for.

Well, the Africans have been declared free; for three months now, they have been left to their own devices, without repressive or coercive laws, and they have neither pillaged nor destroyed nor murdered. The work crews are back in order and are staying that way. The rebels who had been called "brigands" have all gone back to work or have joined the armies of the republic and are fighting for her.

If some plantation crews refused to work, it is because enemies of the public peace gave the field hands false ideas about liberty; it is because landowners and managers continued to treat them like slaves, hiding my proclamations from them, or misapplying them, or telling them that liberty and my proclamations would last only a few days.

If there was vagrancy, if some of those who did stay on the plantations did less work, if almost all field workers believed they could rest on Saturday as well as on Sunday, this is because they wanted to try out their freedom, so to speak, to assure themselves that it was not a dream and that they were really in charge of their own work and of coming and going as they pleased.

We know then what we can fear or hope for from the new freemen. In the initial excitement of their new freedom, they committed errors, not crimes. Their mistakes were the result of errors, ignorance, and poorly understood self-interest. We will help them understand, and they will be like us or even better, because they are less corrupted.

The question of Saturday work seems to be the most important point to them. As slaves, they did not work on Sunday. They almost seem to believe that their status has not changed if they do not have one more day per week.

Africans, listen carefully to me. You can rest on Saturday, on Monday, every day of the week, if you want. No one has the right to force you to work a single day if you don't want to. You are completely free.

But you have to eat and clothe yourselves; you also want occasionally to have a special meal with your friends. You want your women to be well dressed to honor you and to be more attractive. You want to be properly dressed yourself and to have comfortable furniture, to please your women, for your health, theirs, or that of your children.

Only the products of the land will allow you to supply all these needs.

That land does not belong to you. It belongs to those who purchased it, to those who inherited it from its first buyers.

You can lay claim to the products of this land only through agriculture. And I have told you that the portion assigned to you in the revenues of the land will be given to you only *in compensation for your work.*

When I set that portion at one-third of the net revenue, I assumed that you would work six days a week. You want to cut back on Saturday. From the first, I already told you that you have the authority to do this; but look at the results.

To cut back one day of work per week is to cut back one-sixth of the year's work and therefore diminish revenues by at least one-sixth.

Suppose that a sugar estate gives, most years, three hundred *milliers*[5] of sugar in profit through regular work of six days a week. The share of the landowner would be two hundred *milliers;* yours would be one hundred *milliers.*

By resting on Saturday, you reduce the profits by one-sixth; that is, those three hundred *milliers* are lowered to two hundred fifty.

But since it is not the landowner's fault that profits are reduced, it is not fair that his share be reduced. He must still have his two hun-

---

[5]The *millier,* which translates literally as "thousand," was the standard unit used to measure the amount of sugar produced on a plantation.

dred *milliers* in sugar. This will lower your share to fifty *milliers,* and it is fair that this reduction falls on you, since it is your fault that profits are reduced.

What if you wanted another day of rest in addition to Saturday? You still have the power to make this decision. But cutting back two days out of six is one-third of the work, so one-third of the product is cut back. In other words, instead of three hundred *milliers* in sugar, there is only two hundred *milliers,* which is the landowner's share, and nothing will remain for you.

If you wanted to take idleness and refusal to work even farther, the land would not produce even the two hundred *milliers* of sugar for the landowner's share; therefore, it would be clear that you would be abusing your freedom, and the landowner would be free to act by himself.

The freedom of the landowner consists in the ability to have his land worked as he wishes, by whomever he wishes, and in the way that he wishes. He would start by evicting the entire lazy work crew from the plantation and hiring day laborers to work his land. He would no longer have to provide shelter or a provision ground to the field hands. It is quite clear that he would owe nothing to the dismissed Africans, since the right to shelter and provision grounds, like the right to a share of the revenue, is given only to those whose constant and diligent work makes them part of the plantation. He owes nothing like this to the day laborers, who can be considered only transients and who can claim each day only the wages set for one day. . . .

Africans, now you have been educated. Let us see if you will still choose to rest on Saturday with the inevitable poverty [it will bring] instead of the well-being for which I have prepared you.

I must warn you against making other critical errors that may seem to be in your interests. . . .

Today some of you are convinced that, because you have been freed, because measures are being taken to improve your condition, you must have larger gardens than you had when you were slaves. But I tell you that these small gardens were absolutely right and essential for you then. Today, however, they are unnecessary, and there would be no drawbacks or unfairness in taking them away.

Before, you were only given just enough food and clothes to survive. You received no care; nothing was spent so that your lodgings would be clean and healthful, nor for the daily needs of your households. Each of you had the produce from your gardens as an additional means to satisfy the needs that no one would acknowledge, think about, or meet.

Today, you yourselves decide what pleasures you will have; these will become part of the costs of operating the plantation and will be deducted before anything else from the plantation's produce. These things must be decided by the administrative council made up of managers and *commandeurs* that you yourself have chosen.

Before, you had no share in the profits of the plantations. Today each of you will have his share in these profits, in proportion to his work.

Therefore, you now need your provision grounds less than ever. I do not want to take them from you, but I cannot permit them to be any larger than the limits that have always been set: thirty steps by twenty, or an area of six hundred steps, in other words, sixteen gardens for each *carreau*[6] of land. . . .

Finally, your women grumble about the inequality of my proposed system of shares because I have allotted them less than the men. Why give us less than the men, they say? Don't we all go to work at the same time? they ask. Don't we all quit at the same time?

The target of their exaggerated claim is not the landowners, but you, their men. They want us to ignore the natural inequality in the strength of men and women, their usual or regular ailments, and the periods of rest they need for pregnancies, childbirth, and nursing.

Yet these men whose share of the profits they envy are working, saving, and yearning for gold only to spend it on their women.

Africans, if you want these women to be reasonable, be reasonable yourself. This is about your well-being, about the freedom of your fathers, your brothers, your cousins who are maybe this very moment slaves in English, Dutch, Spanish, or Portuguese colonies. This is about the peace of your native land. You hold in your hands the fate of all of Africa. . . .

The following documents, written to Étienne Polverel by managers, over-seers, or military officials in the Cayes plain along Saint-Domingue's southern coast, reveal field workers' varying responses to Polverel's new plantation regulations. The first document, dated February 24, 1794, was written by Pierre Duval, a naval inspector who visited the first Laborde plantation in accordance with Article 22 of Polverel's February regulations on plantation work.

Arriving on the said plantation about nine o'clock in the morning, I found the manager's house locked, and I was told that he had left for

[6]One *carreau* equals 2.79 acres.

Archives Nationales, DXXV 28, Dossier No. 287.

the town of Les Cayes Saturday after dinner. I then asked a cart driver where the field crew was. He answered that they were cutting cane. I went to a cane field, where I found only thirty-three field hands, not counting the two former head slaves [*commandeurs*] and the six cart drivers. I asked the overseers where the other Africans were; they answered that an African had died and that some of the workers were at the burial of this African from the Congo nation.

I ordered the *commandeurs* to bring the field hands to the plantation house and to assemble everyone, men and women, so that I could convey to them the civil commissioner's orders, which I was charged with carrying out. . . . I found the Africans to be in good humor, including the women, most of whom were working and who promised to apply themselves faithfully.

I ordered the overseers and other leaders of the field crew to evict any women and even men who refused to work, and I told these women that I took it upon myself to postpone their punishment and that I would go to ask the civil commissioner to pardon them. But I assured them that all those who were not working after dinner that day would be evicted and not allowed back on the plantation, and that we were awaiting new orders to evict those who refused to work on Saturday but who, at the moment, appeared sorry and wanted to return to work.

The overseers assured me that there had been fifty-five slaves cutting cane this morning and that before I arrived they had sent away some to bury the African who died yesterday and for the ceremonies that were normal in their country; that about twenty women had worked this morning, and that several of those who had stayed in their huts were sick or breastfeeding children.

The next document was written by Lacolle, the manager of the Codère plantation, on March 20, 1794.

I am sending you two African women who refused to work at night after the decision of the plantation's administrative council. Not only did they refuse to work, but they also said the worst things to the *commandeur*, threatening him and saying that he would be the only one working in the sugar mill at night. I therefore ask you to punish them as an example.

Archives Nationales, DXXV 37, Dossier 375.

The next document was written by another manager, Lalesmne, on the Formon plantation on March 17, 1794.

It is my privilege to write and inform you that the so-called Marquis, second *commandeur,* has become more indolent and lazy than ever for the common work of the plantation. Since I arrived on said plantation, there has not been a moment when I have been pleased with his conduct. It appears that he is setting the worst example for the field workers. I must tell you that said Marquis is from the Ibo nation and that three-quarters of the plantation's field workers are from this same country and have sided with him. As for Coridon, the first *commandeur,* he does his duty reasonably well, but he is not supported by his second. . . . The said Coridon always arrives at work with the field hands of his Congo nation an hour before those of said Marquis. I am sorry to trouble you with these problems that exist on this plantation between the senior *commandeurs* as well as among the field hands. . . . My concern is for the common welfare and the good of the republic; I have always been zealous and interested in whatever is my duty and in the good fortune of my fellow citizens.

Archives Nationales, DXXV 37, Dossier 375.

30

JEAN-BAPTISTE BELLEY

The True Colors of the Planters, or the System of the Hotel Massiac, Exposed by Gouli
1795

In late 1794 and early 1795, planters serving in the National Convention began to attack France's emancipation policies. Marie-Benoît-Louis Gouly, a representative of the Indian Ocean colonies, presented a speech claiming that blacks in the Caribbean had reverted to barbarism and

Le Bout d'Oreille des Colons ou Le Système de l'Hôtel de Massiac, mis au jour par Gouli. Belley, Depute noir de Saint-Domingue, à ses collegues (Paris, n.d.).

laziness since the end of slavery. Jean-Baptiste Belley (see Figure 3), who had represented Saint-Domingue since 1794, refuted the assertions of Gouly (whose name he spelled "Gouli") and defended emancipation with a speech that drew on his own experiences as an African-born survivor of the slave trade and slavery.

They tell you, legislators of a free people, they dare write that your sublime decree of 16 Pluviôse [4 February 1794] is disastrous, impolitic, and barbarous. The planters announce from the rooftops that they will have it recalled. You have given back liberty to two million men, torn from their homeland by greed; you have broken their too-heavy chains, the instruments of their misery, of their torture! . . . A man, a tiger who for twenty years devoted himself to torturing Africans in the Île de France, who made himself happy by taking advantage of the sweat and blood of these unfortunates, that man stands up today against the happy day whose light you have brought to these unfortunates . . . His dangerous avarice has made him lose sight of your principles and his duties. . . .

Which one of you was not filled with indignation and pity in reading the bizarre portrait that Gouli has made of the blacks? Is it, indeed, a man that this planter sought to paint? . . . Yes citizens, it is a man, a man without vices, for if he had the vices of his oppressors for two centuries he would have long ceased to exist! But this man brutalized by slavery, the whip always suspended over his head, brought back to childhood by horrible and cruel punishments that degrade humanity and modesty, this man is not without feelings. His withered soul, dead to hope, lived for a long time with the discouragement inspired by his happy and cruel tyrants! Often, in secret, I wiped away the bitter tears of a desperate misery. The development of an energetic thought would surely lead to the death of a slave who expressed it! And their oppressors come here and describe them as brutes, and reproach them for having souls with no shape. . . . Ah! Gouli, you who dare so profane nature, you prove well that it is you that has no soul!

Do you believe, citizen colleagues, that nature is unjust, that it has made some men to be the slaves of others, as the planters assert? Doesn't this unworthy claim show you the principles of these horrible destroyers of the human species? I myself was born in Africa. Brought in childhood to the land of tyranny, through hard work and sweat I conquered a liberty that I have enjoyed honorably for thirty years, loving my country all the while. The torturers of the blacks lie

Figure 3. *Anne-Louis Girodet,* Portrait of Jean-Baptiste Belley, *1798.*
This famous portrait of the African-born Belley presents an intriguing visual analysis of the relationship between prerevolutionary antislavery thought—embodied in the bust of the Abbé Raynal, an eighteenth-century philosopher and historian—and the revolutionary leaders who emerged from Saint-Domingue. How does the painter perceive the connection between Belley and Raynal?

Réunion des Musées Nationaux/Art Resource, NY.

shamelessly when they dare assert that these oppressed men are brutes; if they do not have the vices of Europe, they have the virtues of nature; it is in their name, in the name of all my brothers, who are sensible, thankful beings, who have all been brought back to life by the unexpected appearance of happiness and liberty, that I urge you to maintain your benevolent laws. These laws are, I know, the terror of the slaves' tyrants.

Yes, I attest that what the English and the Spanish possess of the French portion of Saint-Domingue was delivered to them by planters *of all colors,* owners of slaves. The whites especially, born dominators, employed treachery and seduction to drag into their rebellion the property owners of color whose vested interest opened them up to criminal influences. I also attest that, if the English failed to take over all of Saint-Domingue, it is because the blacks who have become free and French have made a rampart with their bodies against this invasion and are bravely defending the rights of the republic. It is certain that if these brave patriots had arms and ammunition, the undeserving blood of the English and the planter traitors would water this land that has been dirtied by their presence for too long.

31

TOUSSAINT LOUVERTURE

A Refutation of Some Assertions in a Speech Pronounced in the Corps Législatif. . . by Viénot Vaublanc

1797

In 1797, several conservative planters were elected to the Corps Législatif, France's parliamentary body. One of them, Vincent Marie Viénot de Vaublanc, delivered a speech that sharply criticized the black leaders of Saint-Domingue and portrayed the situation on the island as one of chaos, violence, and tyranny. Louverture received a copy of this speech

Toussaint Louverture, *Réfutation de quelques assertions d'un discours prononcé au corps législatif le 10 prairial, an cinq, par Viénot Vaublanc* (Le Cap, n.d. [1797]).

and wrote this response aimed at Vaublanc and another detractor of emancipation, General Donatien Rochambeau. The response is organized in the form of refutations of their assertions.

Toussaint Louverture, General in Chief of the Army of Saint-Domingue to the Executive of the Directory

Citizen Directors:

At a moment when I thought I had rendered an eminent service to the republic and to my co-citizens; just when I had proven my gratitude for the justice of the French people toward us; just when I thought I had rendered myself worthy of the confidence the government has placed in me, and that I will never cease to deserve, a speech given in the midst of the Corps Législatif, during the session of May 27, 1797, by Viénot Vaublanc, has been sent to me from the United States. And it has pained me, in reading it, to see that on every page my intentions are slandered and the political existence of my brothers is threatened.

Such a speech, spoken from the mouth of a man whose fortune has been momentarily removed by the revolution in Saint-Domingue, wouldn't have surprised me; he who loses has the right, to a certain point, to complain. But that such a declamation, which cannot calm us or encourage the cultivators to work, but which on the contrary produces the opposite effect by making them bitter, by making them think that the representatives of the French people are their enemies, was approved and sanctioned by the Corps Législatif itself: that is what affected me so profoundly.

To justify myself in your eyes and in the eyes of my co-citizens, whose esteem I desire, I will try to refute the assertions of Citizen Vaublanc and those who furnished him with information, and, finally, I will try to prove that, in this case, the enemies of our liberty have been driven only by a spirit of personal vengeance, and that they have consistently shown contempt for the public interest and scorn for the Constitution.

FIRST ASSERTION

"I will investigate the state of Saint-Domingue; I will examine the acts of the Agents of the Directory, and I will prove that this unfortunate island has arrived at the most extreme degree of misery."

Convinced, in reflecting on the spirit that dictated this report, that Citizen Viénot Vaublanc, representative of the people, wishes to insinuate that the effects of this misery derive from the liberty granted to the blacks, it will be easy for me to demonstrate that liberty itself would have produced only good, if those who had been charged with dispensing it had not used that sacred word to expand their personal power.

The northern region, and particularly the area around Le Cap, were the parts of the colony that suffered the most from the effects of the revolution. The town of Le Cap was always the center of all political discussions and intrigues, particularly during the revolution. There, resistance was stronger, and the blacks of the area, as well as the men of color, witnessing the disastrous projects that certain whites had in store for them, were pushed first by them, then by the need to defend their personal security, to acts of self-defense that led to civil war. But it would be easy for me to prove, if I had more time, that it was the Europeans themselves who first put torches in the hands of my unfortunate brothers and who played the leading roles in the murders and fires that were committed. The neighborhood of Caracole, which was not as directly under the influence of Le Cap and whose residents have also shared in the boon of liberty, has stayed intact through the revolution. Its cultivators, occupied both with pushing back the attacks of brigands and with working the land, have never abandoned their plantations, and today this part of the colony is flourishing as much as it was before the revolution. . . .

And as for the northern part, which truly had suffered a great deal, order—relative to individuals—is as perfectly reestablished as one could desire, and agriculture is making important progress every day. . . .

These results are very different from those Citizen Vaublanc wants to present. . . .

SECOND ASSERTION

"Everything comes together to paint a colony that is in the most horrible state of disorder, suffering under a military government. And what a military government! In whose hands has it been placed? Those of ignorant and crude Negroes, incapable of distinguishing between the most extreme license and austere liberty, guided by laws."

. . . It was the blacks who, when France was threatened with losing the colony, used their arms and their weapons to conserve it, to reconquer most of the areas that treason had handed to the Spanish and the English. It was the blacks who, with the good citizens of the two other colors, rushed to save the general-in-chief [Etienne Laveaux]. . . .

This was the behavior of the blacks in whose hands Citizen Viénot Vaublanc says the military government of Saint-Domingue has been placed; these are the Negroes he accuses of being ignorant and crude. They certainly are, because without education there is nothing but ignorance and crudeness. But must we blame them for the crime of a lack of education or accuse those who prevented them from gaining it by threatening them with the most atrocious punishments? And can only civilized people distinguish between good and evil or have just notions about benevolence and justice? The men of Saint-Domingue have been deprived of education; but precisely because of that they have remained closer to nature, and they do not deserve to be put in a separate class from the rest of humanity, and to be confused with animals, because they have not arrived to the degree of perfection that education provides.

 . . . We can certainly reproach the people of Saint-Domingue, including the blacks, for many mistakes and even horrible crimes. But in the battle between despotism and liberty, have we not seen the inhabitants of France itself, where society's rules are well-established, give themselves over to all the excesses that the enemies of the blacks reproach them for? The fury of the two parties was equal in Saint-Domingue; and if, in these moments of crisis, the excesses of the blacks did not exceed those committed in Europe, must not an impartial judge pronounce himself in favor of the former? According to our enemies themselves, who present us as ignorant and crude, are we not more excusable than those who were not deprived of the advantages of civilization, as we were? Surrounded by furious enemies, by masters who were often cruel; without any supporters other than the benevolent intentions of the friends of liberty in France whose existence we were barely aware of; pushed from error to excess by the opposing parties that were destroying each other rapidly; at first knowing only those laws of the Motherland that favored our enemies' claims and, since emancipation, receiving instructions from our government only every six months or every year, no assistance, and nearly constant insults and condemnations from our former oppressors, how could we not be forgiven for going astray for a few moments, for a few crude mistakes of which we have been the first victims? And most of all, why would anyone wish to burden the vast majority of blacks, innocent men, with the errors of a few who, over time and through the work of the former, have been brought to order and to respect the highest authorities? . . .

FIFTH ASSERTION

"It will be difficult, I think," General Rochambeau continues, "to reestablish order among the looters and destroyers because they control the Africans and will push them to revolt when we want to diminish their influence and take their money; I even do not hesitate to predict that after having armed them, one day we will be forced to wage war on them to force them back to cultivation."

General Rochambeau's prediction will probably come to pass if he returns at the head of an army to re-enslave the blacks, because then, with the Constitution in one hand, they will defend the liberty it guarantees. But the idea that an army is necessary to force them to go back to their field labor has already been completely disproved by what has been done in agriculture during the past year. I will not repeat here what I said at the beginning of my letter; but I will not be refuted when I argue that agriculture is prospering in Saint-Domingue far beyond the hopes of the true friends of this colony, that the zeal of the cultivators is as satisfying as one might desire, and that the effects of their field labor might surprise some, considering that in the middle of a war they are often forced to take up arms for our defense and that of our liberty, to which we are attached more than we are to life itself; and if there are among them some men stupid enough not to understand the necessity of work, their chiefs have enough control over them to make them understand that, without work, there is no liberty. May France be just toward its children of the colonies, and soon its commerce and its inhabitants will no longer resent the riches taken from it during its greatest prosperity. But if the French government is influenced by Vaublanc's projects, it should remember that in the heart of Jamaica, in the Blue Mountains, there exist a small number of men so jealous of their liberty that they have forced the proud and powerful English to respect their natural rights, which the French Constitution still guarantees us. . . .

EIGHTH ASSERTION

"Soon after their arrival, the Agents had the imprudence to welcome the *nègres* who had fought under Jean-François, the chief of the rebels, who had burned the plain and destroyed the most beautiful part of the colony." (And farther down:) "The *nègres* have everywhere abandoned agriculture; today their cry is that this land belongs to them, and that they don't want to see a single white person there. At the same time that they swear to the whites, that is to say to the real French, a ferocious hatred, they fight a cruel war among themselves."

It would not please God if, to improve the cause of the blacks, I denied the fact that some of them have committed excesses. Subterfuge is alien to me; I will tell the truth, even if it speaks against me. I admit that the reproaches that are made here against Jean-François' troop are well-deserved. This is not the first time I have deplored his blindness: but this was the frenzy of a few individuals, and not of all the blacks. Must we use the term "outlaw" both for those who committed these crimes and for those who repressed them, for those who persisted in their guilty conduct and for those who fought to force them to return to their duty? If, because some blacks have committed cruelties, one could argue on that basis that all blacks are cruel, we would have the right to accuse the French in Europe and all the world's nations of barbarism. But the French Senate will not partake of such an injustice; it will be able to reject the passions that the enemies of liberty have stirred up; it will not confuse an uncontained and undisciplined band with men who, since the reign of liberty in Saint-Domingue, have given undeniable proof of their loyalty to the republic, have spilled their blood for it, have assured its triumph, and who, by acts of goodness and humanity, by their return to order and work, through their attachment to France, have certainly paid back the errors into which their enemies pushed them and into which their ignorance carried them. Obedient to the voice of reason, they will always return to it, when their true friends can make themselves heard.

If it was true that the blacks were so unjust as to think that the properties of Saint-Domingue belonged to them, why would they not have made themselves the masters of them, by chasing away men of other colors, who would be very easy to overcome because of their numbers? If they had sworn a ferocious hatred against whites, why is it that the white population of the town of Le Cap today equals that of blacks and men of color? How is it that more than one-half of those leasing sugar plantations on the Cap plain are white?* If union and fraternity do not reign among men of all colors, would we see the whites, the reds [free people of color], and the blacks living in the most perfect equality? . . . The citizen Vaublanc seems attached to stirring up the passions of the men of Saint-Domingue and to reestablishing barbarous prejudices there by publishing that in Saint-Domingue only the whites are truly French! Does this include the traitors paid by the English, those who, after carrying out foul acts of treason, introduced this perfidious nation on the territory of liberty? In that case, we would make it an honor not to deserve this honorable name; but if the friends of liberty classify under this respectable denomination men

*Among the two hundred and fifteen sugar plantations that are in activity in the northern province, about a hundred and seventy have been rented out to seventy people or so, among whom over half are white. . . .

who are submitted, in heart and spirit, to the French Constitution, to its benevolent laws, men who cherish the French, who are friends of their country, we swear that we have and will always have the right to be called French citizens. . . .

Less enlightened than Citizen Vaublanc, we know nevertheless that there must exist among men, whatever their color, only one distinction, that between the good and the evil. Law-abiding blacks, men of color, and whites must be equally protected; when they stray from the law, they must be equally punished. Such is my opinion; such is my wish, and in this matter I call on the justice of Europeans who have stayed in or who return to the colony; sooner or later they will instruct France; they will destroy the crude calumnies of Citizen Vaublanc; they will expose how treacherous, unjust, and impolitic his declamations are.

32

THE COUNCIL OF THE FIVE HUNDRED

Law on the Colonies

1798

In 1798, the Council of the Five Hundred, one of two bodies making up France's Corps Législatif, *passed a law that was meant to solidify the colonial policies of the previous years. It developed the implications of another law from the same period (the law of 4 Brumaire [25 October 1797], mentioned in article VIII of this law), which included the colonies as departments like any others within the territorial limits of France. It also made clear that the French Constitution was to be applied in the colonies.*

A year later, however, the provisions of this law were swept away by Bonaparte's new colonial policy. And the law itself contains many contradictions, combining a generous granting of citizenship with provisions against vagrancy that limited the freedom of former slaves. Nevertheless, it stands as a testament to a radical political project that aimed at erasing the political boundaries between metropole and colony and between black and white.

Archives Nationales, ADVII 20A.

The Council of the Five Hundred, considering that it is of immediate importance to organize the Constitution in the colonies and to take all political, governmental, and legislative measures that will contribute to their reconstruction . . . has passed the following resolution:

Title I: Of Agents

First Article. The Executive of the Directory is authorized to send three agents to Saint-Domingue, three to Guadeloupe and the other islands of the Eastern Caribbean, and one for Cayenne. . . .

VIII. The agents of the Executive of the Directory are charged with executing, on their arrival in the colonies, the law of 4 Brumaire of this month[7] [October 25, 1797] on the division of the territory, and to successively apply all the parts of the Constitution.

IX. They are also authorized to develop, administratively, regulations for cultivation based on the Constitution, which will be provisionally executed until the publication of laws passed on this subject by the Corps Législatif. These regulations will include the reciprocal obligations of property owners and cultivators, means for the education of children and the subsistence of the elderly and the sick; they will favor growth in population by encouraging marriage and rewarding the fertility of legitimate unions. . . .

Title III: Of the Status and the Rights of Citizens

XIV. The declaration of four citizens from a *commune*[8] will be enough to establish the age of individuals whose birth is not inscribed in the public registers that serve to determine the status of citizens; this declaration will be inserted in the registers; the inscription will be considered a birth declaration.

XV. Black or colored individuals who were taken from their homelands and transported to the colonies are not considered foreigners; they enjoy the same rights as an individual born in French territory as long as they work as cultivators, serve in the army, or exercise a profession or trade.

XVI. Any individual convicted of vagrancy by a court of law will be

---

[7]The authors presumably meant "of this year," since the two laws were not passed in the same month.
[8]District.

stripped of the rights granted in the previous article, until they have once again taken up cultivation, a trade, or a profession.

XVII. Any person who cannot provide proof of a domicile or a known status will be considered a vagrant.

XVIII. All black individuals born in Africa or in the foreign colonies and transferred to the French islands will be free as soon as they set foot on the territory of the republic; to gain the right of citizenship they will be, in the future, subject to the conditions prescribed by article X of the Constitution.[9]

XIX. Any citizen who wishes to enjoy the right to vote in the primary assemblies . . . will declare, at the time the population tables ordered drawn up by article XII of the present law, that he wishes to pay a personal contribution equal to three days of agricultural work: he will be required, under pain of having his suffrage rights taken away, to present a receipt showing he has paid it at least ten days before the primary assemblies are held. . . .

XX. It will also be sufficient, to enjoy the advantage granted by article IX of the Constitution,[10] to bring to the municipal administration, ten days before the primary assemblies are held, a certificate from the administrative council that attests that one has served, during the revolution, in one or several campaigns against the enemies of the republic. . . .

Title XVIII: Public Education

LXXXV. The agents of the Directory are charged with organizing public education in the colonies as quickly as possible, according to existing laws.

LXXXVI. Each year on the first of Germinal [21st of March], the day of the Festival of Youth, there will be chosen in each Department, from among the students of the Central Schools, six young individuals without distinction of color who will be transported to France at the expense of the nation and supported during the time necessary for their education in the Special Schools.

---

[9]This article stated that foreigners could become French citizens if, after completing their 21st year and declaring their intention to stay in France, they lived there for seven consecutive years while paying a direct tax. They must also own land, a farm, or a business or have married a French woman.

[10]This article specified that French men who had fought in one or more military campaigns for the establishment of the Republic would be citizens, without any tax requirement.

33

ÉTIENNE LAVEAUX

A Celebration of the Anniversary of Abolition
1798

Several weeks after the Corps Législatif *passed the 1798 Law on the Colonies, Étienne Laveaux and other pro-emancipation leaders celebrated the fourth anniversary of the abolition of slavery with speeches that outlined their vision for the future of the colonies. Laveaux's speech defended Toussaint Louverture at a time when his conduct in Saint-Domingue was being increasingly criticized in Paris.*

Representatives of the People:
I have asked permission to speak to celebrate one of the most illustrious days of our immortal revolution.

It was on 16 Pluviôse, year 2 [February 4, 1794], that the abolition of slavery in our colonies was decreed. Until then liberty, the protector of our republic, had enabled it to triumph everywhere; on that day a grateful republic, in return, made liberty triumph.

What victory could better represent a people? . . .

O, the sublime effect of true philosophy! The republic, on 16 Pluviôse, carried out a conquest of a kind unknown until then. It conquered for the *human race,* or rather it created, though a single strong and precise idea, a million new beings and in so doing expanded the family of man.

My colleagues, let us abandon ourselves for a moment to the pure emotion that we feel and give thanks for 16 Pluviôse: let us give thanks to liberty, which reserved the glory of this great, just, and generous action for the French republic.

The wrenching memory of the abject slavery that darkened our colonies is now far, far from us. Let us fully celebrate this national contribution . . . [I]n our speeches and our deliberations, may we hear talk of only the *mass of the colonial population* and not of this or that color.

Étienne Laveaux, *Discours prononcé par Laveaux, sur l'anniversaire du 16 pluviôse An 2* (Paris, 1798).

In our colonies, *all is French. This system of absolute unity* will make our disconcerted enemies grow pale with rage, and from that moment the metropole will send out the signal that will lead to colonial prosperity; you will soon hear it repeated by our brothers in the colonies: they will cry *"love for the laws, unity, and work!"* . . .

In our colonies, nature is now doing its work of regeneration; it is up to you, fathers of the nation, it is up to the government to assist in this work. . . .

But, citizen representatives . . . your paternal solicitude for all the groups in our vast republic will ask for an account of what our colony of Saint-Domingue has been like since the beginning of the reign of liberty. What has she been doing while the metropole itself has been advancing toward its brilliant destiny? You will permit me, citizen representatives, to avoid all details; I think they will be of no use. I will tell you only, my colleagues, that liberty has lit an electric blaze among these inhabitants; it consumed the rebels and fired the others with a desire to be worthy of the motherland: we saw them come down from the hills immediately to fight the enemies of the republic.

Without a doubt, there were bad citizens among the inhabitants of this colony and even *émigrés;* there were political volcanoes and unforeseen eruptions: but do we forget that our colonies were in *the center of the power* of the implacable enemy of France? Was it surprising that they were devastated by its influence, which has been so dangerous for the metropole itself? Sweet shores, you were destined to suffer because you had to attract to your waters the greedy and Machiavellian English. Repulsed from continental France simply by the shock of its size, they thought they could throw themselves on our colonies as on some helpless prey; they surrounded them with their ships, made them suffer all privations, sowed misery and scarcity there: what wealth, what troops they did use to relieve their rage against Saint-Domingue!

But their efforts, their promises, their gold, everything paled before the loyalty of the men that 16 Pluviôse made into French citizens. These republicans have triumphed over the English, who have been forced to evacuate the land of liberty. It is to the brave general Toussaint Louverture that the republic owes this precious advantage; he mounted a general attack with such wisdom and organization that the frightened English had to surrender in order to retreat; already they have left our lands. Such is the work of this general who is faithful to his oaths, who is tightly tied to the French republic. . . .

I remember with pleasure that already in the year 5 [1797] . . . I tried to describe him to you. I told you, citizen representatives, *"they dare call him a disorganizer!"* Well, it is *thanks to him, thanks to his commitment to pursuing and arresting vagrants that we owe the first agricultural successes; he was able to convince the black citizens of the necessity of work and to respect the property owners; he sincerely wants the reestablishment of the colony and the republic's commercial prosperity. He is guided by article 6 of the Constitution:* The colonies are an integral part of the republic; *he knows he must not and cannot detach himself from it with committing a horrible crime, which would soon be punished by France.* . . .

Five years as a commander in these far-off lands have convinced me that the inhabitants of Saint-Domingue, two thousand leagues away from the metropole, may indeed make errors and commit mistakes, but they have also convinced me that they will never lose sight of the glorious title of French citizens; they have convinced me that they will vanquish the English and all the enemies of the republic to secure their liberty; they are willing to give the republic their virtues, their talents, their tastes, their desires, even the years of their old age. Like the ancient Romans, they will devote the same resources to the most precious and useful art: the cultivation of the land; they will understand that it is the only and unique way to make commerce flourish, as they have made the republic shine through the splendor of their arms and the number of their victories.

5

The Haitian Revolution and the United States

34

THOMAS JEFFERSON

Letters

1797–1802

During the 1790s and early 1800s, Thomas Jefferson's views on slavery and on the possibilities of emancipation were influenced by events in Saint-Domingue, as the following passages show. In the first of these, he responds to a letter from St. George Tucker, an advocate of gradual emancipation who had shared a pamphlet entitled Dissertation on Slavery *with Jefferson.*

To St. George Tucker

Monticello, August 28, 1797

I have to . . . thank you for your pamphlet. . . . You know my subscription to its doctrines; and to the mode of emancipation, I am satisfied that must be a matter of compromise between the passions, the prejudices, & the real difficulties which will each have their weight in that operation. Perhaps the first chapter of this history, which has begun in St. Domingo, & the next succeeding ones, which will recount how all the whites were driven from all the other islands, may prepare our minds for a peaceable accommodation between justice, policy &

Paul Leicester Ford, ed., *The Writings of Thomas Jefferson* (New York, 1896), vol. 7: 167–69, 347–50, and vol. 8, 161–64.

necessity; & furnish an answer to the difficult question, whither shall the colored emigrants go? And the sooner we put some plan underway, the greater hope there is that it may be permitted to proceed peaceably to its ultimate effect. But if something is not done, & soon done, we shall be the murderers of our own children. . . . The revolutionary storm, now sweeping the globe, will be upon us, and happy if we make timely provision to give it an easy passage over our land. From the present state of things in Europe & America, the day which begins our combustion must be near at hand; and only a single spark is wanting to make that day to-morrow. If we had begun sooner, we might probably have been allowed a lengthier operation to clear ourselves, but every day's delay lessens the time we may take for emancipation. Some people derive hope from the aid of the confederated States.[1] But this is a delusion. There is but one state in the Union which will aid us sincerely, if an insurrection begins, and that one may, perhaps, have its own fire to quench at the same time.

Jefferson was concerned that black sailors from the French Caribbean would spread information and ideas that would incite insurrections among slaves in North America. In 1799, the administration of President John Adams, in the midst of a conflict called the Quasi-War with France, opened diplomatic relations with Toussaint Louverture's regime in Saint-Domingue. Congress broke off trade relations with France but made a special exception, sometimes referred to as Toussaint's Clause, allowing the president to continue the very lucrative trade with Saint-Domingue, which his supporters argued was essentially autonomous from France. In addition to diplomatic and trade relations, the Adams administration supplied Louverture with military support, using U.S. Navy ships to blockade ports controlled by his rival in the colony, André Rigaud. These close relations between a black regime and the United States made Jefferson uncomfortable, as the following letters show.

To Aaron Burr
Philadelphia, February 11, 1799

The public papers inform you of everything passing here. Of the proposed navy . . . of our *existing* army of 5,000 men, *additional* army of

---

[1]Jefferson is referring to the other states in the United States.

9,000, *eventual* army of 30,000 (now under manufacture), & *volunteer* army of we know not how many. As it is acknowledged at the same time that it is *impossible* the French should invade us since the annihilation of their power on the sea, our constituents will see in these preparations the utmost anxiety to guard them against even impossibilities. The southern states do not discover the same care however in the bill authorizing the President to admit Toussaint's subjects to a free commerce with them, & free ingress & intercourse with their black brethren in these states. However, if they are guarded against the cannibals of the terrible republic, they ought not to object to being eaten by a more civilized enemy.

To James Madison
Philadelphia, February 12, 1799

The bill continuing the suspension of intercourse with France & her dependencies has passed both houses, but the Senate struck out the clauses permitting the President to extend it to other powers. Toussaint's clause however was retained. Even South Carolinians in the H. of R.[2] voted for it. We may expect therefore black crews, & supercargoes & missionaries thence into the southern states; & when that leaven begins to work, I would gladly compound with a great part of our northern country, if they would honestly stand neuter.[3] If this combustion can be introduced among us under any veil whatever, we have to fear it.

In 1800, a slave named Gabriel in Richmond, Virginia, organized an uprising in which he hoped to bring together black and white artisans to overthrow slavery. The conspiracy was quickly crushed, and Gabriel and other slaves were tried and executed. During the interrogations of the conspirators, it became clear that events in Saint-Domingue had provided inspiration for the uprising. In the following letter, Jefferson reflects on the danger of insurrection in the United States and concurs with other whites who were beginning to advocate a policy of encouraging free people of African descent to emigrate out of the country.

---

[2]House of Representatives.
[3]Jefferson is referring to the possibility of help from the northern states against a slave rebellion in Virginia.

To the U.S. Minister to Great Britain [Rufus King]
Washington, July 13, 1802

The course of things in the neighboring islands of the West Indies appears to have given a considerable impulse to the minds of the slaves in different parts of the U.S. A great disposition to insurgency has manifested itself among them, which, in one instance, in the state of Virginia, broke out into actual insurrection. This was easily suppressed: but many of those concerned, (between 20. and 30. I believe) fell victims to the law. So extensive an execution could not but excite sensibility in the public mind, and beget a regret that the laws had not provided, for such cases, some alternative, combining more mildness with equal efficacy. The legislature of the state, at a subsequent meeting, took the subject into consideration, and have communicated to me through the governor of the state, their wish that some place could be provided, out of the limits of the U.S. to which slaves guilty of insurgency might be transported; and they have particularly looked to Africa as offering the most desirable receptacle. We might for this purpose, enter into negotiations with the natives, on some part of the coast, to obtain a settlement and, by establishing an African company, combine with it commercial operations, which might not only reimburse expenses but procure profit also.

35

REFUGEES IN CHARLESTON, S.C.

Petition

October 25, 1799

Refugees from Saint-Domingue traveled throughout the Americas, but many ended up in ports in the United States, notably in Philadelphia and Charleston. In this petition, refugees tell the story of their escape from Saint-Domingue in late 1793, when the town of Le Cap was burned to the ground. They defend the actions of fellow refugee Alexandre Fran-

"Deposition San Domingo Negro Insurrection of 1793," 1799 in William Clements Library, Haiti Collection.

cis Augustus de Grasse, whose French admiral father had aided General Washington during the American Revolution. In 1799, the United States was in the midst of the Quasi-War with France, and French citizens were therefore eyed with suspicion. The response of the refugees to this context—one also probably calculated to please the slave owners of Charleston and the surrounding region—was to emphasize the ways in which de Grasse had consistently demonstrated loyalty to whites, even when this put him at odds with French officials.

We the undersigned, inhabitants of the town of the Cape, and its dependencies, present at the massacre, and at the burning of this town, the 19ᵗʰ, 20ᵗʰ & 21ˢᵗ June 1793, and the following days, do certify and swear upon the responsibility of an oath, and to render homage to the truth. That M. Alexandre Francis Augustus de Grasse, inhabitant of the dependence of Port au Paix, department of the Cape, Island of St. Domingo, son of the late Count de Grasse, &c., &c., was in the town of the Cape before and during the pillage, massacre, and burning of that town, in the rank of Adjutant General of the army of the whites in activity against the insurgent blacks; that after this fatal event, he was persecuted by the civil commissaries, and by their orders placed under arrest, at the height of the Cape under guard of the negro army, as suspected of having acted against them with General Galbaud, but that after having acquitted himself, he was reinstated in his office, and immediately charged with the command of the barracks; where he has protected with white troops who were under his orders, the men, women, and children, escaped from the sword and from the flames, who had taken refuge there. And that at least, having been forced, in the same manner as a part of the undersigned, to avoid the dangers which still threatened the sad wreck of the white population, he embarked with his wife, a child and several of the undersigned, on the 28ᵗʰ of July 1793, on board the Brig Thomas of Boston, destined for Charleston, South Carolina, where he arrived on the 14ᵗʰ of August 1793, and resides, after having been plundered barbarously by the English privateer the Susanna of Nassau, Captain Ticker, of 150 unhappy fugitives or thereabouts who had no right to consider them, nor treat them as enemies, being otherwise in a neutral vessel, which contained only passengers and their effects, not only of the negro servants who had willingly followed them, but besides a little money, jewels and vessels of silver, which they had saved from the pillage by the assistance of these same servants. This second pillage was held at

Great Inague at the Caicos Islands, where the English privateer detained our vessel two days to complete this exploit. We likewise certify and swear, that M. de Grasse having arrived at St. Domingo before the revolution, has never ceased, from the moment that his efforts were manifested in this unfortunate colony to that of his departure, of being authentically united with the white inhabitants, and in office of a Chief, elected by themselves, was at Port-au-Paix, was at the Cape, to repel the dangers to which their lives and property were daily exposed by the insurgent blacks, and at last, that any circumstances during the course of these fatal events at St. Domingo, having never given cause to form against him the least suspicion contrary to the interests and to the individual safety of the white population of St. Domingo.

In the faith of which we have signed, at Charleston, South Carolina, the 25th October 1799.

36

CHARLES BROCKDEN BROWN

St. Domingo

December 1804

The publisher of The Literary Magazine, *Charles Brockden Brown, has been described as the father of the American novel. Unlike Jefferson, he was an enthusiastic abolitionist, but he nevertheless worried about the possibility of slave uprisings in the United States. In this piece, he reflected on the impact the creation of Haiti might have elsewhere in the Americas.*

When I first heard of the black chief of St. Domingo bestowing on himself the title of emperor of Hayti, I could not help smiling. I thought, at first, it was the device of some wag, who wanted to ridicule the ambition of Bonaparte, but it turned out to be a specimen of that

miserable and childish spirit of imitation, which some think character-
istic of the Negro race.

The affairs of St. Domingo constitute an extraordinary picture. A
sovereign and independent nation of blacks, endowed with the language and many of the arts, especially the military art, of the most
refined nation of the earth, presents itself to our view, in an island separated by a wide ocean from their native or original country. A mob of
slaves have contrived to expel their masters from the finest spot on the
globe, and to form themselves into a political body, probably not less
than twelve or fifteen times more numerous than any other community
of their colour. In Africa, there are doubtless many millions of Negroes,
but the largest community of them probably does not exceed a few
thousands; whereas, at the breaking out of the revolution, the Negro
population of St. Domingo somewhat exceeded 600,000; so that, if the
denominations of empire or emperor are justified by comparative importance, Hayti and its chief are more entitled to these splendid titles,
by their superiority to all other black nations, than France and its new
emperor are, by their pre-eminence above other European nations.

What, says the inquisitive mind, is to be the future destiny of Hayti.
Should it be, in future, left to itself, or should it be able to resist the
external efforts made to subdue it? The blacks are wholly unac-
quainted with the arts of government. They are, by education and condition at least, a lawless and ferocious race, who will bow to nothing
but a stern and sanguinary despotism. For a time, at least, we can
expect nothing but a series of bloody revolutions, in which one military adventurer shall rise upon the ruins of another, till, at length,
some breathing interval will occur long enough to furnish the heredi-
tary principle room to operate, and to engage the affections and obedience of the people to some one fortunate family.

That the blacks of St. Domingo will be left to themselves is, however, by no means probable. They will, no doubt, remain unmolested
till the conclusion of the present war in Europe; but *then,* it is easy
to foresee that the whole power of France will be bent to the recovery
of this valuable colony. Revenge, pride, interest, every motive that
usually governs individuals or nations will combine to stimulate the
efforts of the French towards this quarter. . . . The struggle will be
obstinate and destructive, but the growing superiority of numbers
on the side of the invaders, will render the ultimate event sure. The
blacks will be reduced to a miserable remnant, who will be lost and
confounded with the helpless multitude annually imported from Africa,
to supply the previous waste.

The interest of the European colonists is such that we cannot expect that the French designs upon St. Domingo will meet with any interruption from their neighbors. Such, at least, will be the notions of the British government. A common politician would be included to suppose that the British power in the West Indies would be more endangered by the re-establishment of their great rivals in St. Domingo, than by the independence of the Hayti empire. The wealth and population of all the British isles bear a slender proportion to those of St. Domingo, after a conquest and a peace of a few years, while the latter has over the former the important advantage which attends one compact realm over scattered and disjoined provinces. Against the French, even during peace, a great naval and military establishment must be maintained, which will, by no means, be necessary against the blacks.

Should Hayti continue independent, or should it regain independence at any future period, its history will be a curious chapter in *the book of great contingency,* and such as, I believe, has no parallel in the former history of mankind. A fertile island in America, inhabited by a race of Negroes, derived from a stock in the heart of Africa, who have been raised, by the very slavery of their ancestors, to a similitude in manners, religion, arts, and language with the most potent and refined of the Christian or European nations, is the grand outline of this history.

What indeed will become of the posterity of the Negroes now residing in North and South America? Their present servile conditions cannot possibly continue forever, but the race must necessarily continue, and they cannot fail to go on multiplying to an indefinite extent. They must gradually become personally free, but, no doubt, will, for ages to come, constitute the lowest class of that society to which they belong. They are so distributed throughout the two continents, that no separate community can possibly be generated by their separate interests. Their situation in the islands is somewhat different; and it is by no means impossible, that they may all, at some remote period, become, what St. Domingo has already become, sovereign nations or communities of negroes, by whom the whites shall be tolerated, at one time, as useful guests, and persecuted, at another, as detested enemies.

6

War and Independence

37

TOUSSAINT LOUVERTURE

From *Constitution of the French Colony of Saint-Domingue*

1801

In 1800, Napoléon Bonaparte proclaimed a new constitution for France, which pronounced that henceforth the colonies would be governed by "particular laws" different from those of the metropole and proclaimed from Paris. This was an alarming development for the former slaves of the Caribbean, for planters had long argued that the colonies needed particular laws as a way of defending the institution of slavery. In Saint-Domingue, Toussaint Louverture appointed an assembly, whose members were mostly white planters, which drew up a constitution for the colony. It named Louverture governor-for-life, required ex-slave laborers to remain on their plantations, and encouraged the importation of new laborers from Africa. Bonaparte, far from being pleased about the particular laws produced by Louverture for Saint-Domingue, was enraged by what he saw as a direct challenge to his authority.

The deputies of the departments of the colony of Saint-Domingue, united in a Central Assembly, have decided on and laid out the constitutional foundation of the regime of the French colony of Saint-Domingue, which are as follows:

Constitution de la colonie française de Saint-Domingue (Le Cap, 1801).

Title 1: Of the Territory

Article 1. Saint-Domingue in its entirety, and Samana, la Tortue, la Gonâve, les Cayemites, l'Île à Vache, la Saône, and other adjacent islands, form the territory of a single colony, which is part of the French empire, but submitted to particular laws.

Article 2. The territory of this colony is divided into departments, districts, and parishes.

Title 2: Of Its Inhabitants

Article 3. There can be no slaves in this territory; servitude is abolished within it forever. All men who are born here live and die free and French.

Article 4. All men, whatever their color, are eligible for all positions.

Article 5. There exist no distinctions other than those based on virtues and talents, and no superiority other than that granted by the law to the exercise of a public function.

The law is the same for all, whether it punishes or protects.

Title 3: Of Religion

Article 6. The Catholic, Apostolic and Roman religion is the only one that is publicly professed. . . .

Article 8. The governor of the colony will assign to each minister of the religion the extent of his spiritual administration, and these ministers can never, under any pretext, form a body within the colony.

Title 4: Of Morals

Article 9. The civil and religious institution of marriage encourages the purity of morals, and therefore those spouses who practice the virtues their status demands of them will always be distinguished and specially protected by the government.

Article 10. Divorce will not be allowed in the colony.

Article 11. The status and the rights of children born in marriage will be fixed by laws meant to spread and maintain social virtues and encourage and cement familial ties.

Title 5: Of Men in Society

Article 12. The Constitution guarantees individual liberty and security. No one can be arrested except by virtue of a formally expressed order, emanating from an administrator that the law grants the right to arrest and to detain in a publicly designated location.

Article 13. Property is sacred and inviolable. All persons, either by themselves or through their representatives, are free to dispose of and administer what is recognized as belonging to them. Anyone who attacks this right commits a crime against society and is guilty toward the person whose property they have troubled.

Title 6: Of Cultivation and Commerce

Article 14. Since the colony is essentially agricultural, it cannot be allowed to suffer even the slightest interruption in the work of cultivation.

Article 15. Each plantation is a factory that requires the union of cultivators and workers; it is the peaceful refuge of an active and faithful family, where the owner of the property or his representative is of necessity the father.

Article 16. Each cultivator and worker is a part of the family and receives a portion of its revenues.

All change in residency on the part of cultivators leads to the ruin of cultivation. . . .

Article 17. Since the introduction of cultivators is indispensable to the reestablishment and the growth of crops, it will take place in Saint-Domingue; the Constitution charges the governor to take appropriate measures to encourage and favor this increase in the number of hands, to stipulate and balance various interests, and to assure and guarantee the execution of the respective obligations that will be the result of this introduction.

Article 18. Since the commerce of the colony consists entirely in the exchange of the commodities and products of its territory, the introduction of those of the same kind as its own is and will remain prohibited.

Title 7: Of Legislation and Legislative Authority

Article 19. The administration of the colony will be determined by laws proposed by the governor and pronounced by an assembly of inhabitants, who will meet at fixed dates in the center of the colony, under the title of the Central Assembly of Saint-Domingue. . . .

Article 24. The Central Assembly votes on the adoption or the rejection of the laws that are proposed by the governor; it votes on regulations that have been made and on the application of laws that are already in place, on abuses to be corrected, on improvements to be pursued in all aspects of the services of the colony.

Article 25. On the basis of the report of the tax receipts and spending presented to it by the governor, the Central Assembly determines, if necessary, the amount, the length, and the mode of collection of the tax, and its increase or decrease; these reports will subsequently be printed. . . .

Title 8: Of the Government

Article 27. The administrative reins of the colony are confided to a governor who will correspond directly with the government of the metropole for everything relative to the interests of the colony.

Article 28. The Constitution names as governor the citizen Toussaint Louverture, the general-in-chief of the army of Saint-Domingue and, in consideration of the important services he has rendered the colony, in the most critical circumstances of the revolution, and on the request of its thankful inhabitants, the reins [of government] are confided to him for the rest of his glorious life.

Article 29. In the future, each governor will be named for five years and will be allowed to continue every five years if he has overseen a good administration.

Article 30. To affirm the tranquillity that the colony owes to the firmness, activity, and tireless zeal and rare virtues of General Toussaint Louverture, and as a sign of the unlimited confidence of the inhabitants of Saint-Domingue, the Constitution attributes to him the exclusive right to choose the citizen who, in the unfortunate event of his death, will replace him. This choice will be secret . . .

Article 31. The citizen chosen by General Toussaint Louverture to take over the reins of the government will take an oath before the Central Assembly, at his death, to execute the Constitution of Saint-Domingue and to remain attached to the French government.

38

LOUIS DELGRÈS

Proclamation
1802

In late 1801, soldiers and officers of African descent in Guadeloupe rose up against the Admiral Jean-Baptiste Raymond de Lacrosse, who was trying to arrest several popular officers, and expelled him from the island. An officer named Magloire Pélage took command and sought to negotiate with the exiled Lacrosse and with the French metropolitan government. In May 1802, a convoy of troops under the command of General Antoine Richepance arrived in Guadeloupe with orders to crush the revolt on the island. It was greeted by Pélage, but other officers and soldiers, led by the officer Louis Delgrès, began to resist the French. As he prepared to battle the French, Delgrès issued the following proclamation, which, according to the nineteenth-century historian of Guadeloupe, Auguste Lacour, had been drafted by a white Creole named Monnereau.

To the Entire Universe
The Last Cry of Innocence and Despair

These are greatest days of a century that will always be famous for the triumph of enlightenment and philosophy. And yet in the midst of them is a class of unfortunates threatened with destruction, which finds itself obliged to raise its voice toward posterity so that she will know, once they have disappeared, of their innocence and misery.

The victim of a small number of bloodthirsty individuals who have dared trick the French government, a crowd of citizens, always loyal to the fatherland, has found itself enveloped in an accusation put forth by the author of all its miseries.

General Richepance, the extent of whose powers we do not know, since he has presented himself only as an army general, has so far announced his arrival only through a proclamation whose expressions

---

Auguste Lacour, *Histoire de la Guadeloupe* (Basse-Terre, Guadeloupe, 1855–1858), 3:253–55.

are so broad that, even as he promises protection, he could kill us without departing from the terms he has used. In this style we have recognized the mark of the Admiral Lacrosse who has sworn his eternal hatred of us.... Yes, we would like to believe that the General Richepance, too, has been tricked by this treacherous man, who uses daggers as well as slander.

What are the acts of authority with which we have been threatened? Are the bayonets of those brave soldiers, whose arrival we have been awaiting and who previously were directed only against the enemies of the republic, to be turned against us? Ah! Rather, if we consider the actions the authorities have already taken in Pointe-à-Pitre, they are instead killing people slowly in prisons. Well! We choose to die more quickly.

Let us dare say it. The fundamental principles of the worst tyrants have been surpassed today. Our old oppressors permitted a master to emancipate his slave. But it seems that, in this century of philosophy, there exist men, grown powerful thanks to the distance that separates them from those who appointed them, who only want to see men who are black or who take their origins from this color in the chains of slavery.

First Consul of the Republic, warrior-philosopher from whom we expected the justice we deserved, why have we been abandoned to mourn how far we live from the land that produced the sublime ideas we have so often admired? Ah! Without a doubt, one day you will know of our innocence. Then it will be too late. Perverse men will already have used the slander that they have poured upon us to consummate our ruin.

Citizens of Guadeloupe, you for whom a difference in the color of the epidermis is enough of a title so that you do not fear the vengeance that threatens us—unless they force you to carry arms against us—you have heard what motivates our indignation. Resistance to oppression is a natural right. Divinity itself cannot be offended that we are defending our cause, which is that of humanity and justice. We will not stain it with the shadow of crime. Yes, we are resolved to defend ourselves, but we will not become aggressors. Stay in your homes, and fear nothing from us. We swear solemnly to respect your wives, your children, your properties, and to use all our power to make sure others respect them.

And you, posterity! Shed a tear for our sorrows, and we will die satisfied.

Signed, the commander of Basse-Terre, Louis Delgrès

39

GENERAL JEAN-FRANÇOIS-XAVIER DE MÉNARD

On the Final Stand of Delgrès
1802

After furious battles in the town of Basse-Terre, Delgrès and many of his followers retreated to the heights on the slopes of the Souffrière volcano above the town. The French General Jean-François-Xavier de Ménard, who led some of the French troops in the combat against Delgrès, described the combat against them in a long report on the campaign prepared for the government in France. In this passage, Ménard describes the final stand of Delgrès and his troops at Matouba. One of the most fascinating details is a description of one of the flags flown by the insurgents, which, as he puts it, was meant to symbolize their independence. In 1803, the leaders of the revolution in Haiti would use a similar flag.

The most difficult operation still had to be executed, and the securing of the colony depended on its success. The general-in-chief knew from the reports of spies that the rebels, masters of Matouba, were regrouping and fortifying each day at the d'Anglemont plantation, which they had stocked with all kinds of ammunition, and that Delgrès, after his retreat from the fort, had established his headquarters there and from it threatened the town of Basse-Terre every day.

The general-in-chief, after having gathered information about Anglemont, decided on a plan of attack that aimed to surround the enemy by taking the *Lassale* plantation, situated on a hill that provided the only avenue of retreat. On the night of 7 to 8 Prairial [May 27 to 28], the citizen Cambriel, leader of the second battalion of the sixty-sixth, received the order to leave at dawn to go to this plantation, passing through the woods that are at the foot of the Souffrière. The third battalion was to arrive from the opposite side by going up the Pères and St.-Louis Rivers, while the four grenadier companies were to break

---

"Rapport détaillée des opérations militaires fait au ministre de la Marine et des colonies par le général Ménard, chef d'état-major de l'armée de la Guadeloupe," September 1802, Centre des Archives d'Outre-Mer, C7A 51, 21–37.

through the Constantin passage and two companies of the center the Nosières bridge.

The enemy had advanced posts close to the bridge over the Pères river. As soon as they saw our troops, they retreated behind the St.-Louis River, whose wide crossing, at the level of the Fifi-Massieux plantation, was defended by two cannons. The third battalion of the sixty-sixth performed marvels of bravery to penetrate it, but all its efforts were useless. While the firing was very heavy, the commander Delacroix, with 150 men, crossed the river at its narrowest ford in the area called the horseshoe and took the battery that was stopping his battalion. As he was carrying out this success, the citizen Cambriel, with the second battalion of this demi-brigade, arrived near the Lassale coffee plantation after having overcome incredible difficulties in the woods, which are not pierced by any trails. The enemy, surprised by a maneuver they did not expect, and which put them in a very bad position, hastily retreated to Anglemont. The commander Delacroix took advantage of this to occupy the Parc, which the insurgents could have taken great advantage of. He established communication with the citizen Cambriel, and they both agreed to let their troops take a rest so they would be ready for a vigorous attack. All the bravery of the company of grenadiers was unable to break through the passage of the Constantin hill. The situation of the enemy was so advantageous that, without risking the loss of a single man, they killed all those who presented themselves. Seven grenadiers were killed in this attack. . . . [I]n 1793, the English sacrificed 700 men trying to take this same position without making any progress. The Nosières bridge presents the same difficulties. In any case, the enemy had mostly destroyed this bridge that crosses a precipice 150 feet deep.

The general-in-chief, having visited these two points, ordered that we limit ourselves to harassing the blacks by firing a cannon in their direction. Because of this, the successes of the day were left to the two battalions of the sixty-sixth. At three o'clock in the afternoon, they continued their march towards Anglemont, tightening their line more and more as they approached. The activity, the courage, even recklessness of the *nègres* since the beginning of the attack, the unanimous cry of "Live free or die!" that they often repeated, the care they took to remove the white color from their flag to symbolize their independence clearly announced that their situation was desperate and their resistance would be terrible. It was, in effect, but seeing that it was useless, and with fear beginning to win them over, about 150 men escaped by slipping into the woods that paralleled the pass of the Nosières bridge, and the rest retreated to the d'Anglemont plantation. We charged after them with fixed bayonets. Already a few of the bravest had crossed a ditch surrounding it when a terrible explosion showed us one of the most horrible scenes that war can produce. D'Anglemont had just exploded; its dispersed rubble became a vast pyre whose flames devoured more than 500 corpses, among which we could see women and children.

A surviving prisoner told us that Delgrès, having been wounded in the knee and no longer able to ride a horse, had resolved to die once he saw himself surrounded. He communicated this project to his companions, who adopted it with a ferocious enthusiasm. Immediately, barrels of powder were positioned in such a way as to create the most terrible effect. The blacks, holding each other by the hand, encouraged one another by shouting "No slavery! Long live death!" The signal was about to be given when one of those humanitarian impulses which are sometimes placed in the souls of villains to soften the horror they inspire, pushed Delgrès to save the whites who the fortunes of war had placed in his hands. They exited, but almost all of them were killed by the far-reaching fragments from the explosion.

This act of appalling courage ended the war by destroying all at once, with one blow, the leaders of the revolt, their elite soldiers, and the rest of their ammunition.

40

NAPOLÉON BONAPARTE AND
GENERAL CHARLES-VICTOR-EMMANUEL LECLERC

Letters

1802–1803

In late 1801, Napoléon Bonaparte, now the First Consul of France and its most powerful political leader, began negotiations to secure a peace with the British. After the preliminaries of a peace treaty were signed in October, he set in motion preparations for a massive expedition to be sent to Saint-Domingue. Having learned about Louverture's constitution, and

Paul Roussier, ed., *Lettres du Général Leclerc* (Paris, 1937), 263–74.

*considering it a slap in the face, he had determined to rid himself of the
black general and his partisans in the island.*

*The following selections come from the instructions given to Napo-
léon's brother-in-law, Charles-Victor-Emmanuel Leclerc, by the French
government. Although their intent is clearly to destroy the power of the
black generals of the colony, the instructions claim that the "blacks" of
Saint-Domingue will remain free under a coercive labor regime like that
of Guadeloupe. This statement may have been included to trick the population of the colony, since Bonaparte understood that the threat of a
return to slavery would probably incite massive resistance. Or it may be
that Bonaparte had not yet decided to reestablish slavery in the colony,
as he eventually would.*

Notes to Serve as Instructions to Give to the Captain General Leclerc

CHAPTER I

In order to clearly understand these instructions, it is necessary to
divide the time of the expedition into three phases.

The first is made up of the fifteen or twenty first days that will be
necessary to occupy the key points, organize the national guard, reassure those with good intentions, unite the convoys, organize the
artillery transports, accustom the mass of the army to the habits and
character of the land, and take possession of the plains.

The second phase is that during which, with the two armies prepared, we will pursue the rebels without mercy; we will flush them out
first of the French part and then of the Spanish part. . . .

The third phase is that in which Toussaint, Moyse,[1] and Dessalines
will no longer exist and three thousand or four thousand blacks who
have retreated into the hills of the Spanish part will form what we call
in the islands maroons, and who we will succeed in destroying with
time, steady effort, and a well-organized strategy of attack.

CHAPTER II

The prospect of a black republic is equally disturbing to the Spanish,
the English, and the Americans. The admiral and the captain gen-

[1]Bonaparte is referring here to Moïse, one of Louverture's top generals. Louverture
had accused Moïse of participating in an uprising against him and had executed him a
few months earlier.

eral will write circulars to neighboring establishments to make them know the goal of the government, the common advantage Europeans have in destroying this rebellion of the blacks, and the hope of receiving support. . . . Jefferson has promised that at the instant the French army has arrived, all measures will be taken to starve Toussaint and to assist our army.

CHAPTER III

The French nation will never place chains on men it has recognized as free. There all the blacks will live in Saint-Domingue as they live today in Guadeloupe.

The conduct to follow depends on the three phases talked of above. During the first phase, we will disarm only the blacks who are rebels. In the third, we will disarm them all.

During the first phase, we will not be demanding: we will deal with Toussaint, will promise him whatever he might ask for in order to take possession of the key points, and introduce ourselves into the country.

Once the first goal is accomplished, we will become more demanding. . . . In interviews we might have with Moyse, Dessalines, and the other generals of Toussaint, we will treat them well. We will win over . . . all the blacks who support the whites. During the first phase, we will confirm them in their ranks and their employment. In the third phase, we will send them all to France, keeping them in their ranks if they served well during the second. . . .

Toussaint will be considered subdued only once he has come to Le Cap or Port-au-Prince, in the middle of the French army, and made an oath of loyalty to the republic. On that day, we must, without a scandal, without insults, but with honor and consideration, place him on a frigate and send him to France. We should arrest Moyse and Dessalines at the same time if we can, or pursue them without mercy and then send to France all the whites who are partisans of Toussaint, all the blacks with positions who are suspected of ill will. Moyse and Dessalines will be declared traitors to the fatherland and enemies of the French people. Put the troops on the march and take no rest until we have their heads and have dissipated all their partisans.

If after the first fifteen or twenty days it is impossible to bring back Toussaint, we must declare in a proclamation that if he does not come in a set number of days and make his oath to the republic, he will be declared a traitor to the fatherland, and at the expiration of the deadline we will begin a war without mercy.

Even if a few thousand blacks are still wandering in the hills and seeking refuge in the backcountry, the captain general should still recognize that the second phase is over and promptly move on to the third. This will be the moment to forever assure the colony for France. And on that same day throughout the colony, we must arrest all untrustworthy men in positions of authority, whatever color they are, and place all the black generals on ships, regardless of their behavior, their patriotism, and the services they have rendered, being careful however to maintain not to demote them, and providing assurances that they will be well treated in France.

All the whites who have served under Toussaint and committed crimes in Saint-Domingue will be sent directly to Guyana.

All the blacks who have behaved well, but who because of their rank cannot be left on the island, will be sent to Brest.

All the blacks and men of color who have behaved badly, of whatever rank, will be sent to the Mediterranean and dropped in a port of the island of Corsica.

If Toussaint, Dessalines, and Moyse are taken with weapons in their hands, they will be judged by a military commission within twenty-four hours and shot as rebels.

Whatever happens, we believe that in the course of the third phase we must disarm all the *nègres,* no matter what party they are a part of, and put them back to work in the fields.

White women who have prostituted themselves to *nègres,* whatever their rank, will be sent to Europe.

Little went as Bonaparte planned, however. The resistance of Louverture and his partisans was fiercer and more successful than the French expected, and the war against them dragged on for many months and cost the French significant casualties. Several weeks after writing the following letters, Leclerc died of the yellow fever that had taken so many of his troops. He was succeeded by General Donatien Rochambeau, who took the level of atrocity directed against the blacks to a new level, massacring many black soldiers still fighting for the French.

Leclerc to Bonaparte, October 7, 1802

In Messidor[2] and a part of Thermidor, I held the country without any real forces. At the end of Thermidor, the war began, and it doubled my losses of men. At the end of Fructidor, my army and my reinforcements had been destroyed. Then the blacks, witnesses to my weakness, became audacious. . . .

One battalion of the eleventh colonial regiment that had been merged into the Cap Français Legion had suffered a number of desertions, and so 176 men from this battalion were shipped from Jacmel to Port Républicain.[3] Of this number, 173 strangled themselves on the way, with the leader of the battalion at their head. These are the men we have to fight. . . .

You will perhaps blame me for not having gotten rid of the black chiefs earlier, but remember that I was never in a position to do so and that I was planning on being able to act against them during this season. I have no false moves to reproach myself of, citizen Consul, and if my position has changed from very good to very bad, what is to blame is only the sickness that has destroyed my army, the premature reestablishment of slavery in Guadeloupe, and the newspapers and letters from France that talk of nothing but slavery.

Here is my opinion on this country. We must destroy all the *nègres* of the mountains, men and women, and keep only children under twelve years old, destroy half of those of the plain, and not leave in the colony a single man of color who has worn an epaulette. Otherwise, the colony will never be quiet, and at the beginning of each year, especially after murderous seasons like this one, you will have a civil war that will compromise the possession of the country. If you wish to be the master of Saint-Domingue, you must send me twelve thousand men without wasting a single day. . . .

If you cannot send me the troops that I have asked for, and by the time I have requested, Saint-Domingue will be forever lost to France.

---

[2]Messidor, Thermidor, and Fructidor are months from the revolutionary calendar. Leclerc is describing his situation in July, August, and September 1802.

[3]Port-au-Prince. Revolutionary governments in both Saint-Domingue and France frequently changed place names that had previously referred to the new toppled aristocratic regime.

Roussier, *Lettres,* 253–59.

In another letter written the same day to Bonaparte, Leclerc lamented:

As for me, I have always served you loyally; I will continue to do so and execute all your orders to the letter. I will justify the good opinion you have of me, but I cannot resign myself to stay here for next summer. Since I have been here, I have seen only the spectacle of fires, insurrections, murders, of the dead and the dying. My soul has withered, and no joyful idea can ever make me forget these hideous scenes. I fight here against the blacks, against the whites, against misery and the lack of money, against my discouraged army. Once I have spent six more months in this way, I will deserve some rest.

Roussier, *Lettres,* 259–60.

41

MARY HASSAL

From *Secret History; or the Horrors of St. Domingo*
1808

One of those who witnessed the French debacle in Saint-Domingue was Leonora Sansay, the wife of a Saint-Domingue planter who had left the colony during the early years of the revolution but returned after the arrival of the French expedition, hoping to regain his property. Sansay wrote a letter to Aaron Burr, whom she had met during her stay in the United States, about her experiences during this time. A few years later, under the pseudonym Mary Hassal, she published a book, in the form of a series of letters that described the last days of the French presence in the colony.

Mary Hassal [Leonora Sansay], *Secret History; or, the Horrors of St. Domingo, in a Series of Letters Written by a Lady at Cape François to Colonel Burr* (Philadelphia: Bradford & Inskelp, 1808). Sansay's original letter to Aaron Burr is reprinted in Charles Burdett, *Margaret Moncrieffe; the First Love of Aaron Burr* (New York: Derby & Jackson, 1860), 428–37.

Letter II

What a change has taken place here since my last letter was written! I mentioned that there was to be a grand review, and I also mentioned that the confidence General Leclerc placed in the negroes was highly blamed, and justly, as he has found to his cost.

On the day of the review, when the troops of the line and the guard national were assembled on the field, a plot was discovered, which had been formed by the negroes in the town, to seize the arsenal and to point the cannon of a fort, which overlooked the place of review, on the troops; whilst Clairvaux, the mulatto general, who commanded the advanced posts, was to join the negroes of the plain, overpower the guards, and entering the town, complete the destruction of the white inhabitants. The first part of the plot was discovered and defeated. But Clairvaux made good on his escape, and in the evening attacked the post General Leclerc had so imprudently confided in him. The consternation was terrible. . . .

The ensuing morning presented a dreadful spectacle. Nothing was heard but the groans of the wounded, who were carried through the streets to their homes, and the cries of the women for their friends who were slain.

The general, shut up in his house, would see nobody; ashamed of the weakness which had led to this disastrous event, and of the want of courage he had betrayed: a fever seized him and he died in three days.

Madame Leclerc,[4] who had not loved him whilst living, mourned his death like the Ephesian matron,[5] cut off her hair, which was very beautiful, to put it in his coffin, refused all sustenance and all public consolation.

General Rochambeau, who is at Port-au-Prince, has been sent for by the inhabitants of the Cape to take the command. . . .

Letter III

The so much desired general Rochambeau is at length here. His arrival was announced, not by the ringing of bells, for they have none, but by the firing of cannon. Everybody, except myself went to see him

---

[4] Pauline Bonaparte, the sister of Napoleon.
[5] In *The Satyricon,* the Roman author Petronius tells the story of an inconsolable widow in the Greek city of Euphesus.

land, and I was prevented, not by want of curiosity, but by indisposition. Nothing is heard of but the public joy. He is considered as the guardian, as the saviour of the people. Every proprietor feels himself already in his habitation[6] and I have even heard some of them disputing about the quality of the coffee they expect soon to gather. . . .

The place is tranquil. The arrival of General Rochambeau seems to have spread terror among the negroes. I wish they were reduced to order that I might see the so much vaunted habitations where I should repose beneath the shade of orange groves; walk on carpets of rose leaves and Frenchipone; be fanned to sleep by silent slaves, or have my feet tickled into ecstasy by the soft hand of a female attendant.

Such were the pleasures of the Creole ladies whose time was divided between the bath, the table, the toilette and the lover.

What a delightful existence! . . .

But the moment of enjoying these pleasures is, I fear, far distant. The negroes have felt during ten years the blessing of liberty, for a blessing it certainly is, however acquired, and they will not be easily deprived of it. They have fought and vanquished French troops, and their strength has increased from a knowledge of the weakness of their opposers, and the climate itself combats for them. . . .

The country is entirely in the hands of the negroes, and whilst their camp abounds in provisions, every thing in town is extremely scarce and enormously dear.

Every evening several old Creoles, who live near us, assemble at our house, and talk of their affairs. One of them, whose annual income before the revolution was fifty thousand dollars, which he always exceeded in his expenses, now lives in a miserable hut and prolongs with the greatest difficulty his wretched existence. Yet he still hopes for better days, in which hope they all join him. . . .

Letter IV

Nothing is heard of but balls and parties. Monsieur D'Or gives a concert every Thursday; the General in chief every Sunday: so that from having had no amusement we are in danger of falling into the other extreme, and being satiated with pleasure. . . .

The Creoles complain, and they have cause; for they find in the army sent to defend them, oppressors who appear to seek their de-

---

[6]On his plantation.

struction. Their houses and their negroes are put under requisition, and they are daily exposed to new vexations. . . .

They had supposed that the appearance of an army of thirty thousand men would have reduced the negroes to order; but these conquerors of Italy, unnerved by the climate, or from some other cause, lose all energy, and fly before the undisciplined slaves.

Many of the Creoles, who had remained on the island during the reign of Toussaint, regret the change, and say that they were less vexed by the negroes than by those who have come to protect them.

And these negroes, notwithstanding the state of brutal subjection in which they were kept, have at length acquired a knowledge of their own strength. More than five hundred thousand broke the yoke imposed on them by a few thousand men of a different color, and claimed the rights of which they had been so cruelly deprived. . . .

Letter VI

General Rochambeau has given Clara a proof of his attention to her wishes at once delicate and flattering. She dined with a large party at the Government house, where, as usual, he was entirely devoted to her. After dinner, he led her, followed by the company, to a saloon, that was fitted up for a dining-room. It was ornamented with military trophies, and on every panel was written the name of some distinguished chief.

On one Buonaparte [*sic*], on another Frederick,[7] on another Massena,[8] &c.

Clara said it was very pretty, but that Washington should also have found a place there!

A few days after, a grand ball was given, and on entering the ballroom, we saw, on a pannel [*sic*] facing the door,

Washington, Liberty, and Independence!

This merited a smile, and the general received a most gracious one. It was New Year's Eve. . . .

Letter IX

The most distressing accounts arrive here daily from all parts of the island.

The general in chief is at Port-au-Prince, but he possesses no

---

[7]A reference to the eighteenth-century king of Prussia.
[8]One of Napoléon's most famous generals.

longer the confidence of the people. He is entirely governed by his
officers, who are boys, and who think only of amusement. He gives
splendid balls, and elegant parties; but he neglects the army, and
oppresses the inhabitants.

A black chief and his wife were made prisoners last week, and sentenced to be shot. As they walked to the place of execution, the chief
seemed deeply impressed with the horror of his approaching fate;
but his wife went cheerfully along, endeavoured to console him, and
reproached his want of courage. When they arrived on the field, in
which their grave was already dug, she refused to have her eyes
bound; and turning to the soldiers who were to execute their sentence, said "Be expeditious, and don't make me linger." She received
their fire without shrinking, and expired without uttering a groan.

42

MARIE-ROSE MASSON

Letter to the Marquis de Gallifet
July 27, 1802

*In the confusion of the war in Saint-Domingue, some individuals pre-
pared for the possibility of a return to slavery. In July 1802, when a
French victory seemed likely, Marie-Rose Masson, once a slave of the
absentee landowner the Marquis de Gallifet, wrote him. As she describes,
the death of Gallifet's manager, Odelucq, during the insurrection in 1791
(described in Documents 13 and 14) had left some very important business unfinished that she needed to resolve.*

Marie-Rose Masson to M. Gallifet
July 27, 1802

My name is Mini, daughter of Blanche, of your plantation at Petite
Anse. My father, whom I didn't know, was your esteemed manager

Archives Nationales Gallifet Papers, 107 AP 128.

Mr. Masson, whose successor was Mr. Odelucq, who acted as my father. The fact that he died miserably without having arranged my affairs has often caused me pain and would plunge me into eternal gloom if it were not for the fact that your justice and goodness toward me are assured once I present the facts to you. The time of errors is over . . . those with bad intentions have no support for their destructive influence, a protective government is working to reestablish order, and the result will be that the workers on those of your properties that still exist will have to return to their useful labors by their own will or by force; the rights you have over them, you also have over me and my mother, and if you had not ended them a long time ago, I would be the first to give you the example of my submission. But in 1787, at the request of Mr. Odelucq, you consented that my mother and I would be replaced by two *negrillons*.[9] The difficulty of finding the means for this delayed the conclusion, but once the money had been found, the negligence or other business of M. Odelucq caused him to die without having completed the government procedures, but his receipt of February 13, 1791, which I saved, testifies that the sum of 3342.1 necessary to purchase the two *negrillons* was paid to M. Odeluq by my aunt, Madame Ducatal.

In this situation M. Massu,[10] who is ignorant of the case, is exercising an authority over me that is contrary to your justice; it is therefore necessary that you inform him to let me go once I show him the receipt for 3342.1 livres. I would ask as well that you reassure me with a response explicit enough to assuage my worries. As for the rest, I mean the government procedures, we can wait for a more opportune time.

Please accept, Sir, the respect due a good former master. I ask you to send your response to M. Roquisol, merchant in Le Cap.

[9] Black babies.
[10] Gallifret's new manager.

43

BRIGADIER GENERAL PIERRE CANGÉ

Letter to Delpech

November 1802

In part because of lingering resentments toward Louverture as a result of the War of the South a few years earlier, many men of color joined Leclerc's troops when he arrived. By the middle of October 1802, however, the brutal tactics and open racism of the French leadership led Alexandre Pétion, a leading officer of color, to forge a secret alliance with the black general Jean-Jacques Dessalines, who had led Louverture's troops against Rigaud just a few years earlier. The alliance, predicated on the unification of people of African descent in Saint-Domingue against Leclerc's white army, was a key turning point in the battle for Haitian independence. In this letter, a high-ranking officer fighting in the south of the colony, Pierre Cangé tried to convince another officer of color to change sides by emphasizing the brutality of the French and the promise of racial unity represented by the alliance taking shape in the north.

My dear commander, for a long time I have looked for someone who could explain my way of thinking to you, since you cannot write. When I could not find such a person, I took up arms because I was forced to. I do not fight for the pleasure of making war, but I saw that the newly arrived French government was corrupted and won over by the great planters of Saint-Domingue, the sworn enemies of liberty and equality.

I realized that their goal was to destroy the black and red[11] race from top to bottom, especially the best educated and wealthiest; you, my dear comrade and brother, as well as all the others . . . think you will be spared because they like you. They will only delay destroying you; as soon as they can do it, you will all be finished.

---

[11]The term *red* was sometimes used to refer to those of mixed African and European ancestry.

University of Florida Library, Rochambeau Papers, No. 1331.

Like me, you have seen how this new government tramples the beneficial laws of the French republic to commit acts of cruelty. Like me, you have seen thousands of black and red men, women, and children drowned and hanged; what have they done? How can they accuse children of crimes deserving death? Such things have never been seen under any government. Why have they not hanged and drowned white women and children? It is because of their color. We are the only ones who can get along with each other and bring happiness to our land.

I could not remain calm and quiet after seeing such cruelty. So I took up arms, and my first step was to warn all my black and red brothers that I would not fight them. But I will fight to the death the whites that oppress and kill us. However, because I am on the verge of victory, I will pardon all those who surrender to us. To prove it, I have ordered all my officers to harm no one, even those captured with weapons in their hands.

You know that I attacked Leogane[12] on the twenty-first of the month to permit our brothers to leave and that in fact two thousand men, women, and children did so, especially the young. There are also two whites, Sansfouque and Barthelmy, who are quite pleased to be with us.

So give this some thought, my dear comrade and brother. Take a side that justice and nature have linked to your fate, so that we will fight our enemies together. Surely you know what is happening in the north province; there is no doubt that the great French nation will approve our actions and soon recall these bloody torturers of humanity. You know that the nature of a revolution is that the strongest always wins. It is very clear that we are [strongest] and that we will always be in Saint-Domingue when we are [united] like this.

As for the whites who are with you, I will forget their past conduct if they will surrender to us, and for proof I give my word of honor, which I have never retracted; their persons and their properties will be respected. As for you, you will be as you are now, with the same rank; your properties also will be respected.

Salut et Fraternité, Cangé.

---

[12] A town west of Port-au-Prince.

44

The Haitian Declaration of Independence

January 1, 1804

By November 1803, Saint-Domingue's rebel forces, led by Jean-Jacques Dessalines, had driven the last of the French army out of the colony. Dessalines commissioned one of his secretaries, Louis Boisrond-Tonnerre, to write a declaration of independence. According to tradition, Dessalines chose Boisrond-Tonnerre when he heard him exclaim that this document "should be written with the skin of a white man for parchment, his skull for a desk, his blood for ink, and a bayonet for a pen." The following text was written overnight and read publicly by its author the following morning before a crowd at Gonaïves, a coastal town north of Port-au-Prince.

The Commander in Chief to the People of Haiti

Citizens:

It is not enough to have expelled the barbarians who have bloodied our land for two centuries; it is not enough to have restrained those ever-evolving factions that one after another mocked the specter of liberty that France dangled before you. We must, with one last act of national authority, forever ensure liberty's reign in the country of our birth; we must take any hope of re-enslaving us away from the inhumane government that for so long kept us in the most humiliating stagnation. In the end we must live independent or die.

Independence or death . . . let these sacred words unite us and be the signal of battle and of our reunion.

Citizens, my countrymen, on this solemn day I have brought together those courageous soldiers who, as liberty lay dying, spilled their blood to save it; these generals who have guided your efforts against tyranny have not yet done enough for your happiness; the French name still haunts our land.

Everything revives the memories of the cruelties of this barbarous people: our laws, our habits, our towns, everything still carries the

---

Thomas Madiou, *Histoire d'Haïti* (Port-au-Prince, 1847–1848), 3: 146–50.

stamp of the French. Indeed! There are still French in our island, and
you believe yourself free and independent of that republic, which, it is
true, has fought all the nations, but which has never defeated those
who wanted to be free.

What! Victims of our [own] credulity and indulgence for fourteen
years; defeated not by French armies, but by the pathetic eloquence of
their agents' proclamations; when will we tire of breathing the air that
they breathe? What do we have in common with this nation of execu-
tioners? The difference between its cruelty and our patient moderation, its color and ours, the great seas that separate us, our avenging
climate, all tell us plainly that they are not our brothers, that they
never will be, and that if they find refuge among us, they will plot
again to trouble and divide us.

Native citizens, men, women, girls, and children, let your gaze extend on all parts of this island: look there for your spouses, your
husbands, your brothers, your sisters. Indeed! Look there for your
children, your suckling infants, what have they become? . . . I shudder
to say it . . . the prey of these vultures.

Instead of these dear victims, your alarmed gaze will see only their
assassins, these tigers still dripping with their blood, whose terrible
presence indicts your lack of feeling and your guilty slowness in
avenging them. What are you waiting for before appeasing their spirits? Remember that you had wanted your remains to rest next to those
of your fathers after you defeated tyranny; will you descend into their
tombs without having avenged them? No! Their bones would reject
yours.

And you, precious men, intrepid generals, who, without concern for
your own pain, have revived liberty by shedding all your blood, know
that you have done nothing if you do not give the nations a terrible,
but just example of the vengeance that must be wrought by a people
proud to have recovered its liberty and jealous to maintain it. Let us
frighten all those who would dare try to take it from us again; let us
begin with the French. Let them tremble when they approach our
coast, if not from the memory of those cruelties they perpetrated
here, then from the terrible resolution that we will have made to put to
death anyone born French whose profane foot soils the land of liberty.

We have dared to be free, let us be thus by ourselves and for ourselves. Let us imitate the grown child: his own weight breaks the
boundary that has become an obstacle to him. What people fought for
us? What people wanted to gather the fruits of our labor? And what dis-
honorable absurdity to conquer in order to be enslaved. Enslaved? . . .

Let us leave this description for the French; they have conquered but are no longer free.

Let us walk down another path; let us imitate those people who, extending their concern into the future and dreading to leave an example of cowardice for posterity, preferred to be exterminated rather than lose their place as one of the world's free peoples.

Let us ensure, however, that a missionary spirit does not destroy our work; let us allow our neighbors to breathe in peace; may they live quietly under the laws that they have made for themselves, and let us not, as revolutionary firebrands, declare ourselves the lawgivers of the Caribbean, nor let our glory consist in troubling the peace of the neighboring islands. Unlike that which we inhabit, theirs has not been drenched in the innocent blood of its inhabitants; they have no vengeance to claim from the authority that protects them.

Fortunate to have never known the ideals that have destroyed us, they can only have good wishes for our prosperity.

Peace to our neighbors; but let this be our cry: "Anathema to the French name! Eternal hatred of France!"

Natives of Haiti! My happy fate was to be one day the sentinel who would watch over the idol to which you sacrifice; I have watched, sometimes fighting alone, and if I have been so fortunate as to return to your hands the sacred trust you confided to me, know that it is now your task to preserve it. In fighting for your liberty, I was working for my own happiness. Before consolidating it with laws that will guarantee your free individuality, your leaders, who I have assembled here, and I, owe you the final proof of our devotion.

Generals and you, leaders, collected here close to me for the good of our land, the day has come, the day which must make our glory, our independence, eternal.

If there could exist among us a lukewarm heart, let him distance himself and tremble to take the oath which must unite us. Let us vow to ourselves, to posterity, to the entire universe, to forever renounce France, and to die rather than live under its domination; to fight until our last breath for the independence of our country.

And you, a people so long without good fortune, witness to the oath we take, remember that I counted on your constancy and courage when I threw myself into the career of liberty to fight the despotism and tyranny you had struggled against for fourteen years. Remember that I sacrificed everything to rally to your defense; family, children, fortune, and now I am rich only with your liberty; my name has become a horror to all those who want slavery. Despots and tyrants curse the day that I was born. If ever you refused or grumbled while receiving those laws that the spirit guarding your fate dictates to me for your own good, you would deserve the fate of an ungrateful people. But I reject that awful idea; you will sustain the liberty that you cherish and support the leader who commands you. Therefore, vow before me to live free and independent and to prefer death to anything that will try to place you back in chains. Swear, finally, to pursue forever the traitors and enemies of your independence.

Done at the headquarters of Gonaïves, the first day of January 1804, the first year of independence.

45

The Haitian Constitution

1805

Reflecting the enormous influence of the revolutionary struggle on the structure of the new state, Haiti's first constitution named Jean-Jacques Dessalines emperor, with a council of state comprised of the generals who governed the new nation's six regions. But Dessalines' 1806 attempt to revoke land titles acquired by locally powerful families led to his assassination. Haiti broke into rival states: a republic ruled by Alexandre Pétion comprised of the southern and western regions, and a monarchy under Henri Christophe in the north. Only in 1820, after both men had died, were the two Haitis united into one country.

We, Henri Christophe, Clervaux, Vernet, Gabart, Pétion, Capoix, Magny, Cangé, Daut, Magloire Ambroise, Yayou, Jean-Louis François, Gérin, Moreau, Férou, Bazelais, Martial Besse;

As individuals and in the name of the Haitian people who have legally constituted us the faithful voices and interpreters of their will;

Thomas Madiou, *Histoire d'Haïti* (Port-au-Prince, 1847–1848), 3: 546–53.

In the presence of the Supreme Being before whom all mortals are equal, and who has spread so many different creatures over the surface of the globe only in order to demonstrate his glory and power by the diversity of his works;

Before all of nature, we who have been for so long and so unfairly considered to be its unworthy children, declare that the terms of this constitution are the free, voluntary, and unchanging expression of our hearts and of our constituents' general will;

We submit it to the approval of his Majesty the Emperor Jacques Dessalines, our liberator, for prompt and complete execution.

Preliminary Declaration

Article 1. By this document the people living on the island formerly called Saint-Domingue agree to form a free and sovereign state, independent of all the other powers of the universe, under the name of the Haitian Empire.

Article 2. Slavery is abolished forever.

Article 3. Brotherhood unites Haiti's citizens; equality before the law is irrefutably established; and no other titles, advantages, or privileges can exist, other than those which necessarily result from respect and compensation for services rendered to liberty and independence.

Article 4. There is one law for everyone, whether it punishes or protects.

Article 5. The law cannot be retroactive.

Article 6. Property rights are sacred; violations will be vigorously pursued.

Article 7. Persons who emigrate and become citizens in a foreign country forfeit their Haitian citizenship, as do those convicted of corporal or disgraceful crimes. The former instance is punishable by death and confiscation of property.

Article 8. In cases of bankruptcy or business failure, Haitian citizenship is suspended.

Article 9. No one is worthy of being a Haitian if he is not a good father, a good husband, and, above all, a good soldier.

Article 10. Fathers and mothers may not disinherit their children.

Article 11. Every citizen must know a mechanical trade.

Article 12. No white man, regardless of his nationality, may set foot in this territory as a master or landowner, nor will he ever be able to acquire any property.

Article 13. The preceding article does not apply to white women who the government has naturalized as Haitian citizens or to their children, existing or future. Also included in this are the Germans and Poles naturalized by the government.

Article 14. Because all distinctions of color among children of the same family must necessarily stop, Haitians will henceforth only be known generically as Blacks.

About the Empire

Article 15. The Haitian Empire is one and indivisible; its territory is divided into six military districts.

Article 16. A major general will command each military district.

Article 17. Each of these major generals will be independent of the others and will report directly to the emperor or the general-in-chief named by His Majesty.

Article 18. The following islands are an integral part of the empire: Samana, Tortuga, Gonaïves, Cayemittes, Île à Vache, la Saône, and other neighboring islands.

Article 19. Haiti is governed by a first magistrate who will take the title of Emperor and Supreme Chief of the Army.

Article 20. The people recognize Jacques Dessalines, the avenger and liberator of his fellow citizens, as the Emperor and Supreme Chief of the Army. He is addressed as Majesty, as is his distinguished spouse, the Empress.

Article 21. The persons of Their Majesties are sacred and inviolable.

Article 22. The state will pay a fixed stipend to Her Majesty the Empress as dowager princess.

Article 23. The crown is elective and nonhereditary.

Article 24. The state will allocate an annual stipend to the recognized children of His Majesty the Emperor.

Article 25. Like other citizens, the emperor's recognized male children will be required to work their way up from rank to rank, successively, with the single difference that their military service in the fourth demi-brigade will be counted from the day of their birth.

Article 26. The emperor will designate his successor in the manner he judges most appropriate, either before or after his death.

Article 27. The state will set an appropriate pension for this successor at the moment he comes to the throne.

Article 28. Neither the emperor nor any of his successors will have the right in any situation or for any reason to surround himself with a privileged group under the name of honor guard or any other title.

Article 29. Any successor who strays from either the provisions of the preceding article, or from the course laid out for him by the reigning emperor, will be considered a threat to society and declared as such. In this event, the counselors of state will meet to proclaim his removal and choose their worthiest member to replace him; and if it happens that the said successor tries to oppose this legally authorized measure, the council of state, comprised of the generals, will appeal to the people and the army, which will lend a hand and assist in maintaining liberty.

Article 30. The emperor makes, seals, and promulgates the laws; as he sees fit, he names and dismisses the ministers, the army's general-in-chief, the counselors of state, the generals and other officers of the empire, the officers of the army and navy, the members of local government administrations, the government commissioners in the courts, the judges, and other public functionaries.

Article 31. The emperor directs the collection of state funds and their expenditure and oversees the manufacture of currency. He alone orders coins to be put into circulation and sets their weight and kind.

Article 32. He alone has the power to make peace or war, to maintain political relations and establish contracts with foreign powers.

Article 33. He provides for the state's internal security and defense, and decides on the territorial distribution of the army and navy.

Article 34. In the event of some conspiracy against public security, the constitution, or his person, the emperor will immediately arrest its leaders or accomplices, who will be judged by a special council.

Article 35. Only His Majesty will have the right to pardon a guilty person or to commute his sentence.

Article 36. The emperor will never undertake any project with the idea of conquest or to disturb the peace and the internal regime of foreign colonies.

Article 37. All public deeds will be made in these terms: *The First Emperor of Haiti and the Supreme Chief of the Army by the grace of God and the constitutional law of the state.* . . .

On Religion

Article 50. The law does not recognize any dominant religion.

Article 51. Freedom of worship is allowed.

Article 52. The state does not provide for the expenses of any form of religion or ministry.

General Measures

Article 1. The emperor and the empress will choose the persons who make up the court and set their stipend and support.

Article 2. After the death of the reigning emperor, when it is decided that the constitution needs to be revised, the council of state will meet for this purpose under the leadership of the member with the greatest seniority.

Article 3. Crimes of high treason and the crimes committed by the ministers and the generals will be judged by a special council named and led by the emperor.

Article 4. The army's fundamental duty being to obey, no armed body can make political decisions.

Article 5. No one can be judged without having been heard by legal authorities.

Article 6. Every citizen's house is inviolable.

Article 7. One may enter in case of fire, flood, or a legal complaint from the ministry of the interior or by virtue of an order from the emperor or any other legal authority.

Article 8. He who kills his fellow man deserves to die.

Article 9. No capital punishment or death penalty can be legally carried out unless it has been confirmed by the emperor.

Article 10. Theft will be punished according to the situation preceding and accompanying the crime.

Article 11. All foreigners residing in Haitian territory, as well as all Haitians, are subject to the criminal laws and penalties of the country.

Article 12. All property formerly belonging to a white Frenchman is confiscated for the profit of the state, without appeal.

Article 13. All Haitians who acquired the property of a white Frenchman, but who paid only part of the price specified in the deed of sale, must pay the remaining sum to the state.

Article 14. Marriage is a purely civil deed that is authorized by the government.

Article 15. The law authorizes divorce in certain specific cases.

Article 16. A special law will be passed regarding children born outside of marriage.

Article 17. Respect for leaders, subordination, and discipline are absolutely necessary.

Article 18. A penal code will be published and strictly enforced.

Article 19. In each military district, a public school will be established to educate the youth.

Article 20. The national colors will be black and red.

Article 21. Agriculture, the first, most noble, and most useful of the arts, will be honored and protected.

Article 22. Trade, the second source of a state's wealth, seeks to be free of obstacles. It must be favored and specially protected.

Article 23. In each military district, the emperor will name the members of a commercial court, chosen from the merchant class.

Article 24. Honesty and fairness in commerce will be religiously observed.

Article 25. The government guarantees safety and protection to neutral and friendly nations that establish commercial relations with this island, on the condition that they obey the regulations, laws, and customs of this country.

Article 26. Foreign trading posts and merchandise will be under the protection and guarantee of the state.

Article 27. There will be national holidays to celebrate independence, the birthday of the emperor and of his august wife, as well as agriculture and the constitution.

Article 28. At the first sound of the alarm cannon, the towns will disappear and the nation will rise to its feet.

We, the undersigned representatives, place this explicit and solemn pact of the sacred rights of man and the duties of the citizen under the protection of the officials, of the fathers and mothers of families, of the citizens and the army.

We recommend it to our descendants and recommend it to the friends of liberty, to those who love mankind in every country as remarkable proof of divine goodness, whose immortal decrees have given us the opportunity to break our chains and form a free people, civilized and independent.

A Chronology of Events
Related to the Slave Revolution
in the Caribbean
(1635–1805)

1635 Guadeloupe and Martinique settled by the French.

1660–
1670s Informal settlement of Hispaniola by the French.

1685 *The Code Noir* issued.

1697 Treaty of Rhyswick/Spain officially cedes western half of Hispaniola to the French.

1776 American Revolution begins.

1778 France signs military alliance with the American colonies.

1783 Treaty of Paris ends American Revolution.

1788 Société des Amis des Noirs (Society of the Friends of the Blacks) founded in Paris.

1789 French Revolution begins.

May: The Estates General meets in Versailles.

June: National Assembly is formed.

July: The people of Paris storm the Bastille prison.

August: The National Assembly approves the Declaration of the Rights of Man; slave insurrection occurs in Martinique.

1790 *March 8:* The National Assembly passes the Law on the Colonies.

August: The Saint-Marc Assembly is shut down by royal officials.

October: Vincent Ogé leads a revolt in Saint-Domingue, agitating for the rights of free colored voters.

1791 *February:* Vincent Ogé is executed in Cap Français.

May 15: The National Assembly grants political rights to some free people of color.

June: King Louis XVI attempts to flee France, but is captured and returned to Paris.

August: Slave insurrection begins in Saint-Domingue.

1792 *April 4:* Legislative Assembly grants political rights to all free people of color.

April 20: Legislative Assembly declares war on Austria.

August 10: Revolutionaries in Paris arrest Louis XVI and Marie Antoinette.

September: National Convention proclaims France a republic.

1793 *January:* King Louis XVI is executed for treason.

April: Slave insurrection occurs in Trois-Rivières, Guadeloupe.

June: Léger Félicité Sonthonax offers liberty to those who will fight for the republic in Saint-Domingue.

August–October: Léger Félicité Sonthonax and Étienne Polverel abolish slavery in Saint-Domingue.

September: British troops invade Saint-Domingue.

1794 *February 4:* National Convention abolishes slavery throughout the French empire.

March–April: British troops occupy Guadeloupe and Martinique.

May: Toussaint Louverture deserts the Spanish army and joins the French army in Saint-Domingue.

June–August: Victor Hugues recaptures Guadeloupe for the French.

1798 British troops withdraw from Saint-Domingue.

1799 *July:* War of the South begins between the forces of Louverture and André Rigaud.

November: Napoléon Bonaparte's coup creates a new French regime, the Consulate.

December: Bonaparte's new constitution for France proclaims that colonies will be governed by particular laws.

1801 *July:* Louverture directs the writing of a new constitution for Saint-Domingue, which appoints him governor for life.

October: Soldiers rise up against Admiral Lacrosse in Guadeloupe.

1802 *February:* Napoleonic expedition led by General Leclerc arrives in Saint-Domingue.

March: Treaty of Amiens ends war between France and Britain; Martinique returned to French.

May: Led by Louis Delgrès, soldiers of color revolt in Guadeloupe.

June: Louverture is deported from Saint-Domingue and imprisoned in France.

July: Consulate decrees reestablishment of slavery in Guadeloupe, Guiana, and Saint-Domingue.

November 1: Leclerc dies of yellow fever; General Donatien Rochambeau takes command of French troops.

1803 *April:* Bonaparte cedes Louisiana to the United States; Louverture dies in France.

May: Slavery officially reestablished in Guadeloupe.

November: French troops surrender in Saint-Domingue.

1804 *January 1:* Jean-Jacques Dessalines declares Haitian independence.

1805 First Haitian Constitution issued.

Questions for Consideration

1. What is the role of race in French legislation regarding the colonies (Documents 1, 11, 21, 26, and 32)?

2. What similarities of tone or content can you find between the texts of Mercier and Diderot (Document 2) and other documents in this collection (for instance, Document 4)?

3. Compare Moreau's description of the "mulatto woman" (Document 3) with the portrayals of women provided by Julien Raimond (Document 9) and Laurent Jolicoeur (Document 23). What other documents provide information about the roles and actions of women in the French Caribbean?

4. Compare the arguments and terminology used in Documents 4, 5, 6, 8, and 9, paying particular attention to the use of words such as *nation* and *independence,* as well as the varying use of racial terms such as *black.*

5. What was the relationship between the arguments and actions of Vincent Ogé and Julien Raimond, and the laws declared by the National Assembly in 1790 and 1791?

6. Compare the account of religious practices in Documents 3, 12, and 13. How credible do you think each account is? Why?

7. What strategies did the insurgents in Saint-Domingue and Guadeloupe use between 1791 and 1793? Compare the explanations given by the various authors who described their actions for their success, and explain why each author might have seen things the way he or she did.

8. Compare the responses to the slave revolution in Documents 18, 19, and 20. Which authors believe that the use of violence by the enslaved insurgents is legitimate? Why?

9. What was the relationship between slave revolution and the abolition of slavery in Saint-Domingue and in the French empire?

10. Using Documents 24, 27, 28, and 29, describe the differences between the visions of freedom expressed by administrators such as Hugues, Sonthonax, and Polverel and those expressed by former slaves.

11. Summarize and compare the arguments of Belley, Louverture, and Laveaux in support of emancipation. What were the arguments of their opponents?

12. Compare the interpretations of the Saint-Domingue Revolution presented by North American, Caribbean, and French metropolitan observers. What was each observer most concerned about regarding the impact of the insurrection?

13. What were the French armies sent to Saint-Domingue and Guadeloupe by Bonaparte fighting for? What were the revolutionaries who battled them fighting for? What kinds of symbolism did they use in presenting their cause?

14. Compare Toussaint Louverture's Constitution (Document 37) with the first Haitian Constitution (Document 45). In what ways is the 1805 constitution "democratic"? In what ways is it not? Could Haiti have adopted another form of government in 1805?

Selected Bibliography

GENERAL NARRATIVES

Dubois, Laurent. *Avengers of the New World: The Story of the Haitian Revolution.* Cambridge: Harvard University Press, 2004.

Fick, Carolyn E. *The Making of Haiti: The Saint Domingue Revolution from Below.* Knoxville: University of Tennessee Press, 1990.

Geggus, David P. "The Haitian Revolution." In *The Modern Caribbean,* edited by Franklin W. Knight and Colin A. Palmer, 21–50. Chapel Hill: University of North Carolina Press, 1989.

Geggus, David P. *Slavery, War and Revolution: The British Occupation of Saint Domingue, 1793–1798.* London: Oxford, 1982.

James, C. L. R. *The Black Jacobins: Toussaint L'Ouverture and the San Domingo Revolution,* 2nd ed. New York: Random House, 1963.

SLAVERY AND THE SLAVE TRADE

Geggus, David P. "The Demographic Composition of the French Caribbean Slave Trade." In *Proceedings of the Thirteenth and Fourteenth Meetings of the French Colonial Historical Society,* edited by Philip P. Boucher, 14–30. Lanham, MD: University Press of America, 1990.

Geggus, David P. "The French Slave Trade: An Overview." *William and Mary Quarterly,* 58, no. 1 (January 2001): 119–38.

Geggus, David P. "Sex Ratio, Age and Ethnicity in the Atlantic Slave Trade: Data from French Shipping and Plantation Records." *Journal of African History,* 30 (1989): 23–44.

Geggus, David P. "Sugar and Coffee Production and the Shaping of Slavery in Saint Domingue." In *Cultivation and Culture: Labor and the Shaping of Slave Life in the Americas,* edited by Ira Berlin and Philip D. Morgan, 73–100. Charlottesville: University of Virginia Press, 1993.

Moitt, Bernard. *Women and Slavery in the French Antilles, 1635–1848.* Bloomington: Indiana University Press, 2001.

Stein, Robert Louis. *The French Slave Trade in the Eighteenth Century: An Old Regime Business.* Madison: University of Wisconsin Press, 1979.

Stein, Robert Louis. *The French Sugar Business in the Eighteenth Century.* Baton Rouge: Louisiana State University Press, 1988.

COLONIAL SOCIETY

Geggus, David P. "The Major Port Towns of Saint Domingue in the Later Eighteenth Century." In *Atlantic Port Cities: Economy, Culture and Society in the Atlantic World, 1650–1850,* edited by Franklin W. Knight and Peggy K. Liss, 87–116. Knoxville: University of Tennessee Press, 1990.

Ghachem, Malick W. "Montesquieu in the Caribbean: The Colonial Enlightenment between *Code Noir* and *Code Civil.*" *Historical Reflections/Réflexions Historiques,* 25, no. 2 (1999): 183–210.

McClellan, James E., III. *Colonialism and Science: Saint Domingue in the Old Regime.* Baltimore: Johns Hopkins University Press, 1992.

Moreau de Saint-Méry, Médéric Louis Élie. *A Civilization That Perished: The Last Years of White Colonial Rule in Haiti,* edited and translated by Ivor D. Spencer. Lanham, MD: University Press of America, 1985.

Ogle, Gene E. "'The Eternal Power of Reason' and 'The Superiority of Whites': Hilliard d'Auberteuil's Colonial Enlightenment." *French Colonial History,* 3 (2003): 35–50.

Peabody, Sue. *"There Are No Slaves in France": The Political Culture of Race and Slavery in the Ancien Régime.* Oxford: Oxford University Press, 1996.

FREE PEOPLE OF COLOR

Garrigus, John D. *Before Haiti: Race and Citizenship in French Saint-Domingue.* New York: Palgrave MacMillan, 2006.

Garrigus, John D. "Color, Class and Identity on the Eve of the Haitian Revolution: Saint-Domingue's Free Colored Elite as *Colons Américains.*" *Slavery and Abolition,* 17 (1996): 20–43.

Garrigus, John D. "Redrawing the Colour Line: Gender and the Social Construction of Race in Pre-Revolutionary Haiti." *Journal of Caribbean History,* 30 (1996): 28–50.

Geggus, David P. "Slave and Free Colored Women in Saint Domingue." In *More Than Chattel: Black Women and Slavery in the Americas,* edited by Darlene Clarke Hine and David Barry Gaspar, 259–78. Bloomington: Indiana University Press, 1996.

King, Stewart R. *Blue Coat or Powdered Wig: Free People of Color in Pre-Revolutionary Saint Domingue.* Athens: University of Georgia Press, 2001.

Socolow, Susan M. "Economic Roles of the Free Women of Color of Cap Français." In *More Than Chattel: Black Women and Slavery in the Americas,* edited by Darlene Clark Hine and David Barry Gaspar, 279–97. Bloomington: Indiana University Press, 1996.

ASPECTS OF THE REVOLUTION

Dubois, Laurent. *A Colony of Citizens: Revolution and Slave Emancipation in the French Caribbean, 1787–1804.* Chapel Hill: University of North Carolina, 2004.

Geggus, David P. *Haitian Revolutionary Studies.* Bloomington: Indiana University Press, 2002.

Howard, Thomas Phipps. *The Haitian Journal of Lieutenant Howard, York Hussars, 1796–1798,* edited by Roger Norman Buckley. Knoxville: University of Tennessee Press, 1985.

Pachonski, Jan, and Reuel K. Wilson. *Poland's Caribbean Tragedy: A Study of Polish Legions in the Haitian War of Independence 1802–1803.* Boulder, CO: East European Monographs, 1986.

Pérotin-Dumon, Anne. "Ambiguous Revolution in the Caribbean: The White Jacobins, 1789–1800." *Historical Reflections/Reflexions Historiques* (Canada), 13, nos. 2 and 3 (1986): 499–515.

Stein, Robert Louis. *Léger Félicité Sonthonax: The Lost Sentinel of the Republic.* Rutherford, NJ: Fairleigh Dickinson University Press, 1985.

Thornton, John K. "African Soldiers in the Haitian Revolution." *Journal of Caribbean History* (Barbados), 25, nos. 1 and 2 (1991): 59–80.

Thornton, John K. "'I Am the Subject of the King of Congo': African Political Ideology and the Haitian Revolution." *Journal of World History,* 4, no. 2 (1993): 181–214.

Tyson, George F., Jr. *Toussaint L'Ouverture.* Englewood Cliffs, NJ: Prentice-Hall, 1973.

HAITIAN HISTORY AFTER THE REVOLUTION

Cole, Hubert. *Christophe: King of Haiti.* New York: The Viking Press, 1967.

Dayan, Joan. *Haiti, History, and the Gods.* Berkeley: University of California Press, 1995.

Logan, Rayford W. *The Diplomatic Relations of the United States with Haiti, 1776–1891.* Chapel Hill: University of North Carolina Press, 1941.

Nicholls, David. *From Dessalines to Duvalier: Race, Colour and National Independence in Haiti.* New Brunswick, NJ: Rutgers University Press, 1996.

Sheller, Mimi. *Democracy after Slavery: Black Publics and Peasant Radicalism in Haiti and Jamaica.* Gainesville: University of Florida Press, 2000.

Trouillot, Michel-Rolph. *Haiti; State against Nation: The Origins and Legacy of Duvalierism.* New York: Monthly Review Press, 1990.

EFFECTS OF THE HAITIAN REVOLUTION

Gaspar, David Barry, and David P. Geggus, eds. *A Turbulent Time: The French Revolution and the Greater Caribbean.* Bloomington: Indiana University Press, 1997.

Geggus, David P., ed. *The Impact of the Haitian Revolution in the Atlantic World.* Columbia: University of South Carolina Press, 2001.

Hunt, Alfred N. *Haiti's Influence on Antebellum America: Slumbering Volcano in the Caribbean.* Baton Rouge: Louisiana State University Press, 1988.

Trouillot, Michel-Rolph. *Silencing the Past: Power and the Production of History.* Boston: Beacon Press, 1995.

CLASSIC FRENCH LANGUAGE STUDIES

Ardouin, Beaubrun. *Études sur l'histoire d'Haïti.* 11 vols. 1853–1865. Reprint, Port-au-Prince: Dalencourt, 1958.

Auguste, Claude B., and Marcel B. Auguste. *L'Expédition Leclerc, 1801–1803.* Port-au-Prince: Henri Deschamps, 1985.

Debien, Gabriel. *Les esclaves aux antilles françaises.* Basse-Terre: Société d'histoire de la Guadeloupe, 1974.

Fouchard, Jean. *Les marrons de la liberté.* Paris: Ecole, 1972.

Madiou, Thomas. *Histoire d'Haïti.* 8 vols. 1847–1848. Reprint, Port-au-Prince: Henri Deschamps, 1989.

Index